More praise for

The Politically Incorrect Guide™ to
English and American Literature

"Not only does Elizabeth Kantor know what they don't want you to learn from English literature, but she is ready, willing, and able to tell you. Her book itself instructs and delights, as she reminds us of literature's noblest functions."

> **—J. O. Tate**, Professor of English, Dowling College

"A sane, sound, and sensible overview that helps the reader unlock the treasure trove of great literature, where courage and cowardice, love and hate, death and justice and joy, all spring to life through the words of great writers. Unlike the 'foul and pestilent congregation of vapours' that cloud our literature departments, this book provides a dose of pure oxygen. Read, learn, and enjoy!"

> **—David Allen White**, Professor of English, U.S. Naval Academy

"Like plumbers and dentists, English teachers can be divided into the good and bad. However, when the plumber and the dentist don't know what they're doing, your toilet overflows and your tooth aches. English teachers can cover up a radical failure to understand their discipline by diverting the attention of students from the work of literature itself to biographical materials; sources and analogues; and, most recently, deconstructionism, a formulaic approach that is little more than shameless indoctrination. *The Politically Incorrect Guide™ to English and American Literature* redirects the attention of the student to the text—with a renewed respect for its integrity and a mean wit that makes the study of poetry and fiction fun again, as it was intended to be all along."

> **—Tom Landess**, former Professor of English and Academic Dean at the University of Dallas

The **Politically Incorrect Guide**™ to
English and American Literature

The **Politically Incorrect Guide**™ to

English and American Literature

Elizabeth Kantor

Since 1947
**REGNERY
PUBLISHING, INC.**
An Eagle Publishing Company • Washington, DC

Excerpt from THE COCKTAIL PARTY, copyright 1950 by T.S. Eliot and renewed 1978 by Esme Valerie Eliot, reprinted by permission of Harcourt, Inc.

Excerpts from "The Waste Land" and "Sweeney Among the Nightingales" from COLLECTED POEMS 1909-1962 by T.S. Eliot, copyright 1936 by Harcourt, Inc., and renewed 1964 by T.S. Eliot, reprinted by permission of the publisher.

Cataloging-in-Publication data on file with the Library of Congress

ISBN 10 1-59698-011-7

ISBN 13 978-1-59598-011-2

Published in the United States by
Regnery Publishing, Inc.
One Massachusetts Avenue, NW
Washington, DC 20001
www.regnery.com

Distributed to the trade by
National Book Network
Lanham, MD 20706

Manufactured in the United States of America

10 9 8 7 6 5 4 3 2 1

Books are available in quantity for promotional or premium use. Write to Director of Special Sales, Regnery Publishing, Inc., One Massachusetts Avenue NW, Washington, DC 20001, for information on discounts and terms or call (202) 216-0600.

This book is dedicated
with gratitude and affection
to
Mary Hills Baker Gill
and
Mark L. Reed,
the best readers I know

CONTENTS

Introduction: Why This Book Is Needed   xiii

Part I: **What They Don't Want You to Learn from English Literature (An Introduction to the Canon, from *Beowulf* to Flannery O'Connor)**   **1**

Chapter 1:   **Old English Literature: The Age of Heroes**   **3**

Beowulf: The hero and the poem

The Dream of the Rood

"This life on loan"

The Battle of Maldon

Chapter 2:   **Medieval Literature: "Here Is God's Plenty"**   **23**

Middle English poetry

The politically incorrect world of the Middle Ages

The Canterbury Tales vs. *The Handmaid's Tale*

The dreary world of *The Handmaid's Tale*

The fecundity of medieval art

A pre-classical aesthetic

In the light of eternity

Christianity and freedom

Separation of church and state, medieval style

The argument from authority

The invention of chivalry

Chapter 3:   **The Renaissance: Christian Humanism**   **49**

Christopher Marlowe

William Shakespeare

The tragedies

The comedies

The sonnets

Chapter 4: **The Seventeenth Century: Religion as a Matter of Life and Death**   **85**

John Donne

John Milton

Chapter 5: **Restoration and Eighteenth-Century Literature: The Age of Reason**   **103**

Dead white male #1: John Dryden

Dead white male #2: Alexander Pope

Dead white male #3: Jonathan Swift

Dead white male #4: Samuel Johnson

"The proper study of mankind is man"—or is it?

Chapter 6: **The Nineteenth Century: Revolution and Reaction**   **119**

Revolutionary repeat

Wordsworth and Coleridge

Byron and the Shelleys

Keats

Jane Austen: Without a room of her own

Celebrating "patriarchal values"

Women who are bossy (and talk too much)

Men who aren't patriarchal enough

The benefits (to *women*) of "sexist" conventions

Victorian literature

Dickens

Chapter 7: **The Twentieth Century: The Avant-Garde, and Beyond**   **153**

Decadents and aesthetes

Modernism

Chapter 8: **American Literature: Our Own Neglected Canon**   **167**

Big country, short attention spans

The mystery of evil

The possibility of escape

Why we should still read *Huckleberry Finn*
(despite the ugly racial epithets)

Literature from the Deep South

"A hillbilly Thomist"

**Part II: Why They Don't Want You to Learn about   187
             English and American Literature**

Chapter 9:   **How the PC English Professors Are Suppressing English   189
             Literature (Not Teaching It)**

English professors teach anything and everything...
except English literature

Why they don't want you to read English and American
literature

"Theory"—Marxism, feminism, deconstruction, and
bashing dead white males

Postmodernist jargon: hideously ugly, mentally crippling

Reality-denial as a critical stance

Chapter 10: **What Literature Is *For*: "To Teach and Delight"**   203

What literature is really for

Which literature is truly great?

Truth, beauty, and goodness

**Part III: How You Can Teach Yourself English and   213
             American Literature—Because Nobody Is
             Going to Do It for You**

Chapter 11: **How to Get Started (Once You Realize You're Going to   215
             Have to Read the Literature on Your Own)**

"Close reading"

Reed's Rule

What seems like an ordinary line of poetry

The nuts and bolts of literary analysis

The words themselves (what they mean, what they sound
like, where they come from)

A use for English grammar, after all

Meter, verse forms, genres, and beyond

Chapter 12: **Learn the Poetry by Heart—See the Plays—Gossip about**   **229**
the Novels (That's Just What Jane Austen Did)

Learn the poetry by heart

See the plays as often as you can—or, better yet, *act* in
them

Read the great novels, lend them to your friends, and
gossip about the characters

Notes   243

Acknowledgments   261

Index   265

WHY THIS BOOK IS NEEDED

Why a *Politically Incorrect Guide™ to English and American Literature*? Well, for starters, English professors are so politically correct they're beyond parody. PC English professors believe (and write, and teach) truly amazing things: That Jane Austen was a feminist subversive whose novels express her rage against the patriarchy... that Stalin was valiantly struggling to turn the Soviet Union into a democracy... that Shakespeare wrote *Macbeth* to domesticate women.

Too many of the folks who teach English in college are out of touch with reality and bored with their subject. Enroll in an English class at an American university, and you might find yourself studying Marxist theory, or the history of ballet. You could be treated to an investigation of pornography through the ages. Or you might spend the semester watching foreign films. What is far too *unlikely* to happen is that you will be taught to understand and appreciate great literature in the English language.

These days English professors seem to be teaching anything and everything *but* classic English Literature—from "gender theory" to Freud to "Latino/a popular culture." PC English professors are busy replacing the "dead white males" of the traditional literary canon with the authors of '80s bestsellers that hit all the politically correct themes. Departments of

English are staffed by professors dedicated to suppressing English literature, not to teaching it.

The problem isn't just that English professors waste their students' time, though they certainly do. And it's not just that they do their best to indoctrinate their students into leftist politics, turn them into bitterly unhappy feminists, or recruit them for the antiwar movement—though they do all those things too. The real problem is that they *don't* teach great English and American literature. After all, why would a PC professor *want* his students to learn about Chaucer, Shakespeare, Milton, and the rest of the much-abused dead white males who used to make up the now deconstructed canon of great literature in English? The politically correct line is that Western civilization is the root of all evil. Why on earth would PC English professors want to help perpetuate it?

The departments of English in our universities were established to preserve our literary and linguistic heritage and transmit it to future generations. We've allowed those departments to come under the control of people who hate and fear that heritage. The result? English and American literature are full of things that are worth learning, but that English professors can't be bothered to profess. This *Guide* is an introduction to what you should have learned in college, but your professors didn't want you to know.

This book will teach you what every well-educated, well-read, literate, and humane American should know about English and American literature, but—through little fault of his own—probably doesn't: the great stories, the delightful plays, the powerful and sometimes achingly beautiful verse. It will give you the tools (formerly taught in departments of English, now neglected by PC English professors) that you need to be able to get the most out of this literature—to enjoy it more intensely, to learn from it in a way you can't learn from anything else, and to make it your own. The *Guide* will also show you how to pick your way through the minefield of "literary theory," which can quite effectively cut you off not just from great literature, but from all the wellsprings of Western culture.

The fact is, even if you sign up for a course with "Shakespeare" or "Faulkner" in the title, there's absolutely no guarantee that you're going to be taught English or American literature. On the contrary, the professor is all too likely to make use of the literature to indoctrinate you in some ideology that's worse than irrelevant—that's positively hostile—to the literature you're ostensibly studying. The professor will be interested in the novels or plays not as great works of art that speak to the human race on themes of universal importance, but as cultural artifacts that "privilege" white males over "marginalized" groups such as women and racial minorities. The professor's own politics (Marxism, "deconstruction," or some other radical agenda) will be the real content of the course.

Imagine that you've just arrived at Ivy University and discovered that your English class is being taught by a professor who takes the position that "[t]he question is not whether Shakespeare studies need feminism, but whether feminism needs Shakespeare." She's assigned the following readings, all from *A Feminist Companion to Shakespeare*:

→ "Made to write 'whore' Upon?: Male and Female Use of the Word 'Whore' in Shakespeare's Canon" by Kay Stanton

→ "Sycorax in Algiers: Cultural Politics and Gynecology in Early Modern England" by Rachana Sadchev

→ "...in the Lesbian Void: Woman-Woman Eroticism in Shakespeare's Plays" by Theodora Jankowski

→ "Misogyny Is Everywhere" by Phyllis Rackin.[1]

She plans to spend the rest of the semester proving to the class that Shakespeare doesn't deserve to be read by women.

As far as I know, there is not a university Shakespeare course built around *A Feminist Companion to Shakespeare*. But that volume is a fair sampling of opinions you might encounter in any university's department of English: the essays are written by respected scholars with responsible positions in our universities, and the opinions, assumptions, and modes of analysis that appear in those essays are typical of the attitudes your own professor or T.A. is all too likely to bring to the literature you're studying. If you're a recent college graduate—or if you've spoken to one— you know all about this trend.

When Shakespeare isn't being arraigned by feminist professors for propping up "the patriarchy," he's being searched for evidence of complicity in the slave trade and the rape of the Americas. *Othello* and *Macbeth* and *The Tempest* no longer have anything to say about human nature—only about racism, sexism, and colonialism. Or, rather, the folks teaching English in college seem strangely ignorant of the fact that there *is* any content to human nature beyond racism, sexism, and similar modes of oppression.

Their ignorance seems particularly odd when you consider that they have an enormous body of evidence to the contrary at their disposal. That is, it would be at their disposal if they could bring themselves to pay real attention to the great literature they ought to be teaching, instead of projecting postmodernist ideologies onto it—or simply avoiding the literature entirely and teaching other subjects. English and American literature make up an unparalleled introduction to the wide breadth of human concerns, human capacities, and human wisdom. What you learn in English classes these days is, in contrast, a handful of pinched and bankrupt ideologies, not one of which has as much truth or humanity in it as a single Shakespeare play.

The story of one recent graduate is instructive in several respects.[2] Megan Basham reports on what it was like to major in English at Arizona State University—and also on the surprising things that began to happen to her when, despite the best efforts of her professors, she managed to get beyond the superficialities of postmodern literary education and into the literature itself.

Arizona State, as Basham herself points out, is more famous as a party school than as an intellectual powerhouse. The attitudes and ideas she describes are not the eccentricities of some cutting-edge innovators. The ideologies that have wrecked the study of our literature were first taken up in our elite institutions, but today they're mainstream, pervasive across the country and throughout all the ranks of our higher education system, from elite universities to community colleges.

Basham learned to "deconstruct the racist, misogynistic, homophobic subtext" of the literature she studied. She noticed that "appreciation for John Donne's subtle, metaphysical metaphors has been replaced by appreciation for Adrienne Rich's obvious, sexual ones." English Literature, as it was taught to her, "left a lot of room for would-be intellectuals to take up class time debating the homoerotic interpretations of *As You Like It* and *Richard III.*" Her epiphany came during a survey class that covered medieval and Renaissance literature. She'd decided there was "[n]o point examining the actual texts"—she was doing fine giving the professor back the same line he was feeding the class: Chaucer's "Wife of Bath's Tale" was "enlightened" because of its bold treatment of sexual themes; Spenser's poetry was marred by "unhealthy self-denial and recrimination." This system broke down when she was writing a paper on Sir Thomas Malory's *Morte D'Arthur.*

For the Malory paper, she made the mistake of actually reading the literature, and the sources behind it. She then made the further mistake (at least, from the point of view of PC English professors) of taking what those texts said seriously, instead of dismissing it all as so much unenlightened "self-denial and recrimination" from our misogynist past. She discovered that the story of Lancelot's guilty relationship with Guinevere offered some insight into the lives she and her peers were living. Like

Lancelot, they had at their command opportunities beyond most people's dreams. And like him, they were infected by a certain "sickness of soul." "An encounter with Christ's sacred chalice changed Lancelot's heart," explains Megan Basham. "An encounter with Lancelot changed mine."

Self-criticism and Christian faith are by no means the only valuable things you can discover in English and American literature. You can learn to recognize and admire certain qualities that that literature paints in all their glory (and solid worth): military valor, mental balance, chastity. You can catch the Romantic poets' passion for exploring the capacities of the human mind and heart, or the Victorian novelists' fascination with character. Or you can simply learn to love beauty, and despise ugliness—to admire skill, and know the difference between consummate achievement and lazy bungling. What all these lessons have in common is that it's hard to imagine politically correct English professors' being pleased that their students were learning them.

This *Politically Incorrect Guide*™ will introduce you to the grand range of things that you can learn from literature in English, and that you won't have picked up from your college professors. I've tried to provide at least a taste of the greatest literature from every historical period, but there are inevitable omissions and imbalances. Oscar Wilde, for example, probably gets more space than his literary accomplishments warrant, and Edmund Spenser certainly gets much less than he deserves, because of the need to cover some important themes from the end of the nineteenth century on the one hand, and the abundance of fine Renaissance poetry on the other.

The lists at the beginning of each chapter include the literature discussed as well as additional works; together they add up to a curriculum for a self-taught survey of English and American literature. The literary works, themes, and modes of analysis treated in this *Guide* will give you a solid start and help you figure out where you want to go next, but no survey can possibly be exhaustive. There's an almost infinite variety of wonderful literature written in our language—and of life-changing lessons that you can take from it.

The one lesson that you can't learn from great English and American literature is the politically correct point of view: the idea that the culture of the West is nothing but a source of injustice, and that only perpetual vigilance against all its "ism"s and "phobia"s can protect us against the return of oppression and misery. If you could learn from our great literature to despise and fear Western civilization, the PC professors wouldn't have quit teaching it.

Part I

WHAT THEY DON'T
WANT YOU TO LEARN
FROM ENGLISH LITERATURE

An Introduction to the Canon, from
Beowulf to Flannery O'Connor

Chapter One

OLD ENGLISH LITERATURE
THE AGE OF HEROES

Heart must be the hardier, courage the keener,
Spirit the greater, as our strength lessens.

—*The Battle of Maldon*

English literature begins with *Beowulf.* Or it used to, before PC professors decided that 1) Heroism is irrelevant to modern life; 2) It's impossible to know the truth about the past (nothing scholars said about *Beowulf* before the dawn of postmodernism communicates the objective truth about the poem, its author, or the Anglo-Saxon England that it was written in—their understanding of the poem only betrays *their* agendas); and 3) Studying the Old English language is a waste of graduate students' time, which could, after all, be better employed reading more "literary theory"—Marxism, feminism, and so forth.

Study of the language *Beowulf* was written in—Old English (also known as Anglo-Saxon)—was, until quite recently, part of the standard curriculum for serious students of English.[1] Old English is closely related to German, and more distantly to the Scandinavian languages. It was spoken by the barbarian Germanic peoples, known collectively as the Anglo-Saxons, who had conquered and settled England when the Roman Empire was collapsing. Old English is almost entirely opaque to modern

The Old English literature you must not miss

Cædmon's Hymn

Beowulf

The Dream of the Rood

The Battle of Maldon

English-speakers, but there are words and sometimes even whole phrases—"þæt wæs god cyning"[2] (that was a good king), for example—that seem to jump off the page to remind you that *Beowulf* is, after all, written in an earlier incarnation of our own language.

Students of English literature (even if they didn't plan to become specialists in Old English poetry) used to learn to read Anglo-Saxon. By studying the development of the English language over time, they also used to learn something about the mechanics of all speech: which sounds are made in which parts of the mouth, how the different sounds are physically related to one another. That way, even scholars concentrating in Renaissance drama or Romantic poetry had an acquaintance with the nuts and bolts, as it were, of the English language.

Beowulf: The hero and the poem

Eliminating the Old English requirement was one of the first triumphs of the fans of "literary theory" ("deconstruction" and its ilk) in departments of English. Graduate students in English don't read *Beowulf* as they used to, and they're missing something well worth knowing. *Beowulf* is full of all kinds of fascinating things, but this is what the central plot boils down to:

The hero, Beowulf the Geat, travels to Denmark to help Hrothgar, King of the Danes, get rid of a lake-bottom-dwelling monster called Grendel. Heorot, the beautiful hall Hrothgar built, has been unusable (at least at night) since its inaugural feast, when Grendel, disturbed by the music at the celebration, came to the hall, killed thirty warriors, and carried them off to eat. Grendel hasn't left Heorot alone since, and Hrothgar and his wise men have despaired of a solution—until Beowulf arrives. The hero and his men stay the night in Heorot to wait for the monster. Grendel shows up looking for supper, kills and eats one of the Geats, and makes the mistake of grabbing Beowulf for his second course. The monster escapes from the warrior's grip only by leaving one of his arms behind, torn out of its socket at the shoulder. A blood-trail to a lake reveals where Grendel has crept off to die.

Hrothgar thanks and rewards Beowulf, but it turns out that Heorot still isn't safe. Grendel's mother visits the hall the next night, kills a Dane, and escapes with Grendel's arm. Beowulf goes into the lake after her and kills her with an ancient sword he finds in her lair. Richly rewarded for his deeds, the hero returns to the land of the Geats, where he eventually becomes king.

Finally, fifty years later, Beowulf kills a dragon that is ravaging the Geatish countryside—but only with the help of a young kinsman; and Beowulf himself is killed in the accomplishment of this last great feat. The Geats burn Beowulf's body and build a tower to house the ashes and the treasures he won from the dragon. Without their great king, the Geats must look forward to defeat at the hands of the many enemies Beowulf kept at bay during his lifetime.

That's the basic plot, but it's far from being the whole story. Looming behind and peeking around the corners of the main plotline are a number of other stories which give extra depth—whole other dimensions—to the poem. The *Beowulf* poet (we don't know his name, and we have only guesses about what sort of man he was, and where and when exactly he lived) tells us about a dragonslayer named Sigemund, whose adventure was already an old story in Beowulf's day—and who shows up in Wagner's *Ring* cycle. He refers to obscure episodes from the wars of the

Can You Believe the Professors?

"Anglo-Saxon England is *nothing other than what it has been perceived to be* by historically grounded human beings, from the time of the Anglo-Saxons to the present moment."

John D. Niles, denying the objective reality of the subject to which he's devoted his career. "Appropriations: A Concept of Culture," *Anglo-Saxonism and the Construction of Social Identity*, ed. Allen J. Frantzen and John D. Niles, (Gainesville: University of Florida Press, 1997), 209.

Danes and the Geats with other Germanic peoples: Franks and Frisians, Swedes and Heathobards. The poet sheds light on his characters by comparing them to other figures of history and legend. And he hints at what will happen after the end of the poem. It's foreshadowed, for example, that Heorot will one day be destroyed by fire, and that Hrothgar's sons will be killed by their father's trusted nephew.

It's a great adventure story, exactly the kind of poem you'd think—if it were in the right professorial hands—would stand a decent chance of turning the thousands of *Lord of the Rings* movie fans at our nation's universities into aficionados of great English poetry. But English professors approach *Beowulf* from a great ideological distance. Not many would go as far as John Niles, who flatly denies that Anglo-Saxon England has any reality beyond people's ideas about it. But they do worry that *Beowulf* is "too masculine and too death-haunted"[3] or otherwise out of step with the world as they see it.

And no wonder. *Beowulf* is full to the brim with ideas and attitudes that are exactly opposite to the postmodernist intellectuals' beliefs about the world. The typical English professor hardly wants his students learning the kinds of things you can learn from *Beowulf*: for example, to admire war heroes, to prefer the tried and true to the trendy and radical, to see Christianity as a powerful civilizing force, and—possibly worst of all—to ask what's wrong with the clever man who hates the warrior (who's a better man than he is).

Your average college professor is not a great admirer of all things military. He tends to think of soldiers as bloodthirsty

Can You Believe the Professors?

"The epic poem, as Marx once observed, requires historical conditions which the steam-engine and the telegraph put paid to.... In any case, we no longer believe in heroism...."

Terry Eagleton explains why heroism and *Beowulf* are irrelevant to modern people (in an article that appeared in the *London Review of Books* a little less than two years before September 11, 2001). "Hasped and Hooped and Hirpling," *London Review of Books* 21, no. 22 (November 11, 1999): 16.

killers or deluded dupes. And *Beowulf* is one long hymn of praise for the warrior. It's also—which may be even worse, from the look-down-your-nose-at-those-ROTC-idiots point of view—a defense of the necessity of military heroism.

Beowulf takes place in a world that's dangerous, and not just because it's inhabited by monsters and fire-vomiting dragons. The ordinary dangers that fill up the background of the poem—dangers to men from other men—are quite realistic. The circumstances of the remembered historical conflicts may have been changed to make a better story. But real situations in which the choice was kill or be killed were an inescapable feature of life among the ancient Germanic tribes, the ancestors of the Old English.

The *Beowulf* poet continually reminds us that peace is fragile; that deadly conflict can break out on any occasion; and that attempts at peacemaking are especially dangerous. For example, as Beowulf explains to his own king on his return from Hrothgar's court, Hrothgar plans to patch up the Danes' feud with the Heathobards by giving his daughter in marriage to a Heathobard prince. Inevitably, as Beowulf predicts, Hrothgar's plan will end in disaster. Violence will erupt when, at the wedding feast, an old Heathobard warrior points out to a young companion that it's his father's sword that some Dane is wearing, and reminds him of how his father died fighting the Danes. The Heathobards won't be able to resist the opportunity for revenge, and the feast will end in more killing.

The Roman historian Tacitus, writing about the Germanic tribes in the first century A.D., described men like these: warriors whose lives were defined by pride, fidelity, and violence, who measured themselves and one another by their valor in battle and their fierce loyalty to their own. The culture Tacitus described in his *Germania* has some unique features, but a lot of what he wrote about is common to societies as distant from each other in time and space as the Bronze-Age Greek heroes of Homer's *Iliad* and the warlike Indians the French and English encountered in

North America. In these cultures, which we may call *heroic* or *primitive,* men of standing don't do productive work, which is the province of women and slaves. Except for hunting (the leisure activity of the warrior) what the hero contributes to society, his full-time job, is the defense of his own people against other men like himself—or, alternately, the conquest and plunder of other peoples for the enrichment of his own. His other activities, whether singing and competing in drinking contests (among the Germanic tribes) or decorating the backs of his cattle by rubbing ashes into their hair (among the Nuer people that anthropologist E. E. Evans-Pritchard studied in twentieth-century Sudan),[4] are ritual or ornamental.

> ## What They Don't Want You to Learn from *Beowulf*
>
> Heroes deserve our respect and gratitude; if we don't admire them, there's something wrong with *us.*

But the warrior's defense of his own people by his heroism is not merely decorative; it's absolutely necessary. The strategic insertion of a few conflict resolution experts via time machine would not have changed the dynamics of the heroic age, allowed the ancient Danes and Heathobards to realize that they were irrationally demonizing each other by viewing outsiders as "Other," and ironed the violence out of their culture. Ancient Germanic tribesmen didn't fight because they despised their enemies. When Beowulf talks about the Heathobards who will wreak havoc at the wedding, he considers them not as "Other"—inexplicable, alien, or monstrous—but as great-hearted warriors, too proud to forgo their opportunity for revenge.

The primitive ancestors of the English fought against men they respected and even identified with—because in the absence of what used to be called civilization there is no way to be sure of freedom, prosperity, or self-respect except to determine to die rather than yield. And, despite what some modern people seem to think, the civilizing element absent from the primitive or heroic society is not the insight that these things simply aren't worth dying and killing for. There were many men living in heroic-age cultures who didn't easily take offense, who didn't consider revenge a duty, and who didn't think their reputations were worth defending with their lives: they were known as slaves.

The virtues of the heroic age have always been necessary. Wherever and whenever civilization begins to fray among us, you can see the dynamics of the heroic age begin to reassert themselves—as in gang and drug-lord culture, where men risk death and kill for their honor. And we all depend on heroic virtues in our soldiers, to defend our civilization against barbarism from outside.

Beowulf affirms the two aspects of the heroic life that are most offensive to the modern intellectual: the unavoidable waste of men, and the necessary structure of military command. In Old English poetry, to be lordless is to be hopeless.[5] Beowulf's own death is a disaster because he leaves his people at the mercy of their many enemies. The Geats without Beowulf will be in the fix the Danes are in in the poem's "Finn episode" after their leader Hnæf is slain by the Frisians: forced into a humiliating and untenable subjection to their enemies. Military command is a necessary condition of freedom—and the death of some is necessary for the security of others. As the poet argues after one of Beowulf's companions is killed by Grendel, Grendel would have killed more, if Beowulf's courage (and a wise God) had not prevented that fate.

But courage in *Beowulf* is not just something necessary for safety, like burglar alarms, vaccines, or paying your income taxes. Heroism is glorious; it's good in itself; it deserves praise. It's self-evidently valuable—like gold, which is its natural reward. Bravery is preeminent among the things the *Beowulf* poet continually brings to our attention as deserving our respect. It's the quality that determines the worth of a man. To the extent he has it, he's worthy of praise. To the extent he lacks it, he has to hear the humiliating things that the man who "wants to speak the truth" (wyle soð sprecan) must say: Men who are faithless in battle have no reward, no glory, no honor, nothing left but their lives—and they'd be better off dead.

The *Beowulf* poet is interested not just in who's brave and who's not, but also in who wants to tell the truth about these things, and who doesn't. The man who wants to speak the truth "in accordance with what is right" (æfter rihte) will distinguish what's good from what's base. He'll recognize nobility wherever he sees it—in the courage and faith of a hero, or in the generosity of a king who rewards warriors with gold. But not everyone tries to know the truth.

We can only guess what the Anglo-Saxons would have thought of the modern antiwar intellectual, but the *Beowulf* poet does address a similar phenomenon. Bravery like Beowulf's naturally inspires wonder and praise, telling and retelling. But there is one man in the poem who refuses to acknowledge Beowulf's courage. Hrothgar's courtier Unferth dismisses Beowulf's past exploits and predicts he'll fail against Grendel.

The *Beowulf* poet makes it clear that while Unferth's attitude has something to do with one positive capacity the courtier has—his "wit" (a capacity he, interestingly enough, shares with our intellectuals)—the underlying motivation for his grudging attitude is nothing more or less than envy: "It vexed him greatly, the adventure of Beowulf, that high-spirited seafarer. For he did not admit that any other man on earth might ever achieve more glory under heaven than he himself." Unferth attacks Beowulf with words for almost exactly the same reason that Grendel attacks the Danes with his murderous claws. He hates a good that's beyond him. Our intellectuals tend to ask why our soldiers' lives are spent in vain, or who benefits from the glorification of the military hero.

The *Beowulf* poet was interested in a different question: What's wrong with the man who won't give the hero the glory he's earned?

The Dream of the Rood

By the time *Beowulf* was written, the heroic culture of the Anglo-Saxons was being transformed by the civilizing power of Christianity. We're used to thinking of the very first Christians—the disciples Jesus called from their fishing nets—as poor, unlettered men from a provincial backwater of the Roman Empire. But the Apostles were urban sophisticates compared to the Germanic barbarians who invaded the Roman Empire and began to convert to Christianity as it was collapsing.

There's a story told about Clovis, King of the Franks,[6] that illustrates the almost unbridgeable gap the Germanic tribesmen had to reach across to accept the gospel. Clovis is said to have been much moved when he was first told the story of the Crucifixion. "If I had been there with my Franks," he exclaimed, "I would have avenged His wrongs!"[7] It's hard to think of anything more alien to the Crucifixion as it's portrayed in the New Testament than the duty of revenge among the German tribes. You can make a pretty good case that these barbarians misunderstood Christianity completely. And yet there was something they saw and loved there, not really understanding it; and it changed them. *Beowulf* is a fruit of that transformation.

Beowulf's battles are not just the exploits of an ordinary hero in defense of his people against warriors from some other tribe. And they're not the timeless contests of pagan

What They Don't Want You to Learn from *Beowulf* and *The Dream of the Rood*

Christianity is a powerful transformative—and civilizing—force.

myth, either. Grendel isn't a fairy tale bogey or a mythological monster. When Grendel first appears, the Danes are rejoicing and a poet is singing the story of God's creation. The poet makes clear that Grendel represents the kind of evil you can read about in the Bible. He's descended from Cain, the first murderer. And Cain's murder of his brother was a result of the original disobedience of Adam and Eve, which itself came about because of Lucifer's rebellion against God. Grendel's hostility to men is part of the eternal enmity of mankind's original Enemy.

And in Beowulf's character there is a glimpse of virtue that transcends the ethic of the heroic age. Behind the hero, you can see the shadowy image of a Man who is stronger, braver, and more patient than any other man, and Who faces death and emerges with a different kind of victory.

But to get the full flavor of the intersection between Christianity and the heroic pagan culture of the Anglo-Saxons, you have to read another Old English poem: *The Dream of the Rood.* This poem begins with a dream in which the poet sees the Cross (the Rood), sometimes as a sign of victory, covered in gold, but alternately wet with blood. Then the Cross itself begins to speak. It tells its story, which is the story of the Crucifixion.

Except that in this telling of the passion of Christ, all the passion—that is, the suffering—is attributed to the Cross itself, while Christ is shown as a victorious warrior. The Cross is the one manhandled, wounded, and bound by enemies. Then the Rood sees Christ coming toward it—not as a beaten prisoner, but as a brave warrior, eager to do a great deed: "The young hero ungirded himself, Who was almighty God, strong and stout-hearted. He took His stand on the lofty gallows, courageous in the sight of many, since He would free mankind."

The Cross speaks as if it is the hero's loyal retainer, duty bound, in the heroic tradition, to hold the ground, not daring to flee the battle. But then comes the poem's most poignant moment: "A shadow went forth, dark under the sky. All created things wept; they mourned the fall of the king. Christ was on the Cross." This is the moment at which the hero of the poem, the brave warrior, is no longer able take an active role, to play the Germanic hero. Or, if you look at it another way, this is a window on the crisis in which the pagan culture of the Anglo-Saxons encountered a heroism that was beyond its reckoning, and was broken and changed by it.

"This life on loan"

Christendom—the civilization of Christian Europe—was the eventual result of the encounter that the Anglo-Saxons and their Germanic cousins had with Christianity. We're the heirs of that civilization, in an unbroken line, never interrupted by a catastrophe as total as the barbarian invasions and the breakdown of order, technology, and culture that ended the Roman Empire.

Not that there aren't some among us who seem to be looking forward to such a catastrophic breakdown—Marxist professor Terry Eagleton among them. Here's Eagleton (the fellow who thinks *Beowulf* is irrelevant because heroism is passé) anticipating the long overdue, but still somehow inevitable, collapse of the capitalist system and rallying the socialists that, even now he fondly imagines, will play a vital role in shepherding us all through the crisis:

> The system undermines its own hegemony, without much need of help from the left. What is to be feared is...the prospect that it will begin to unravel while the left is disheveled, disorganized and incapable of steering ragged, spontaneous revolt into productive channels. The problem then is that a lot more people are likely to get hurt than might otherwise be the case.[8]

Our intellectuals' tendency to look forward to a great clearing of the decks and a fresh start is yet another way in which they're hopelessly out of sympathy with Old English literature. The Anglo-Saxons, who were living in the aftermath of just such a clearing of the decks and in the midst of just such a fresh start—the last really fresh start Western civilization has seen—were backward- rather than forward-looking. In *Beowulf,* everything good is old. The best roads (the only ones that are actually paved) are the old Roman roads. The only kind of sword that's any good is an old one, the work of ancient smiths. And the best sword in the poem, the one Beowulf takes off the wall of Grendel's lair and uses to kill Grendel's mother, is the oldest of all, with the history of the primordial war between good and evil and the destruction of the antediluvian children of Cain engraved on its hilt.

One of the first things that you notice when you start to read Old English poetry is a pervasive feeling of what you might call nostalgia, if nostalgia weren't far too weak a word. "Þis læne lif"—this life on loan—is a phrase that recurs in Anglo-Saxon poetry in the same way as "wine-dark sea" keeps showing up in Homer. Old English literature is drenched in a terrible grief for the loss of the past, a passionate longing for what's gone, and a keen awareness of how fragile every human good is.

Loss and sorrow figure heavily in the surviving poetry of the Anglo-Saxons. J. R. R. Tolkien—Old English literature scholar (and, in his off hours, the author of a prose epic, recently turned into three major motion pictures)—famously disagreed with the usual classification of *Beowulf* as

What Else They Don't Want You to Learn from *Beowulf*, and the Rest of Old English Literature

Prosperity is self-correcting.

an epic like Homer's *Iliad* or Virgil's *Aeneid*. According to Tolkien, *Beowulf* is an elegy, the first 3,000-plus lines of which are merely a prelude to Beowulf's funeral dirge.[9] Many of the shorter Anglo-Saxon poems are complaints about painful losses. But the elegiac note in Old English poetry is about more than individual unhappiness. There's a larger grief that pervades the whole literature. The Anglo-Saxon poets are acutely aware that all things are passing away. "Swa þes middangeard" (Thus this middle-earth), says the Wanderer, "ealra dogra gehwam dreoseð ond fealleþ" (each and every day declines and falls).[10] Life is on loan; peace is fragile and short-lived; warmth and companionship are fleeting; valuable goods are rare things, too easily lost.

This sense of the fragility of things was intensified—if it wasn't created in the first place—by the history and situation of the ancient English. The Germanic tribes inhabiting Western Europe, including the Anglo-Saxons, were still relatively primitive peoples living in the ruins of a civilization that their ancestors had helped to destroy. Remnants of that civilization—particularly the ruins of stone buildings—seemed so much beyond the capacity of the Anglo-Saxons that they spoke of them as *enta geweorc*—"the work of giants." And yet they pictured the old buildings as they must once have been, full of light and people, before enemies, disease, time, and weather emptied and wrecked them.[11]

The early English lived in conditions of scarcity that we can hardly imagine: there wasn't enough of anything. People, pleasures, skills, useful objects, and beautiful things were all rare and valuable. Perhaps it's natural that the Anglo-Saxons should have appreciated so keenly what they had, and mourned so intensely for what they knew had been lost.

And perhaps it's natural that our intellectuals, living in conditions of unexampled abundance, should be impatient with a teeming world population and a bewildering array of material goods, and that they should feel an irresistible urge to sweep the board clean and start again from scratch. One of the things you might pick up from reading *Beowulf*—but only from really *reading* it, not picking through it hunting for signs of racism, sexism, and homophobia—is that the material prosperity we live in cannot be taken for granted as the universal birthright of mankind. Professor Eagleton's assertion that the left's demand for "conditions in which everybody in the planet can get enough to eat and have a job, freedom, dignity and the like" is a "remarkably modest" proposal[12] would have dumbfounded the Anglo-Saxons. Among the early English, as among most people in most times and places, the basic necessities of life were hardly won. Objects of desire came at a high price, even for the king or the hero.

Among us, on the other hand, even the very poorest suffer not so much from a lack of things as from a kind of squalor arising from badly managed abundance. The homes of our "underclass" are strewn with broken objects of an intricacy and usefulness beyond the wildest imaginings of the *Beowulf* poet. What wouldn't have been beyond his imaginings, though, is the connection between what a Marxist would call the "material conditions" of our lives and the mental and moral attitudes of our intelligentsia.

That prosperity should breed overweening pride, violent urges, and (ultimately) self-destructive behavior would come as no surprise to the Old English. Here's how the *Beowulf* poet has the Danish king Hrothgar warn Beowulf, after his great triumph, against just such an ending to his so-far successful story: Don't be like Heremod, he warns. God gave Heremod power and glory, but he became violent toward his own people. As Hrothgar explains, prosperity isolates a man from the hardships that ordinarily keep men in check. The successful man enjoys unalloyed power and pleasure; he can let his pride grow, and his conscience sleep. And he becomes dissatisfied with what he has. Things are bound to end badly for him. Prosperity never lasts forever, and men who, like Heremod, are spoiled by it are likely to go on making ever larger errors of judgment until they bring on a final disaster, that it's too late for them to learn from.

This is not the kind of analysis of the economic underpinnings of thought that Marxist critics are typically interested in. But it's a line of inquiry they might profitably pursue (before, as for Heremod, it's too late). Our intellectuals are spoiled by and at the same time impatient with our unprecedented abundance, whether of objects or of knowledge or of people. But prosperity can't last forever—largely because it does spoil people. In our lifetime the population of Europe will begin to shrink for the first time since the Middle Ages. And our own country has been attacked by men who behave more barbarously than the Germanic

The Anita Hill of the Dark Ages?

Besides Heremod, the proudest and most wantonly destructive character in *Beowulf* (among the ordinary human beings, that is) is the beautiful princess Modthryth, who specializes in false accusations. She gets any man who dares to raise his eyes to look at her killed.

Remember the feminist activists who couldn't seem to work up any interest in whether Anita Hill was telling the truth about Clarence Thomas? After all, the only important thing was that sexual harassment should always be taken *very seriously* (never mind whether it had actually happened in this particular case or not).

Well, there's a feminist professor who writes as though Modthryth's story is really about *male* violence against *women*. To Professor Gillian Overing of Wake Forest University, Modthryth's murders amount to "complicity—also a form of mimicry—in the masculine objectifying, destructive mode."

Gillian R. Overing, *Language, Sign, and Gender in* Beowulf (Carbondale and Edwardsville: Southern Illinois University Press, 1990), 105.

tribes who overran the Roman Empire. It is by no means certain that our civilization, which has continued unbroken since the Anglo-Saxons were civilized, is, finally, any less fragile than the one the Anglo-Saxons helped destroy.

The Battle of Maldon

It's instructive to put the twenty-first-century intellectual's attitude toward the hero side by side with the attitude of his heroic-age counterpart. After the September 11 attack on America, Arizona Cardinals safety Pat Tillman turned down a $3.6 million contract and trained as an Army Ranger—finding a new use for the extraordinary combination of intelligence and determination that had made him such a remarkable football player. On May 22, 2004, serving in Afghanistan with the Rangers, he was killed by friendly fire.

Five months later, John Jota Leaños, assistant professor of Chicana and Chicano studies at Arizona State University (where Tillman had played college football)—and self-styled "Xican@ public artist, performance artist, and cultural worker"—distributed posters calling Pat Tillman's heroism into question.[13]

Leaños suggested that while Tillman was a hero "to many of you," his death was more a shame than an achievement. "FRIENDLY FIRE" screams the headline across the top of the poster. Next to Tillman's picture, Leaños, speaking as if in Tillman's own voice, complains:

My death was tragic

My glory was short-lived

Flawed perceptions

of myself

my country

and

the War on Terror

resulted in the disastrous

end to my life.

In the last decade of the tenth century, Vikings sailed ninety-three ships to England and ravaged the Essex coast. At Maldon the earl Byrhtnoth and his men opposed their landing, Byrhtnoth was slain, and the Vikings won the day. *The Battle of Maldon,* written soon after this disaster, celebrates the heroism of the English in their defeat.

The unknown author of this poem could, like John Leaños, be described as a kind of "public artist, performance artist, and cultural worker"—the public intellectual of his day. Also like John Leaños, he believed that at least some of the deaths he memorialized were unnecessary: the results of mischance, of the cowardice of fellow soldiers, and even of a disastrous mistake arising from a flaw in the character of the English commander.

Both the beginning and the end are missing from the surviving manuscript of the poem. The fragment we have of *The Battle of Maldon* begins with the men's dismissal of their horses (the English were to fight the Vikings on foot). One young man lets his beloved hawk go—by which sacrifice, the poet tells us, we can know the boy will not fail in the fight. The hawk flies to the woods; the boy steps to the battle. The earl's men are letting go of the pleasures and responsibilities of their ordinary lives and steeling themselves to face the invader and, very possibly, death.

Byrhtnoth orders his men for the battle, and they listen as the Viking herald offers peace if the English are willing to pay tribute. The earl refuses, and the men wait what seems like "too long" for the battle to be joined. The tide between the mainland where the English are mustered and the island where the Vikings have landed goes out, and the Vikings attempt to come across, but the English cut down the first man over: the ford is narrow, and the attackers are at a disadvantage.

What They Don't Want You to Learn from *The Battle of Maldon*

It *is* noble to die in battle, even if your death was caused by your own side's mistake

Here's where Byrhtnoth makes the fatal mistake. The Vikings ask leave to cross unmolested onto the mainland and fight the English there, and the earl, as the poet explains, "because of his pride" (for his ofermode) lets the enemy come across the ford. Now the odds are against the English, and they begin to fall. Their case becomes hopeless soon after the earl himself is hit by a thrown missile and then cut down. In the crisis, some of Byrhtnoth's men flee, betraying their lord and breaking their oaths; one Godric takes the earl's own horse and flees from the battle, confusing loyal soldiers, some of whom think that it is Byrhtnoth himself quitting the fight, and turn to run. The shield wall is broken. But those who know the earl is dead and who are true to the end shout out to each other to remember the vows they made to their lord, and keep them. They know now that their only choice is disgrace or death.

Anglo-Saxon loyalty and heroism by no means depended upon uncritical enthusiasm for leaders, à la the Hitler Youth. As a matter of fact, the King of England at the time of the Battle of Maldon, the man Byrhtnoth refers to as his own lord, was a man known to later generations of schoolboys as "Ethelred the Unready," a rough translation of Aethelræd Unræd: Ethelred the Badly Advised, or Ethelred the Poorly Judging. This unflattering nickname is evidence that the English of a millennium ago were not blind to their rulers' flaws. And the *Maldon* poet places the blame for defeat squarely on the shoulders of Earl Byrhtnoth.

But it doesn't occur to the poet that the catastrophic mistake of the earl—any more than the poor judgment of the king, or the cowardly betrayal of Godric, or the ultimate futility of the English defense—diminishes the warriors' heroism. Quite the opposite. Their deaths, their defeat, and even their betrayal by some of their companions (and in another sense by the pride of their own lord), make their loyalty and their courage more powerful. That's not because Old English poetry celebrates the unthinking obedience that our intellectuals associate with traditional loyalties (but that really has its home in modern totalitarian movements, including Marxism). And it's not because the "death-haunted" Anglo-Saxons had some kind of sick, "Goth"-style fascination with death and disaster. It's simply because the hardest conditions are the ones in which the hero's mettle is truly tested. In the last speech we have from *The Battle of Maldon,* the old warrior Byrhtwold encourages his fellows thus:

> Heart must be the hardier, courage the keener,
> Spirit the greater, as our strength lessens.

If Pat Tillman's "glory was short-lived," as John Leaños so confidently claims, who's to blame?

→ Is it Tillman, who, like those heroes of old, let go of the thing he loved and sacrificed his youth and his strength, his native intelligence and his hard-won skill, because of his loyalty to something greater than himself?

→ Is it President Bush, the generals, or Tillman's fellow soldiers, who—as rulers and commanders and soldiers always have done and always will do—made mistakes, misjudged things, failed in the moment of crisis and confusion?

→ Or is it our artists and "cultural workers," our critics and our poets, who don't feel the generous impulse that propelled the *Maldon* poet to hold up such heroism for our emulation, who no longer recognize the nobility of such a sacrifice—who can't see how it shines?

Chapter Two

MEDIEVAL LITERATURE
"Here Is God's Plenty"

Man, please thy Maker, and be merry,
And set not by this world a cherry.

—William Dunbar, *Of Covetousness*

J ust a few decades after *The Battle of Maldon* was written, a more momentous battle changed England—and its language and literature—forever. In 1066 William, Duke of Normandy (afterwards known as William the Conqueror), invaded and conquered England. Harold, the last Anglo-Saxon king of England, was killed at the Battle of Hastings. William had an arguably legitimate claim to the English throne, but to many of the English the Norman Conquest seemed like an enemy occupation. William put down revolts against his authority with great brutality; he dispossessed the Anglo-Saxon nobility in order to reward his Norman followers with landed estates. The Normans imposed an alien legal system on the English people, and Norman French, not English, became the language of the law and the ruling class. Sir Walter Scott's *Ivanhoe* is a romantic fictionalized account—great fun to read—of the dislocated and oppressed Saxons during the time between the Conquest and the assimilation of the Norman conquerors into English society (as are

The medieval English literature you must not miss

Chaucer,
The Canterbury Tales

William Langland,
Piers Plowman

Gawain and the Green Knight

Thomas Malory,
Morte d'Arthur

many treatments of the Robin Hood legend, which originated during this turbulent period).

Middle English poetry

By the time of the great flowering of English poetry in the fourteenth century, English was a hybrid language, somewhere in between Anglo-Saxon and Norman French. In some places (in the king's court, and in London generally) it had more French in it. In places remote from the center of power—in the West Midlands, for example, where the author of *Gawain and the Green Knight* lived—it was closer to the language of *Beowulf,* and nearly as incomprehensible to the modern reader. Geoffrey Chaucer, on the other hand—court poet, government bureaucrat, and sometime diplomat—wrote his *Canterbury Tales* in a language that readers today can understand with just a little practice.

Some old-fashioned poets in Chaucer's day were still using the alliterative verse of Old English poetry. *Piers Plowman,* for example, is probably the greatest poem in Middle English *not* by Chaucer. Its author was a man as different from the wealthy and urbane Chaucer as a poet living in London at the same time could possibly be. William Langland (if that was even his name) was so obscure that we're not sure exactly who he was. He seems to have been a desperately poor man, originally from the West Midlands, who had studied for the priesthood but never been ordained, and who used his spare time making verses that annoyed the corrupt clergy of his day. From a few apparently autobiographical bits in his poetry, it appears that he lived in London with his wife and daughter, scraping out a bare living for his little family by saying prayers for the dead.

The lines below, from *Piers Plowman,* are modernized for easier reading; but you can see that it's written in the old alliterative verse. The lines don't rhyme, and they don't share a precisely measured rhythm (they don't even have the same number of syllables per line). Instead, each line has four stressed syllables, at least three of which begin with the same sound. *Piers Plowman,* like many other poems written around this time, begins with a vision the author claims he saw in a dream. In this case, Langland reports seeing a tower on a high hill with a dungeon in the valley beneath it. In the middle:

> A fair field full of folk found I there between—
> Of all manner of men, the mean and rich,
> Working and wandering as the world asketh.

The famous beginning of Chaucer's *Canterbury Tales,* on the other hand, is written in the kind of meter that we're used to from Shakespeare, Wordsworth, or Tennyson—patterns made of fixed numbers of stressed and unstressed syllables that make up rhyming lines.[1] Here are the opening lines of Chaucer's "Prologue," where we'll meet his pilgrims—Knight and Squire, Wife of Bath and Prioress, Monk and Friar, Miller and Cook, and so forth—who will tell the different stories that make up Chaucer's masterpiece, purportedly to entertain each other in the course of their pilgrimage to the shrine of St. Thomas Becket at Canterbury. Chaucer's sound is more difficult for us to make out than his meaning. The "great vowel shift" that drastically changed the pronunciation of English, gave us the silent e, and made English spelling so difficult, has intervened between his day and our own. But if you remember that Chaucer's final e's weren't usually silent, but sometimes they were run into the following word, you can see that the opening lines of *The Canterbury Tales* do rhyme, and have roughly the same rhythm as a typical line in Shakespeare:

> Whan that Aprill with his shoures soote
> The droghte of March hath perced to the roote...

That is, *When April with its sweet showers has pierced the drought of March to the root.* What happens then? *People long to go on pilgrimages, and especially from end to end of every shire in England, they go to Canterbury, to visit the holy, blissful martyr, who helped them when they were sick.*

The politically incorrect world of the Middle Ages

The Canterbury Tales and *Piers Plowman* are *very* different poems. Langland's dream-vision ranges over a landscape that's as deep the human psyche, as high as the hope of heaven, and as wide as the universe itself: his "fair field full of folk" whom we see from a great distance, moving around like the small figures in a Brueghel painting, is this world and all our business here, suspended in a little space between heaven and hell. *The Canterbury Tales,* on the other hand, is a delightfully realistic story from contemporary life. The pilgrims set out from a particular inn in Chaucer's own London (the inn's host, Harry Bailey, was a real person). And the stories they tell are full of more characters that seem just like real people. Reading "The Miller's Tale" or "The Wife of Bath's Prologue," you almost think you've been in fourteenth-century England.

But either poem is a doorway into a world that was *very* politically incorrect. Middle English literature shows us a society that was thoroughly—even officially—Christian. People actually believed that they had immortal souls, and they took a lively interest in the question of whether they (and other people) were going to be spending eternity in heaven or hell. In medieval England, religious conformity actually *was* enforced by the government. Everybody knew, as the narrator of *Piers Plowman* men-

---

What They Don't Want You to Learn from the English Literature of the Middle Ages

A thoroughly (even officially) religious society doesn't have to be a brutally repressive theocracy.

tions, that you could be burned for heresy. Relations between the sexes were organized on startlingly unenlightened principles, backed up by religious authority. Men and women were understood to have been created with different natures, for different roles: wives were supposed to obey their husbands.

Fourteenth-century England ought to be the real-life version of the horror story that the secularists warn is imminent whenever the de-Christianization of American society is slowed down a little (when anyone suggests mentioning Intelligent Design in biology class, say, or some minuscule percentage of our tax burden is diverted into "faith-based" programs). And yet the England we glimpse in Middle English literature is nothing like our modern intellectuals' fears about what a really Christian society would look like. Our chattering classes routinely put conservative Christianity in the same "religious fundamentalist" category as the Taliban. And one reason they can get away with it is because of widespread ignorance about the past of Western society—an ignorance due, in no small part, to English professors' neglect of English literature.

The Canterbury Tales vs. The Handmaid's Tale

Among the many third-rate books that English professors waste their students' time on (when they could be teaching truly great English literature) is Margaret Atwood's 1986 *The Handmaid's Tale,*[2] whose title is modeled on the names for the individual tales within Chaucer's *Canterbury Tales*—"The Merchant's Tale," "The Nun's Priest's Tale," and so forth. *The Handmaid's Tale* is the quintessential expression of our intellectuals' fears about what a truly Christian culture would look like. It is set in a dystopic near future, after a coup by fundamentalist Christians has turned the United States into the Republic of Gilead. In Gilead, abortionists and heretics are executed, feminists are exiled to the colonies to clean up radioactive waste, and ordinary *Cosmo*-girl types are, after a brutal reeducation, reduced to serving as "handmaids" in (otherwise) traditional families suffering from infertility. As a "handmaid," a young woman is subjected to joyless and impersonal sex with the man of the household—in the presence of his wife, no less—for procreative purposes.

To anyone who's read many stories of the victims of real totalitarian regimes, *The Handmaid's Tale* is disappointing, to say the least. The trials of the heroine, Offred (*of Fred,* that is; her identity has been erased; she's known only by the name of the man whose household she belongs to), are mostly familiar, and gruesome enough. She's subjected to many of the horrors you can read about in Aleksandr Solzhenitsyn's accounts of life in the Soviet prison and labor camp system. The man she loves is shot and her child is torn from her arms; she spends years not knowing whether they are alive or dead. She is physically abused, and she sees friends and strangers brutalized and killed. She is forced to choose between dying in a labor camp and selling her body (and soul) for survival and a little physical comfort.

But her response to these events is anticlimactic. The heroine of *The Handmaid's Tale* remembers panty hose and nail polish with longing. She risks brutal punishment to hide butter in her shoe, to use in lieu of the forbidden moisturizing lotion. The man whose "handmaid" she is seduces her into an illicit relationship outside the limits of the prescribed procreational sex and rewards her by allowing her to read his secret stash of outlawed women's magazines, *Vogues* and *Mademoiselles,* and she finds them more fascinating than ever. The sense you get from reading Solzhenitsyn—or Frederick Douglass's *Narrative* of his life as a slave—that great suffering lays bare significant realities neglected in prosperity—is conspicuous by its absence.

English professors, I'm sorry to report, write scholarly articles and books on *The Handmaid's Tale.* They teach the novel in college classes. And they join "the Margaret Atwood Society," "an international association of scholars, teachers and students who share an interest in Atwood's work."[3] At the most recent meeting of the Modern Language Association (the big annual conference for professors of literature in English and other modern languages), there were three sessions devoted to Atwood's works—coincidentally, the exact same number as were devoted to the works of Geoffrey Chaucer. One web-published study guide to *The Handmaid's Tale,* by Washington State University's English professor Paul Brians, illustrates just why it's such a bad idea for English departments to replace classic English literature with PC novels from the 1980s.

Brians doesn't appear to be an especially radical professor. In fact, compared to the folks on the real cutting edge, he's a model of common sense, particularly on the subject of English usage.[4] The English department at Washington State University is no top-ranked magnet for the latest fads in postmodernism, like Yale in the '70s or Duke in the '80s. Brians's study guide to *The Handmaid's Tale* is a pretty typical example of what college students today can expect to learn from their English professors. What's deplorable is how that typical lesson *widens* the gulf between the students and the culture of the West, instead of transmitting Western culture to the next generation.

The dreary world of *The Handmaid's Tale*

Below are selected questions and information from Professor Brians's study guide to *The Handmaid's Tale.*[5] Brians does a fine job of bringing out the themes of Atwood's novel, such as they are. As he shows, Atwood's dystopia combines aspects of radical Islam with elements of twentieth-century conservative Christianity and features of the pre-feminist past of Western, Christian Civilization—of the Middle Ages, in particular.

> Serena Joy's speechmaking on behalf of housewifery is a clear satire on the career of Phyllis Shlafley [sic]. . . .

In what era were Bibles routinely sequestered from the general population?

Why is women's pleasure in sex no longer valued?

The Soul Scroll machines . . . are also reminiscent of the old Catholic practice of paying priests to say prayers for the repose of the dead.

The law prohibiting the ownership of property by women reinstates the law as it stood in the nineteenth century and earlier. Many of the extreme aspects of Giladean culture have actually existed in the past.

Arranged marriages seem hopelessly exotic to many Americans, but in Western civilization they were the rule rather than the exception until a couple of centuries ago.

The reference to Iran is of course the most pointed, because of that nation's conservative Islamic revolution which involved strenuous demodernizing and drastic restrictions on the freedom of women.

Prof. Pieixoto's talk is of a type familiar to literary historians: the attempt to connect a the [sic] author of a text with some historical person known from other records, particularly in Medieval studies.

Students whose knowledge of the Middle Ages and the nineteenth century is derived from lessons like this—as it will be, if they study English with professors who prefer Margaret Atwood to Chaucer and Jane Austen—will have their ignorance of our past confirmed, rather than corrected. They'll leave college under the impression that life in the Middle

Ages resembled life in the Republic of Gilead: Bibles were "routinely sequestered from the common people" and used for oppressive purposes by theocratic elites. Women's sexual pleasure was not "valued" in an era of arranged marriages. Women's inability to own property made them the powerless dependents of men. Medieval religious practices were meaningless, inhuman rituals that contributed to soul-destroying conditions under which women led wretched lives pretty much like those of Atwood's suicidal "handmaids."

But if instead of being taught *The Handmaid's Tale* college students read *The Canterbury Tales* under the guidance of professors as sympathetic to Chaucer as Professor Brians is to Atwood, they'd get a very different impression of the Christian Middle Ages. Medieval literature is nothing at all like what you expect if you go into it with the impression that an explicitly Christian society must be some kind of totalitarian nightmare.

The English literature of the Middle Ages creates an overwhelming impression of irrepressible bounty, a kind of burgeoning fullness that won't be contained within any bounds. *The Canterbury Tales* are everything that's diametrically opposed to the bleak, flattened world of *The Handmaid's Tale,* and Chaucer's pilgrims are nothing like Atwood's dreary, pinched characters. The tales Chaucer's pilgrims tell, and the story he tells about them, do certainly contain ugly realities: bitter poverty, violence (including, certainly, violence between men and women), and every vice known to human nature. But these things are only parts of a rich and lively picture of the enormous variety of human experience. The seventeeth-century English poet John Dryden wrote the most accurate description of what reading Chaucer is like: "Not a single character has escaped him.... There is such a variety of game springing up before me, that I am distracted in my choice, and known not which to follow. 'Tis sufficient to say, according to the proverb, that here is God's plenty."[6]

The fecundity of medieval art

The abundance that readers find in *The Canterbury Tales* is due in part to Chaucer's individual genius: what Dryden calls his "most wonderful comprehensive nature." But Chaucer was most definitely a man of his own age (though also most definitely not a man only *for* his own age). His excellences are highly characteristic of his own time and his own country. *Piers Plowman* has a very different flavor from *The Canterbury Tales,* but it too is huge, teeming with life. In some ways it seems to be painted on even a broader canvas than Chaucer's, and to be populated by an even wider range of lively and expressive characters. The world of *Piers Plowman* is outsized, gargantuan, apocalyptic, taking in the whole world, all of human history, even heaven and hell—and it always seems to be opening up a new window onto yet higher heights, deeper depths, or wider vistas.[7]

You could say this kind of beauty—of layers within layers, a great plethora of things that can't be contained or ever accounted for, of detail that continues to surprise and delight because there can be no end to discovering more of it—was in the air of late medieval Europe, especially in the northern countries. The excellence characteristic of this literature has something in common with the aesthetic appeal of some of the pictures in the *Tres Riches Heures du Duc de Berry,* the first of which were painted in France about ten years after Chaucer's death, and of the paintings by Hieronymus Bosch or of Pieter Brueghel the Elder in the next two centuries. In contrast to the great art of the Italian Renaissance, these northern European paintings are appealing by virtue of an abundance of tiny individual figures—some of which are beautiful or interesting in themselves, others of which (especially in Bosch) are definitely nasty, but all of which together make up a great, glittering, endlessly fascinating panorama.[8]

A pre-classical aesthetic

But why is this particular kind of aesthetic pleasure characteristic of the art, music, and literature originating in this time and this place? One possible answer is that medieval art is, in a sense, a pre-classical art.[9] There's *room* in medieval English literature for things that no literature written according to classical rules of unity, restraint, and harmony could contain. In the first stages of the growth of an art, complexity is difficult to achieve, and people prize intricate decoration. As time goes on and the art is refined according to classical canons, artists aim for discrimination and elegance, instead.[10] All art requires *some* selection or streamlining of life, but the critical inquiry that reduces that selection to rules comes late in the development of an artistic tradition.

Both the perils and the characteristic excellences of a pre-classical aesthetic are illustrated by Chaucer. Chaucer himself pokes fun at the formlessness of medieval tragedy in his "Monk's Tale." Until the Knight finally stops him (with the Host's enthusiastic support), Chaucer's monk seems set to tell the entire history of the world (beginning with Lucifer and Adam) as an unrelievedly monotonous series of stories about falls from prosperity and happiness.

The rules of classical tragedy—the unity that limits its scope, and the structure that gives it shape—would exclude "The Monk's Tale." But they would also exclude Chaucer's beautiful *Troilus and Criseyde.* The classical definition of tragedy is in Aristotle's *Poetics.* According to Aristotle, tragedy is about the reversal in the fortunes of a man of high estate (Oedipus, for example, the king of Thebes who discovers that he has killed his father and married his mother and blinds himself when he sees the truth). But Troilus doesn't suffer a sudden and dramatic reversal in fortune. Instead, C. S. Lewis points out, *Troilus and Criseyde,* succeeds in capturing, as no classical tragedy does, a bitterly painful kind of sorrow that

A Book You're Not Supposed to Read

The Allegory of Love: A Study in Medieval Tradition by C. S. Lewis, Oxford University Press, 1959.

ordinary people experience in the normal course of life.[11] Troilus discovers slowly, with increasing misery—as he waits for Criseyde, and she never comes to meet him—that she must be unfaithful.

Troilus's tragedy is just one thing that there's room for in medieval literature because its standards are so free and easy. The sheer number, and many different kinds, of people—if we define "people" very loosely—that populate medieval literature also add enormously to its richness.

In the light of eternity

You might think the moralism and otherworldliness of medieval Christianity would suck all the color, vigor, and interest out of life in this world. Christians in the Middle Ages insisted on seeing everything *sub specie aeternitas,* that is, considered in the light of eternity. This life on earth, they believed, is as the twinkling of an eye compared with our eternal life after death, and the happiness or misery we feel here is as nothing compared with either the inexpressible joys of heaven or the endless pains of hell. Medieval literature constantly underlines this fact—as, for example, in the late medieval morality play *Everyman*. The entire plot of the play is that Everyman discovers that everything he has in the world— his earthly goods, his fellowship with his friends, his family—deserts him in the hour of his death.

Christians in the Middle Ages also insisted on thinking and talking perpetually about morality. And the literary device they used for writing about this favorite topic of theirs was allegory. Allegory is *the* typical medieval literary device. Sometimes it's very thoroughgoing. Of the *dra-*

matic personae of *Everyman*, for example, only a handful are even arguably concrete individuals (and most of *them* are sketchy and anonymous enough). Besides God, there's an unnamed angel, an unnamed learned doctor, an unnamed messenger who introduces the piece, and Everyman's unnamed cousin. The rest of the cast are Everyman himself, plus Death, Fellowship, Kindred, Goods, Good Deeds, Knowledge, Confession, Beauty, Strength, Discretion, and Five Wits.

But rather than reducing everything to monotone abstraction , allegory in medieval literature makes available a whole new cast of characters who seem as concrete and lively as flesh-and-blood people. "Cousin" can't accompany Everyman to the Final Judgment because she's stubbed her toe. The thugs in Chaucer's "Pardoner's Tale" envision "Death" as a dishonest rogue who has murdered their evil-living friends, and on whom they plan to take revenge. (They do find him—but finding Death turns out to be different from what they thought.) "Gluttony" in *Piers Plowman* sets out to go to Confession, but he gets sidetracked when an alewife tells him what she has on offer in her pub. "Sloth" in the same poem falls asleep in the middle of his prayers (in any case, he doesn't really know even the Our Father properly—though he knows lots of ballads about Robin Hood).

Medieval otherworldliness adds yet another cast of characters. The Devil makes regular appearances—in Chaucer's "Friar's Tale," for example—as do angels and saints. Paradoxically, the medieval fascination with the afterlife and fondness for moral allegory people medieval literature with extra layers upon layers of robust and fascinating characters.

Alongside the visitors from heaven and hell are quite realistic human beings (some of them contemporary, many of them drawn from Bible stories and from classical history), plus a host of other kinds of persons we hardly think of and never tell stories about: pagan gods and goddesses, and animals who (as you learn if you wear the magic ring that gives you the power of understanding the language of birds) turn out to have very human love lives. All these characters mix freely with one another in medieval literature. And the poets aren't worried by anachronisms or other incongruities. Old Testament characters in medieval plays refer to the Blessed Virgin Mary, and to Christ's death on the Cross (which it's hard to see how they could have known about). In Chaucer's "Merchant's Tale" the ancient pagan goddess Proserpina swears by "very God, that nys but one"—that is, the one true God.

Christianity and freedom

But the overwhelming sense of freedom and burgeoning life in medieval literature is about more than this cast of thousands, and more than the pre-classical looseness of form and flexibility about historical accuracy. It's also about a certain kind of freedom of thought that Christianity made possible. We're so skittish about the repressive potential of Christianity that we're reluctant to "impose our religion" on other people even to the extent of telling what them we believe. Religious and moral questions are relegated to the private sphere. Our public religious disputes are all meta-arguments—about, say, whether allowing manger scenes on public property is compatible with religious freedom. We appeal to scientific expertise for solutions to our practical problems, without reference to what the ultimate purpose of human existence may be, if any.

Things were very different in the Middle Ages. Argument about the fundamental things was the characteristic activity of the medieval mind. Medieval people didn't just quarrel, they also argued from reason and authority. The Wife of Bath argues from experience, but also from Scripture, that marriage (even up to five times) is a good thing. Pluto and Proserpina in "The Merchant's Tale" disagree about women's virtue and appeal to the Bible and the lives of the virgin martyrs. The cock and hen in "The Nun's Priest's Tale" engage in a learned dispute about the significance of dreams. And Chaucer's two long prose tales—

"The Tale of Melibee" and "The Parson's Tale"—are intricate arguments, the first on the morality of revenge and forgiveness, and the second on penance for sins, with each subject considered from every possible point of view.

Chaucer's characters are often rationalizing when they argue, and sometimes they're engaging in cynical bids to manipulate other people. But they live in a world where people believe that rational argument *cannot* always be reduced to rationalization. Medieval people took it for granted that the human mind was capable of reaching the truth on moral and religious matters. They believed in reason, and they saw debate as a legitimate method for sorting out what the truth was.

Their belief in the power of reason to arrive at the truth—and also, hard as it may be for us to understand, their belief in religious authority—gave the English of the Middle Ages a kind of freedom that's the opposite of totalitarian oppression. We think of authority as some power imposing on us despite our free will; a medieval man was more likely to think of

A Book You're Not Supposed to Read

The Victory of Reason: How Christianity Led to Freedom, Capitalism, and Western Success by Rodney Stark, Random House, 2005.

authority as a solid place to stand, even as a secure defense against arbitrary power. When the author of *Piers Plowman* brings up the fact that heretics can be burnt at the stake, it's in order to say, essentially: Go ahead and burn me if I'm wrong about this; what I'm saying is right here in the Bible. The religious authorities might make mistakes or abuse their office; they could persecute the wrong person, who would be vindicated later (as they did Joan of Arc, for example, in the century after Chaucer). But their authority was grounded in a truth that was greater than their own power, and that was, in some sense, accessible to every individual, even the most powerless.

Separation of church and state, medieval style

The political situation in medieval England reflected these beliefs. While the English in the Middle Ages certainly didn't have religious freedom, they did have a very practical kind of separation of Church and State. The king of England was, in theory, a vassal of the pope. But the king and noblemen—the State—had the real and overwhelming power on the ground. Then again, if the king exceeded his authority or behaved viciously, he could be rebuked and even disciplined by the Church. The disapproval of the religious authorities was an actual check on government power: If the king was condemned by the pope he could lose the loyalty of his subjects.

Throughout the Middle Ages, State and Church in England were in a low-intensity conflict that occasionally erupted into a major confrontation. Thomas of Canterbury (a.k.a. Thomas Becket), the saint whose shrine Chaucer's pilgrims were on their way to, was the most famous casualty of this long-running conflict. Thomas asserted the rights of the Church too strongly for Henry II's taste and was killed at the behest of the king, who later—to get himself back into the good graces of the Church, and of his own Christian people—did public penance at Thomas's tomb. The tug of war between State and Church authority in England never entirely ended until Henry VIII succeeded in breaking the Church's power: naturally, he had St. Thomas's shrine at Canterbury destroyed.

It's fatal to any totalitarian project for people to believe that there is an authority that they can appeal to over the heads of the political power. That's why totalitarian governments cannot tolerate religion.[12] The postmodernist pretense that all authority is just a mask for raw power and that all reasoning is only rationalization is no defense at all against oppression—in fact, it can be a justification for it. Christianity, in contrast, is a guarantor of individual human freedom, not a threat to it. And the "plenty" of medieval English literature testifies to that freedom.

John Ruskin, writing in the nineteenth century, theorized about the differences between classical and medieval architecture.[13] Both the Parthenon and the cathedrals of the Middle Ages are great works of art. But, Ruskin argued, the slave culture of the ancient world was necessary to create the particular *kind* of great work the Parthenon is. Its perfection depends on a division of labor that allows creative freedom only to the greatest artists. In ancient Greece the master craftsman made all the really delicate and creative work on a great building. His was the only hand that was really free. Lesser craftsmen followed the master's designs slavishly, accomplishing only the simpler tasks that they could be trusted to bring to perfection.

The medieval cathedrals, Ruskin explained, were built differently. Even the humblest craftsman had free rein for his skills—if only to carve an ugly gargoyle in a dark corner. ***The perfection of the work as a whole was sacrificed for the freedom of the individual craftsman***. And yet the many individual and imperfect creations, which cause the whole building to fall short of perfection, somehow give it a kind of beauty that's different from perfection. It's the same beauty as medieval literature has: a reflection of the amazing variety of the human race and the infinite value and interest of each of its members—each individual created in God's image and redeemed by His Son, each one, no matter how humble, capable of knowing the truth with his own reason, and each one moving through this life toward infinite sorrow or, with the help of God's grace, toward eternal bliss.

The argument from authority

In their hammer-and-tongs arguments, medieval characters are always appealing to ancient wisdom. They took *very literally* the advice in the fifteenth chapter of the Epistle to the Romans, paraphrased thus by Chaucer's Nun's Priest at the end of his tale: "For St. Paul saith that all that written is, / To our doctrine it is yrwrite, iwis [I know]." When St.

Paul recommended everything written in the past as valuable for our learning, he seems to have meant the Holy Scriptures. But when the Nun's Priest applies St. Paul, he's recommending *literally* "all that written is"—including the beast fable he has just told about a rooster, his hen, and a marauding fox—as material to learn from.

Sometimes the characters in medieval literature appear to be trying to live by the advice of everyone who lived before them in world history. It's very easy to look down your nose at medieval people's uncritical respect for ancient wisdom—until you start comparing some of the actual advice they picked up from their authorities to the things people believe today. Take, for example, the question of what we now call "date rape." The conventional wisdom today is "'No' means no." Anyone who says a word against getting drunk and going to a young man's dorm room is "blaming the victim." The medieval advice to young women was quite different: If you want to stay chaste, don't get drunk: "For wine and youth doth Venus encrease / As men on fire will cast oil or grease."[14] Which bit of wisdom is more likely to help a young woman who is in danger of sleeping with a man and feeling used afterwards?

The characters in medieval literature—Chanticleer and Pertelote in "The Nun's Priests's Tale," or Melibee and his wife in "The Tale of Melibee"—who quote Seneca, the Book of Job, and Ovid's love poetry at each other a mile a minute whenever a marital disagreement or a personal decision comes up, can seem pretty silly. But are they really any sillier than twenty-first-century people who change their exercise plans, their brands of make-up, and their childrearing practices according to the tips

What Else They Don't Want You to Learn from Medieval English Literature

The wisdom of the past beats the latest expert opinion, hands down.

in women's magazines? Seneca and the Book of Job are at least time-tested. Those ancient authorities might introduce us to ideas (new and different to us) that we'll never stumble across in *Self* or *Redbook*.

The invention of chivalry

In Chaucer's day women were (at least theoretically) subject to all those traditional constraints the feminists try to frighten us with, whenever anyone questions whether feminism has been a net gain for human happiness: arranged marriage, wifely obedience, the husband's control of the marital property. But somehow these conditions have not flattened and bleached Chaucer's women à la *The Handmaid's Tale*—or the feminists' fantasies about the "erasure" of female desire. *The Canterbury Tales* are full of female characters (the Wife of Bath, among the pilgrims, and characters in several of the tales) who choose husbands or lovers, are disobedient, exert control over their husbands' money, and have a very healthy interest in sex.[15] There is, admittedly, talk in the *Tales* about women whose shrinking from love and sex is in some sense typically feminine;[16] but some of it's tongue-in-cheek. As the Man of Law explains, *Though wives are very holy things, they must take patiently at night the kinds of things that are pleasing to the folk that have wedded them with rings, and lay their holiness aside, a little, just for the time.*

Chaucer pokes fun at the kind of man who is so deluded about a woman's innocent, shrinking-violent nature as to imagine that his physical attentions will be too much for her. The aged and ridiculous January in "The Merchant's Tale" fantasizes that his lovemaking will overpower his fresh young bride May: "Alas," he says to himself as he watches May at the wedding feast, "O tender creature, now I would to God you might well endure all my courage—it is so sharp and keen, I'm afraid you won't be able to sustain it." In the event, May is underwhelmed. After a vigorous wedding night—in part thanks to the "spices hot" (the medieval

What They Don't Want You to Learn from *The Canterbury Tales*

Traditional sex roles did not silence women, erase their sexuality, or blot out their personalities.

approximation of Viagra) that January has swallowed to increase his "courage"—the old man sits up in bed to sing. As he sings, the slack skin around his neck shakes, and the narrator lets us know exactly what his bride, seeing him in his nightcap, thinks of his lovemaking: in her opinion, it's not "worth a bean."

The tender creature that January was so afraid of hurting is much more enthusiastic about Damian, a young squire. January goes blind and keeps May with him constantly, out of jealousy. But she manages first to arrange for Damian to hide in January's private walled garden, then to persuade her husband to take her there for a private picnic, and finally to get January to help her up into a pear tree on the pretense of picking some fruit—where Damian is waiting to take immediate advantage of the situation. Unfortunately for the lovers, January regains his eyesight at the worst possible moment. How May is able to persuade her husband to believe her story, rather than his own eyes, beggars belief; you have to read Chaucer himself to get the full flavor of his delightful portrait of female ingenuity—more than that, of serene feminine self-confidence—in a very tight spot.

Chaucer's tales are full of resourceful women who seem quite competent to manage the men in their lives, despite the disadvantages they labor under. Their husbands' superior physical strength, ownership of all the marital property, and positions as the heads of their households (with the right to command their wives' obedience, backed up by the religious endorsement of their husbandly authority)—none of it seems to be a match for the women's psychological and verbal cleverness.[17]

But not all the marriages in *The Canterbury Tales* are conducted along these battle-of-the-sexes, survival-of-the-fittest lines. Something else students of English literature might be learning about from Chaucer, if more of them were studying him, is the value of chivalry, the uniquely Western arrangement between the sexes.

Feminists, of course, pretend that putting women on a pedestal somehow really demeans them. The courtesy that distinguishes women for the special attention and respect of men is supposed to be an insidious tool for keeping women subordinate to men. But the extraordinary respect and freedom that women enjoy in the Western world is difficult to explain according to this feminist criticism of chivalry. It's in the West that—for some centuries, now—a man has been seen as a real man only insofar as he is gentle with women.[18] If courtesy helps enslave women, we ought to be less, not more, free where it prevails. But we're not.

And one crucial reason that we're not is something you can actually see happening in the literature of the Middle Ages. The emergence of chivalry in the West is one case in which Shelley's grandiose statement that "poets are the unacknowledged legislators of the world" seems to be literally true. The chivalric attitude toward women didn't begin as an ideal for marriage, much less as a set of rules for the treatment of all women by all men. In Chaucer's time chivalrous love was still more a literary fad than a pervasive feature of society. You get a feel for its faddish quality in the person and tale of Chaucer's Squire, who dresses and behaves according to the latest fashion,[19] and talks about love as something that only the smart set knows all about. The Squire assures us, *A dull man would not even be able to describe the subtle looks and dissemblings that the young people in his story engage in; only a man who knows love and love's service would know what was really going on.*

Courtly love was originally almost a hobby, a kind of game for the leisured upper class. What inspired it in the first place is murky. Courtly love clearly would never have been invented without Christianity: the special role of the Blessed Virgin Mary doubtless played a part in its development, as did the Christian insistence on monogamy and on *male*

A Feminist Explains (Away) Chivalry

"As the sociologist Hugo Beigel has observed, both the courtly and the romantic versions of love are 'grants' which the male concedes out of his total power. Both have had the effect of obscuring the patriarchal character of Western culture and in their general tendency to attribute impossible virtues to women, have ended by confirming them in a narrow and often remarkably conscribing sphere of behavior."

Kate Millett, *Sexual Politics* (Garden City, New York: Doubleday, 1970), 37, citing Hugo Biegel, "Romantic Love," *The American Sociological Review* 16 (1951): 331. Millett is a well-known "second-wave" feminist whose work is cited by English professors—for example, Washington State University English professor Michael Delahoyd (see http://www.wsu.edu/~delahoyd/medieval/love.html viewed 7/4/2006)—for the feminist take on courtly love.

chastity, both of which tend to elevate women. Just as clearly, courtly love has something to do with the feudal organization of medieval Europe, which in its turn had been shaped by the old code of loyalty between the barbarian Germanic warrior and his lord.

The rules of courtly love are clearer than its origins. In its original conception, it had nothing to do with courtship in the ordinary sense. The courtly lover aimed not at marriage but rather at an adulterous liaison with a woman high above him, almost certainly beyond his reach. The fact that the lady was married added to the hopelessness (or near hopelessness) of his passion. The courtly lover was his lady's abject slave. He was mortally injured by the sight of her beauty, and only her favor could save him. From an attitude of perfect humility, the lover begged his lady to take pity on him, lest he die of love for her.

What Chaucer shows us in *The Canterbury Tales* is not courtly love in its pure form, but courtly love trickling down into the rest of society, and especially into the institution of marriage. It's not hard to see why the humble service of the courtly lover—once it was invented in the first place—should be something that a wife (especially a medieval wife pledged to obedience) might like to see in her husband. And that's what Chaucer shows us in his *Tales*: women who see courtesy as a great improvement over the traditional, pre-chivalrous arrangements between men and women.[20] From our point of view, the really fascinating thing about the mixture of courtly love with marriage is how different the resulting hybrid institution—which we could call the courteous or chivalrous marriage—is from the modern feminist-inspired ideal: the marriage of equality.

Take, for example, the ideally chivalrous marriage between Dorigen and Arveragus in "The Franklin's Tale." Dorigen seems to possess what the old woman in "The Wife of Bath's Tale" claims is every woman's dearest wish: *Women desire to have sovereignty over their husbands just as over their lovers.*

Dorigen is quite impatient with courtly love in its classic form. When a young squire named Aurelius gets up his courage to express his secret passion for her, she tells him he's making a fool of himself. In her practical feminine way she finds the whole thing incomprehensible: *What pleasure can it possibly be to him,* she asks, *to go and love the wife of another man, who can have her body whenever he wants?*

But Dorigen's marriage to Arveragus seems to have come into being in the first place on some higher and less practical plane. Arveragus has won Dorigen's love, and her hand in marriage, by just the kind of feelings and behavior that a lover owed his unattainable lady in the courtly love tradition. Arveragus "did his pain / To serve his lady in his best wise / And many a labour, many a greet emprise / He for his lady wrought, ere she were won." But finally she had pity on him—because of his worthiness, but also because of his "obeysaunce." And then the two of them came to a private agreement. She agreed to take him as her husband and her lord. And he agreed that he would never exercise his right as her husband to command her against her will. He would obey her in everything, as any lover would his lady, except that he would keep up the outward appearance of mastery, as a husband. Arveragus's generosity as a lover inspires Dorigen to promise to be a meek wife: "Sir, I will be your humble true wife." "Thus," the Franklin tells us, "been they both in quiet and in rest."

The modern ideal for marriage, sold to us by the feminists, is that no one should have to obey anyone in a marriage. Power and hierarchy, they tell us, can be escaped altogether; men and women can relate to one another on an equal footing. Everything about sex is infinitely negotiable at the whim of the participants: there are no fixed roles for men or women, and the terms of a relationship can be reworked as necessary, to suit both parties' changing feelings. The relationship itself should last only as long as both parties find that it fulfills their individual needs and aspirations.

The medieval mind was hierarchical rather than egalitarian, and communal rather than individualist. The people of the Middle Ages believed that relationships required a hierarchical structure in order exist at all. (Thus the necessity for obedience in any religious community.)

They also had a greater respect for the inherent power of sex than we do. The feminist mantra, "Rape isn't about sex; rape is about power," would have made very little sense to them. Sex itself is pretty clearly "about power" in *The Canterbury Tales*—and not just about the power of men over women, or of women over men. There are also some ugly power plays in the *Tales* between old and young ("The Merchant's Tale"), attractive and nerdy ("The Miller's Tale"), sadistic and patient ("The Clerk's Tale"), powerful and weak ("The Physician's Tale"), and clever and brutal ("The Reeve's Tale"). Medieval people saw sexual experience as something with the power to change people forever.[21] And, living before the invention of effective contraception, they naturally had more trouble than we do forgetting about the procreative power of sex.

There are some obvious disadvantages to the modern equality-style sexual relationship. It doesn't keep up connections between people (men and women, children and fathers) as well as traditional marriage. Also, it has become painfully clear, women are at a disadvantage competing for what we want out of love and sex on an absolutely equal playing field: apart from anything else, we're fertile and sexually attractive for a shorter period of time than men. The one unanswerable selling point for the equality model, despite its wretched failures, is that there's no acceptable alternative. Do we really want (the feminists ask) to go back to the bad old days when men had all the power and women were their slaves?

The Canterbury Tales reveals that there once *was* an alternative solution—and that chivalry, when it was first applied to marriage, was something different from the traditional ideal of wifely obedience,[22] and also different from the breakdown of that ideal into the battle of the sexes. The courteous marriage Chaucer gives us in "The Franklin's Tale" is not about the traditional arrangement in which men command and women either obey or scheme to deceive. Nor is it about equality. It's about mutual service, obedience, and obligation. It doesn't pretend, as we sometimes do, that men and women are just the same, or that people can live in a sexual relationship without truly giving or absolutely losing anything—even without changing one another at all.

We pretend that *no one* will have to be obedient in order to love. In the marriage of courtesy, *both* husband and wife have to. The chivalrous marriage is a marriage based on *more* service and *more* obedience than a simply traditional marriage.

Because Arveragus shows Dorigen that he will serve and obey her as her lover, she can trust him enough to obey him as his wife. He is her "Servant in love and lord in marriage," and both husband and wife are pledged to patience with each other, and rewarded with happiness. Something very much like this scheme (a man was supposed to treat his wife with the courtesy and respect due a lady, and she was supposed to respect his authority) was the prevailing ideal for marriage in the West until—well, until feminists in the twentieth century sold us on their theory that chivalry was really just a tool for oppressing women. Why would feminist English professors want us to know any more about it?

> ## What Else They Don't Want You to Learn from Chaucer
>
> Chivalry is one of the great inventions of Western culture, and it has contributed enormously to women's happiness.

Chapter Three

THE RENAISSANCE
Christian Humanism

What a piece of work is man! How noble in reason! How infinite in faculty! In form and moving, how express and admirable! In action how like an angel! In apprehension, how like a god! The beauty of the world, the paragon of animals....

—Shakespeare, *Hamlet*

Humanism is, in some sense, essential to Christian culture. After all, the central claim of the gospel is that in order to save us from our sins God became Man. The Incarnation has enormous implications for the dignity of the human being, and those implications weren't missed in the Middle Ages. Thomas Aquinas, the great thirteenth-century philosopher and theologian—not often thought of as a humanist—said, "In fact, the only-begotten Son of God, wanting us to be partakers in His divinity, assumed our nature, so that He, made Man, might make men gods."[1]

But "humanism" is a term we usually use to describe the Renaissance attitude toward man. In Italy beginning in the 1300s, and across the rest of Europe in the next two centuries, man seemed to become larger somehow. He was suddenly more interesting to himself. He could spread himself in a way that he hadn't been able to afford in the Middle Ages. Man suddenly seemed to fill the whole world stage.

This change had many causes. The economy, technology, and cultural achievements of Europe had been growing, sometimes steadily, sometimes

The Renaissance literature you must not miss

Edmund Spenser, *The Faerie Queene*

Philip Sidney, *Defense of Poesy*

Chrisopher Marlowe, *Doctor Faustus* and *The Jew of Malta*

William Shakespeare, *The Taming of the Shrew, As You Like It, Twelfth Night, The Merchant of Venice, The Tempest, Henry IV (Parts I and II), Henry V, Hamlet,*

continued on p. 50

The Renaissance literature you must not miss (continued)

Macbeth, Othello, King Lear, and *Sonnets*

by leaps and bounds, since the Dark Ages. Techniques in the arts were continually improving, and these successes eventually reached a kind of critical mass. Most dramatically, painting, sculpture, and architecture went from strength to strength. There came a point at which artists thought of what they were doing less in terms of continuation or gradual improvement and more in terms of making something really new. Eventually, Italian painters and sculptors (Leonardo da Vinci and Michelangelo among them) equaled and even surpassed their Greek and Roman models in the realistic representation of men and women. Scholars no longer worked to preserve the wisdom of their fathers or carefully add to it, but rather to correct the errors and scrape away the accretions of the recent (medieval) past in order to get back to the language and the models of classical times.

This sense of a break with the past and a revolution in the direction of classical culture was not as dramatic in northern Europe. But by the time the Renaissance arrived in England,[2] the English had experienced another break with their past that was, in part, an attempt to recover the original Christian faith of classical times: the Protestant Reformation. Henry VIII introduced the Reformation (or such elements of it as he found convenient to his ends) into England beginning in 1534. By the time Shakespeare was writing, England had suffered through half a century of bloody changes back and forth between Catholicism and Protestantism. What was the state religion under Henry's son Edward was heresy under Henry's daughter Mary, and then the state religion again under his younger daughter Elizabeth; the loyalty to the pope that made you a good Catholic subject to Queen Mary made you a traitor to Queen Elizabeth.

The Reformation had complex and various effects on the English people, but it's fair to say that both English Protestants (the majority, when all the changes finally shook out) and English Catholics (reduced to a persecuted minority under Elizabeth) ended up with a religious experience that feels stripped down and simplified in comparison with medieval Christianity: the Reformation faith and the Counter-Reformation faith, each in its own way, was focused in a more concentrated way on the Man Jesus. The Reformation both disturbed[3] and inspired[4] the imaginations of English poets, as did something else that had intervened between the dawn of the Renaissance in Italy and the English Renaissance: the discovery of the New World.

The discovery of America seemed to enlarge the world.[5] And the people the Europeans found there inspired them to think about *themselves* in a different way. Shakespeare's *The Tempest* is one fruit of European man's novel self-consciousness. Meeting (relatively) uncivilized human beings set the Europeans thinking about civilization and human nature— about what is natural to man, what artificial.

And it wasn't just the New World that Renaissance man saw as an object for conquest. He conceived the ambition to discover nature's secrets and harness her great powers for his own use. The Renaissance fascination with magic was one expression of this ambition; the new experimental science was another. Francis Bacon, for example, advised his contemporaries to put nature on the rack to make her tell her secrets. Bacon, like Machiavelli, wanted to redirect people's attention from the question of what they *should* do to the question of what they *could* do. Bacon's *Advancement of Learning* and *New Organon* suggested that resources devoted to theology, philosophy, and the subjects we now think of as the humanities could be more profitably devoted to what was at first called "the new philosophy" (which we call science)—the project to master nature for "the relief of man's estate," the improvement of living conditions in this world. This strain of Renaissance humanism that is about man's ambition for mastery was an especially powerful influence on the work of Christopher Marlowe, the great playwright who was just two months older than Shakespeare, but whose career is contemporaneous only with Shakespeare's early plays—because of Marlowe's mysterious death at age twenty-nine.

Christopher Marlowe

Christopher Marlowe is popular with the kind of English professor whose highest term of praise is "transgressive." These folks believe that the main point of art is to break taboos, to violate boundaries, to upset conventions (and the kind of people who live by them), and to call into question any limit—especially any moral limit—that confines us.

Marlowe's (alleged) atheism is one reason for his appeal to these folks; his (probable) homosexuality is another; his (nearly certain) involvement in the shady underworld of Elizabethan England is yet another. But the literature he wrote—especially his plays, which are second only to Shakespeare's in their power and the fineness of their poetry—is well worth knowing even if you don't share these interests. In the six short years before his violent and untimely death, Marlowe wrote a handful of dramatic masterpieces, each one built around a villain-hero who defies God and man in pursuit of some overreaching ambition or stubborn passion. These protagonists are Renaissance men who have got the bit between their teeth. They speak their defiance of all restraints in what Ben Jonson called "Marlowe's mighty line," the powerful blank verse that Marlowe made the standard for English dramatic poetry.

Tamburlaine the Great, Marlowe's first hit on the stage, exhibits the progress of the Scythian conqueror as he cuts down every obstacle in his path. Tamburlaine ruthlessly reduces kingdoms to his will and cages conquered royalties (he makes the emperor of Turkey his footstool, literally). In Marlowe's sequel, Tamburlaine kills his son with his own hand, bridles and drives captive kings before his chariot, defiantly burns the Koran (daring Mohammed to work a miracle to put a stop to his blasphemy), and finally dies after his doctor has warned him that the heat in his veins has dried up the moisture of his blood.

To introduce *The Jew of Malta,* Marlowe brings on the soul of Machiavelli with a few choice words of atheist and immoral philosophy: "I count religion but a childish toy / And hold there is no sin but ignorance." Barabbas,[6] the play's protagonist, betrays and kills almost everyone he knows, including his own daughter—and he doesn't mind poisoning an entire convent of nuns to accomplish her murder. Eventually he falls into a boiling cauldron, caught in a trap of his own making. *The Jew of Malta* is almost as anti-human race as it is anti-Semitic: Jews and Muslims and Christians in the play outdo one another in dishonesty and nastiness: Barabbas's daughter is the one innocent creature in this Machiavellian world. And despite the extremes Barabbas and the rest of the characters in *The Jew of Malta* go to, Edward II (in Marlowe's play of the same name) may be the most "transgressive" of all Marlowe's heroes. Edward prefers the affections of another man to those of his wife, and dies horribly at the behest of her lover.

But of all Marlowe's portraits of men who reach beyond the limits of nature, law, and religion, *Doctor Faustus* gives us the quintessentially Renaissance villain-hero. Faustus is a scholar who turns to magic after having mastered all the more ordinary subjects. He sells his soul to Lucifer in exchange for twenty-four years of power and pleasure, during which time he is to be assisted, waited on, and entertained by the devil Mephistopheles. Mephistopheles negotiates the original pact with Lucifer; arranges for Faustus to enjoy

Can You Believe the Professors?

"Queer theory insists that all sexual behaviors, all concepts linking sexual behaviors to sexual identities, and all categories of normative and deviant sexualities, are social constructs, sets of signifiers which create certain types of social meaning. Queer theory follows feminist theory and gay/lesbian studies in rejecting the idea that sexuality is an essentialist category, something determined by biology or judged by eternal standards of morality and truth."

Mary Klages, professor of English at the University of Colorado at Boulder, in a webpage on "queer theory" that Professor Klages apparently posted for English 2010 Modern Critical Thought, offered in the fall of 1997. http://www.colorado.edu/English/courses/ENGL2012Klages/queertheory.html viewed 7/28/2006. See http://www.colorado.edu/English/courses/ENGL2012Klages/index.html viewed 7/28/2006.

unheard-of knowledge (he takes him on a dragon-drawn-carriage tour of the universe), power, and reputation; and persuades the magician to ignore all his urges to repent. Faustus's final speech, in the last hour before damnation, shows him trying to save himself by commanding the planets to halt in their orbits: "Stand still, you ever-moving spheres of heaven, / That time may cease and midnight never come."

But Faustus has reached the point at which his will can no longer control events—as Marlowe's villainous heroes all eventually do. After the magician's horrible final struggle, the devils take him off to hell. The chorus closes the play with a summation of Faustus's tragic career, in Marlowe's poignant verses: "Cut is the branch that might have grown full straight / And burnéd is Apollo's laurel bough. . . ."

Marlowe seems to have had a lot in common with his villain-heroes. His short life ended almost as violently as any of theirs—he was stabbed in the face by a government agent in highly mysterious circumstances reminiscent of Barabbas's plots. There's good evidence[7] that he was an atheist, a spy working for the secret service that Francis Walsingham ran

"Quenchless Thirst"

The Duke of Guise in *The Massacre at Paris* expresses the consuming ambition that grips all Marlowe's villain-heroes:

> That like I best that flies beyond my reach.
> Set me to scale the high pyramides
> And thereon set the diadem of France;
> I'll either rend it with my nails to nought,
> Or mount the top with my aspiring wings,
> Although my downfall be the deepest hell.

for Queen Elizabeth, and a proponent of pederasty. Government informers testified that Marlowe proselytized for atheism and sexual vice. And Marlowe's poetry itself is evidence of the fact that he found atheism, magic, male sexuality, and Machiavellian scheming all powerfully attractive. If Marlowe was an atheist, his atheism wasn't in the mold of the calmly superior Enlightenment and nineteenth-century rationalists. He was disseminating an outrageously blasphemous alternative story about Christ and his Apostles: something like *The Da Vinci Code,* only much, much more so. And if Marlowe liked men rather than women, his homosexuality wasn't along the lines of the I-only-want-equal-civil-rights-so-I-can-visit-my-long-time partner-in-the-hospital folks—it was more in the style of the "Ten percent is not enough. Recruit! Recruit! Recruit!" crowd.

It's easy to see why the devotees of the "transgressive" in general, and of "queer theory" in particular—the school of postmodernism dedicated to using literature to undermine all distinctions between the normal and the deviant—would be enthusiastic fans of Marlowe. From what we can infer about his life, you'd guess that Marlowe was just their kind of artist. The witnesses who testify about his unorthodox opinions paint Marlowe as a man eager to propagate them. Marlowe's friends and associates make him sound as outrageous as a character in a Marlowe play. The man who, Thomas Kyd testified, "would suddenly take slight occasion to slip out" nasty ideas comes across as just as clever and unsavory as the priest in *The Jew of Malta* who assures a nun he'll keep her last confession secret; listens to her dying plea that he try to save her father—"Convert my father that he may be saved, / And witness that I die a Christian!"—and then remarks, the minute she's dead, "Ay, and a virgin too; that grieves me most," just before setting off to blackmail her father with the contents of her confession.

But outrageous or nasty Marlowe-like characters are not *all* there is in Marlowe's plays. And the plays themselves are not simply angry attacks on the moral and religious structure of the Elizabethan world view or

The Dan Brown of the Sixteenth Century?

Richard Baines, a government informer who may at one point have worked undercover with Marlowe on the Continent, reported that Marlowe had argued, among other things:

That "Christ deserved better to die than Barabbas....though Barabbas were both a thief and a murderer."

That Marlowe himself could invent a better religion than Christianity "and that all the New Testament is filthily written."

"That the woman of Samaria and her sister were whores and that Christ knew them dishonestly."

"That St. John the Evangelist was a bedfellow to Christ and leaned always in his bosom, that He used him as the sinners of Sodom."

"That all they that love not tobacco and boys are fools."

It's hard to get more transgressive than that.

attempts to "queer" the audience's understanding of right and wrong, vice and virtue, love and hatred, the normal and the deviant—those "binary opposites" that the queer theorists maintain are mere artificial constructs. There *are* plays in English that are about nothing but "challenging" morality and religion. But they're not anything like as good as Marlowe's plays. There are many reasons that *The Jew of Malta* and *Doctor Faustus* are great works of literature, while, say, Tennessee Williams's *Night of the Iguana* is not—to take an example from a very different time and place, but one by a playwright who shared Marlowe's hostility toward religion and conventional standards of right and wrong. Chief among the reasons that Marlowe's play is great, while Tennessee Williams's isn't, is that the things that Marlowe's blaspheming characters rage against don't all get knocked down in his plays.

The art of blasphemous revolt against religion and morality yields diminishing returns. Marlowe could get lots of bang for his buck partly because he was writing when almost everyone still took God, His commandments, and the salvation of their own souls very seriously. Tennessee Williams, almost four hundred years later, was writing when skepticism about religion was widespread and sexual morality was increasingly a matter of convention and prudence, rather than of religious belief. The Reverend Shannon's argument in *The Night of the Iguana* that "all your Western theologies, the whole mythology of them, are based on the concept of God as a *senile delinquent*"[8] may have seemed profound to audiences in the early 1960s,[9] but its power has faded, and there's not much else in the play to make a deep impression.

The Vagina Monologues was written almost forty years after *The Night of the Iguana* and is several rungs below even it on the scale of literary value. It was created in the era of *Piss Christ* and the notorious exhibition of an elephant-dung-studded collage of the Virgin Mary at the Brooklyn Museum of Art. By the end of the twentieth century, when writers and artists could no longer depend on their audience to *have* any definite religious or moral beliefs, they were reduced to attempting to get attention by violating whatever residual religious sensibilities or taboos about public sexual display might still exist.

But Marlowe wrote his plays in a thoroughly moral and religious world. And some of their most powerful moments are about what Marlowe's characters lose by embracing atheism and vice. The poignancy of this loss is the real focus of interest in *Doctor Faustus.*

Marlowe could hardly have made Faustus's choice to damn himself seem more foolish, even if he'd been earnestly intent on writing a warning against dabbling in the black arts. In the opening scene, Faustus speaks as if he's deciding to become a magician because he's run out of

What They Don't Want You to Learn from Christopher Marlowe

"Transgressive" will take you only so far—in life and in art.

subjects worthy of his attention. He runs through philosophy, medicine, law, and theology; claims he's already mastered all of them; and turns at last to what his "Bad Angel" calls "that famous art / Wherein all nature's treasure is contained." "A sound magician is a mighty god," Faustus tells himself, as he looks forward to the "world of profit and delight / Of power, of honour, of omnipotence" that necromancy promises.

But it's obvious that he hasn't so much mastered theology as run away from it. "Divinity," which Faustus calls "[u]npleasant, harsh, contemptible, and vile," is uncongenial to him because he doesn't like contemplating the doctrine that the reward of sin is death: "That's hard," he complains.

Faustus gets very little in exchange for his soul, and that little seems like less and less as the play progresses. When he's considering taking up magic, he imagines that the spirits at his command will "[r]esolve me of all ambiguities" and "search all corners of the new-found world"; they will read him "strange philosophy" and tell him "the secrets of all foreign kings." These grandiose plans don't come to much. Faustus tours the universe, learns all kinds of exotic sciences, and entertains himself extravagantly: "Have not I made blind Homer sing to me / Of Alexander's love and Oenon's death?" But these exotic pleasures are increasingly useful only in Faustus's frantic efforts to distract himself from reconsidering his bargain and saving his soul.

The knowledge Faustus sought is no more use to him than power or pleasure. Mephistopheles tells him the truth about the physical universe, and even about the importance of his soul—the heavens were made for man. He also tells Faustus the truth about hell and damnation, but Faustus seems incapable of believing him:

Faustus: I think hell's a fable.

Mephistopheles: Ay, think so still, till experience change thy
mind.

Certainly Faustus has no profit from learning what Mephistopheles
knows, any more than Mephistopheles himself. Some of the most poignant language in the play is in Mephistopheles' speeches about the devils'
loss of Heaven:

Faustus: Was not that Lucifer an angel once?

Mephistopheles: Yes Faustus, and most dearly loved of God.

But Mephistopheles doesn't like talking about God, or Heaven, and he
positively refuses to acknowledge the creation of the world. At Faustus's
question, "Now tell me, who made the world?" he balks: "I will not." But
God is in the play, nevertheless. He's there in the heavens Faustus can't
see without beginning to repent. He's there in the counsel of Faustus's
Good Angel and in the warning Faustus reads on his own arm when he
cuts himself to sign away his soul in his own blood. And He's there,
finally, in Faustus's last speech:

See, see, where Christ's blood streams in the firmament!

One drop would save my soul, half a drop. Ah, my Christ!

Ah, rend not my heart for naming of my Christ!

Yet will I call on him!

But he doesn't. Instead, he calls on Lucifer:

Oh spare me Lucifer!

Where is it now? 'tis gone: and see where God

Stretcheth out His arm, and bends His ireful brows.

In Marlowe, we're still seeing God, even if we're seeing Him from hell.
The lost bliss of Heaven and the theological truth in Doctor Faustus aren't

just there to satisfy the censor. And they don't just give the play a way to end; they give it shape and structure, weight and meaning. They're artistically necessary. We don't know whether Marlowe, like Mephistopheles, really knew better than to be a thoroughgoing materialist, or if he simply was a better artist than Faustus, not to mention Dan Brown. We do know that while Marlowe the man may have agitated against God, religious truth, and virtue; Marlowe the artist saw that he couldn't do without them.

William Shakespeare

If Marlowe's life doesn't overshadow his work, it's at least a fascinating distraction. With Shakespeare, it's just the other way around. Nothing we know about Shakespeare's life is really important; almost nothing about it is even memorable. Marlowe's work, like his life, is an interesting foil for Shakespeare's. While Marlowe was interested in rebellion, in pushing things up to and if possible beyond their limits, Shakespeare was interested in what *is.*

Shakespeare's plays are at once incredibly delightful and breathtakingly *real.* For more than three hundred years after his death, the most critically astute members of Shakespeare's audience said essentially the same thing about him, all from their own very different perspectives and in their own very different critical vocabularies. Shakespeare's plays, they agreed, have universal appeal because they reflect (or even simply express) nature in a way no other literature does.[10] "He was not of an age, but for all time," as Ben Jonson put it in his introductory verses to the First Folio of Shakespeare's plays. Shakespeare's particular genius—described variously as his "most comprehensive soul," as a "deep and accurate science in mental philosophy," or as a sort of "Negative Capability"[11]—is a capacity that enabled him to create unequalled representations of the enormous variety of human nature and human experience.

"Our myriad-minded Shakespeare," as Coleridge called him[12] created characters as unique as human individuals, and almost as real.[13] As Dr. Johnson put it, "Shakespeare has no heroes; his scenes are occupied only by men."[14]

This estimate of Shakespeare held up, more or less intact, through the middle of the twentieth century. A pre-"theory" academic writer such as Mark van Doren sounds pretty much the same notes as Dryden, Pope, and Johnson, Coleridge, and Keats: "... he is the kind of story-teller who can be judged by the most general standards we have" and "Shakespeare loved the world as it is. That is why he understood it so well; and that in turn is why, being the artist that he was, he could make it over again into something rich and clear.[15]

But our English professors take a very different attitude toward Shakespeare. The main point of their scholarship seems to be to establish that Shakespeare was most definitely a man of his own age, and *not* for all time. For them, *The Tempest* is interesting for what it can tell us about European colonialism, or the state of gynecology in Renaissance England. *The Merchant of Venice* interests them chiefly as a piece of testimony about Christian anti-Semitism, or, alternately, about the depredations of capitalism. They see *Othello* as so much evidence about race relations in early modern Europe. They point to *Macbeth* as a part of the cultural conspiracy to domesticate women. They comb through *The Winter's Tale* looking for missing links in the history of lesbianism.[16] The very features of Shakespeare's work that convinced earlier readers of his intuitive understanding of universal human nature seem to the postmodernist English professor to be evidence that Shakespeare belonged to a culture that's alien to their aspirations, a culture that we will have to escape to be truly free.

The concept of "nature," which the first critics of Shakespeare's works continually referred to in their attempts to explain his greatness, is the key to understanding his works—and also the key to understanding why the postmodernist critics want to cut Shakespeare down to size. Shakespeare's plays may mirror nature, but that doesn't mean that they reflect real-world experience in a photo-realistic, slice-of-life, stream-of-consciousness kind of way—which is one of many reasons that a Shakespeare play is infinitely more delightful than, say, a John Updike novel, not to mention than anybody's twenty-four-hour live webcam site. Shakespeare's works seem *real* and *natural* without being "realistic" or "naturalistic." But the difference between the unretouched photo or the webcam and what you get in Shakespeare is not the difference between warts-and-all reality and some airbrushed ideal. Shakespeare shows you the warts, but he makes them fascinating. He does it by getting at the nature of things, especially of human nature.

Hamlet, for example, is more than a depressed and confused young man. He's the very picture of self-aware intellectual youth: highly intelligent, enormously sensitive to the moral failings of his elders, alive to all the implications of everyone's actions, but tragically unable to shoulder responsibility, to get control of events. In the same way, Richard III is not just a nasty little man who resents other people's happiness and plots to ruin them for his advantage. He's the quintessentially crooked plotter, whose villainy is more outrageously successful (for a while) than the schemes of the most brazen real-life villain, and whose success unravels in exactly the way that that kind of success inevitably does unravel. Iago is not just an envious man bent on revenge. He's practically spite incarnate—except that, at the same time, he's a believable individual, not an allegorical stick figure. When you see a Shakespeare play, you recognize the characters. They're real, only more so. You know them from your experience—though

What They Don't Want You to Learn from Shakespeare

There really is such a thing as human nature.

you have never known a human individual whose speech and actions were so characteristically right for his character. You think, *That's just how it really is.* Somehow the play seems more intensely real than the ordinary reality you live in.

Shakespeare got these effects because he knew what the seventeenth- and eighteenth-century critics called nature (and especially human nature): exactly what it is about things (and particularly about people) that makes them the kind of things, and people, they are. He was fascinated by the structures under the surface of human life. This interest in the nature or essence of things is what Dr. Johnson was talking about when he claimed that Shakespeare created "just representations of general nature": "a species" rather than "an individual." But he doesn't mean that Shakespeare's characters are vague or abstract; after all, this is the same Dr. Johnson who argued that Shakespeare's characters are men, not heroes. He's pointing out that Shakespeare gives us characters who seem to show us more about what human beings are really like even than the ordinary men and women we meet do.

Shakespeare's creation of human characters at once more real and more delightful than any before or since is analogous to the Italian Renaissance painters' creation of human figures that seem to combine the natural and the beautiful to a degree that no other artists ever equaled. Renaissance painting, unlike the art of the medieval painters, was informed by anatomy. Renaissance painters knew more about what was inside the flesh they were painting, about the bones and muscles that made a face or a body what it was, than any artists in history had ever known. And unlike the Impressionist painters at the end of the nineteenth century, who aimed at painting only the appearance of the surfaces of things, Renaissance artists were interested in painting human figures, in representing the actual bodies they understood so much about. In the same way that those Italian painters were interested in what shapes human figures, Shakespeare was interested in what makes human characters—and human history, and all the things that human beings think about, from the justice of God to the mechanics of lust—*what they are.*

Shakespeare's poetic technique is itself a kind of exploration of reality. Whether he's writing a single speech or creating a five-act tragedy, he tends to work by looking at a thing from many different angles. Shakespeare's characters don't just talk about things, they define them and redefine them, piling one illuminating comparison on top of another. His plays are full of famous speeches in which a character takes some particular aspect of human experience and riffs on it. It might be something as large as jealousy or reputation, or as specific as how men who survive a battle may celebrate its anniversary in future years or the particular psychology of a man who's experiencing a violent physical attraction to a modest girl precisely because of her innocence, though he's immune to the more obvious sexual stimulants.[17] Portia's speech in *The Merchant of Venice* about the "quality of mercy" is one example. Henry V's speech on the "ceremony" of kingship is another.

Hamlet's famous "To be or not to be" speech is yet another—Hamlet considers the possibility of death from all sides, it seems. But this is only one of many speeches exploring death in the plays, and particularly in *Hamlet* itself.[18] Every possible angle on this theme seems to have some place in Shakespeare's best-known play: why we long for death and why we fear it; what it does to our bodies and what it does to our souls; what we know about death and how it's a mystery; how many different ways there are to die, and how many different reasons for dying. There's a ghost in the play. There's a disinterred skull, too. And there's almost every kind of violent death you can name: There's a girl who goes mad and kills herself. And a rash young man who throws his life away in a duel over his sister's honor and life. And a scheming courtier who's exterminated like a rat as he hides eavesdropping. And college friends who betray their schoolmate and agree to bring about his death, only to fall into their own trap. And a fratricide who's wracked by guilt but can't bring himself to give up his brother's wife and his brother's kingdom. Not to mention a number of poisonings, both purposeful and by accident.

And *Hamlet* isn't the only Shakespeare play with a theme running through it. *Henry V*, for example, seems to ring every possible change on successful kingship—or even simply on success. As the play's epilogue sums up Henry's career: "Small time, but in that small most greatly lived / This star of England: Fortune made his sword; / By which the world's best garden he achieved. . . . " The play is full of scenes and characters that set you thinking: What is a king? And what are the qualities that make for greatness? How many parts generosity, courage, leadership, and humility is it? How many parts ruthlessness? And what are its costs? And despite its heavy costs, despite even the fact that it's never permanent, isn't the achievement of a great man a very good thing indeed?

Shakespeare does something similar with wealth in *The Merchant of Venice*. Every thing, incident, and person in the play seems to have something to do with money. There's Antonio, a merchant who has grown rich by risky ventures in trade. There's Shylock, a Jew who lives by lending money at interest and hoards coins and jewels at home. There's Shylock's daughter, who elopes, taking large amounts of his portable wealth with her, and spends it prodigally. There are two marriages made at least partly for money. There's Portia, an heiress whose father's will specifies that she'll be awarded to the man who guesses rightly among three treasure chests.

There's Bassanio, a charming young man with large debts (another Shakespeare character we instantly recognize from our knowledge of human nature—the quintessential child of good fortune: the charming, lucky, promising, handsome, spendthrift, disingenuous, careless man whom everyone loves) who asks his friend, from whom he's already borrowed money he can't pay back, for a large and very risky loan, on the grounds that throwing good money after bad is like losing an arrow and then shooting another in the same direction and watching where it lands—that way, you might find both. There's also a lawsuit over a defaulted loan, in which the moneylender claims the right to cut a pound of flesh from the merchant's chest. There are wives who pretend to have been unfaithful because their husbands gave away the rings their wives gave them. And boatloads of beautiful and endlessly fascinating poetry about almost any question you can think of, involving wealth and treasure: where it comes from, where it goes, and what it does to men and women and their relationships.

Of course *The Merchant of Venice* isn't *only* about money, and *Hamlet* is about much more than death. The plays can't be reduced to the themes you find running through them (any more than you can boil Shakespeare's achievement down to his realistic and fascinating characters, his moving scenes and satisfying plots, or his gorgeous poetry). But those themes—like the lineaments of Shakespeare's characters—are the bones and muscles underneath the surface of the drama. They're taken from the actual structure of human experience. They're elements of the underlying patterns and hierarchies that give shape to the individual moments of our lives just as our anatomy gives shape to our bodies. Shakespeare was an expert in what Coleridge called "the common fundamental laws of our nature."[19]

There wasn't an ideological bone in Shakespeare's body. His art isn't about forcing human experience into predetermined patterns. He goes to work precisely the opposite way. Shakespeare pokes and prods at reality, he throws characters and ideas together and makes them combine and recombine in every possible way. He's not concerned about apparent contradictions, which abound in his plays as they do in our experience. Shakespeare doesn't impose alien structures on his material; he notices the structures in the material of human life, and they fascinate him.

Naturally, all of this goes over like a lead balloon with the PC English professors, who hate the very idea of human nature, deny that it has any fundamental laws, and believe that even the manifestly natural differences between men and women are artificial "social constructs." If you're a feminist professor who can't admit that men and women are different by nature, you'll miss what Shakespeare noticed, and shows us in *Macbeth*: that ambition tends to work differently on men and women. To you, *Macbeth* will look like part of the patriarchal plot to define male and female by "binary opposites" such as brutal vs. verbal and tough vs. brittle. Or imagine you're a Marxist professor of "cultural studies" who believes that human culture is determined by economic conditions. You won't want to admit that *The Tempest* is an endlessly fascinating drama exploring universal truths about the human condition. Instead, you'll prefer to see is as a blueprint for colonizing non-Western cultures and enslaving people "of color."

The closeness to nature that made Shakespeare's contemporaries—and critics for three and a half centuries—see his insights as universal is the very thing that makes it imperative for the postmodernist professor to show that they're *not* universal. Shakespeare was living at a time when people took morality and the stubborn limits of human nature for granted. We're living in a very different age—the era of "It depends on what the meaning of 'is' is"; of "What right do you have to impose your morality on me?"; and of "At the heart of liberty is the right to define one's own concept of existence, of meaning, of the universe and the mystery of human life."[20] The idea that human nature has any God-given definition, any inherent limitations, or even any universal features is offensive to the postmodernists' belief in their right to cast off the shackles of reality and define themselves. The feminists and "queer theorists" deride any recognition of sex differences as

Can You Believe the Professors?

"Instead of accompanying her husband into battle like the ancient Scotswomen in the chronicle, Lady Macbeth waits at home for his letter and his return like a good, modern wife. In fact, the domestication of women appears to be a major project of this play."

Phyllis Rackin, professor emerita of English at the University of Pennsylvania and former president of the Shakespeare Association of America. *Shakespeare and Women* (Oxford and New York: Oxford University Press, 2005), 130.

the heresy of "essentialism." The Marxists refuse to admit that their project to drastically remake human nature has failed—much less to acknowledge that project's horrific costs. They're still pinning their hopes on the possibility of creating "other worlds."[21] But those of us who still love the world we actually live in, love Shakespeare.

The tragedies

Shakespeare's histories and tragedies are satisfying in part because of their sense of a natural order (of structures behind or underneath human experience, and the nature of the world itself) that are defied only at great cost. All the ugliest things we know—greed, lust, violence, envy, betrayal—show up in Shakespeare's plays. Like everything else, they're looked at from every side and the patterns they make in human lives are illuminated. Those patterns, unlike the ugly things themselves, are beautiful. Each human shipwreck is delightfully individual, and yet representative of wider truths about human nature, and the nature of the world. There are, it seems, as many fascinating ways for human beings to come to grief as there are different kinds of people.

Macbeth, for example, is something like a laboratory experiment in what unbridled ambition does to human beings. It makes Macbeth into a progressively more paranoid and isolated thug, piling murder on murder—a sort of proto-Stalin. By the end he's a figure almost like Hitler in the bunker. Lady Macbeth, in whom ambition takes a recognizably female form, is all strength, confidence, and resolve (and very effective taunts about her husband's manhood) when she's pushing Macbeth to commit the initial murder. But she cracks under the weight of the responsibility, once the deed's done and she has to live with it. In *Macbeth,* as in the history plays, there's the sense that the tyrant's crimes have set in motion destructive forces that will eventually encompass the tyrant himself—and that won't be laid to rest until the legitimate order is restored.

Othello looks at jealousy[22] from every possible angle—what its sources are, what kind of thing it is, what it does to people. The title character is a dark-skinned Moor who is commanding the forces of Venice in their war against the Turks. The main plot is the story of how Othello's ensign Iago, envious of Cassio (whom Othello made his lieutenant—a position Iago wanted, and thinks he deserved), tricks Othello into murdering Desdemona, Othello's virtuous wife, by persuading Othello that she's been unfaithful with Cassio. The play is full of scenes, minor characters, and speeches that, even when Othello's distrust of his wife isn't in question, illuminate the nature and effects of jealousy, "the green-eyed monster which doth mock the meat it feeds on." In the play's opening scene for example, Iago and Roderigo, a disappointed suitor to Desdemona, wake her father in the middle of the night to break the news that she has eloped with Othello. The way Roderigo talks about the marriage is ugly enough: he says Desdemona is in "the gross clasps of a lascivious Moor." But Roderigo's language is mild compared with Iago's nastiness: "I am one, sir, that comes to tell you, your daughter and the Moor are now making the beast with two backs." Jealousy and envious hatred color the world, making the conjugal act look depraved, even monstrous.

What They Don't Want You to Learn from Shakespeare's Tragedies

Some choices are inherently destructive (it's just built into the nature of things).

King Lear, which is often felt to be Shakespeare's most profound play, almost seems to be about nature itself. *Lear* is set in the remote past of pagan Britain, before human nature had been baptized by sacramental grace. And its plot turns on the most basic natural relationship—the bond between parent and child.

Lear abdicates his kingdom to his daughters, trusting his support in his old age to their natural affections. Lear's attempt to hang onto the perquisites of power while giving up the responsibilities may be doomed from its inception. It's difficult to see, though, what other choice he—or any of us—has. It's grievous if we're cut off in our prime, and then again it's a terrible thing if we outlive our mental and physical strength to suffer the indignities of a dependent old age. But Lear makes things worse by indulging in a tendency that's natural to old men: doting on those of his children who feed his appetite for affection. He divides everything he has between Goneril and Regan. They satisfy his craving for filial love with insincere and extravagant speeches. Cordelia, who really loves her father, looks into her heart and can't find it in her own honest nature to flatter Lear: "What must Cordelia speak? Love, and be silent."

The characters in *Lear* are forever talking about nature and about what's unnatural, and soon enough Lear himself is reduced to experiencing nature in its rawest form: he's homeless and wandering out of doors in the rain and wind, raging against the ingratitude of the "unnatural" daughters he's discovered don't really love him, and speculating that "unaccommodated man" is no more than "a poor, bare, fork'd animal." More than any other play, Lear makes us feel that we're seeing the tragedy at the heart of human existence—the mortality and the sorrow that define our lives.

The comedies

Shakespeare's tragedies may make up the greatest body of drama in the English language. But there's a way in which his comedies are even more impressive. There are other plays—*Oedipus Rex*, *Agamemnon*, the great works of Euripedes—that you could at least argue are in the same rank with Shakespeare's best tragedies. But as Ben Jonson claimed in his introduction to the First Folio, Shakespeare's comedies are in a league of their own.

It's not that *The Merchant of Venice* or *The Tempest* is a better play than *Hamlet* or *King Lear*. But you can make a persuasive argument that in creating his greatest comedies Shakespeare succeeded in doing something that's even more difficult to pull off than writing a great tragedy. Shakespeare's seem almost to be *an entirely different kind of play* from other playwrights' comedies. It's difficult to say why Shakespeare succeeds where no other playwright has. You might speculate that there's something about the human condition—or about the nature of drama—that makes happy endings harder to pull off than sad ones. Or that no other playwright figured out how to make a comedy seem almost as weighty, as full of import, as a tragedy. What's clear is that Shakespeare's comedies seem to aim at a different target from most great comedy, and that (unlike the writers of, say, Victorian melodrama) Shakespeare nails it.

The work of Ben Jonson is the obvious contemporary example of successful sub-Shakespearean comedy. Like most great comic dramatists, including his classical models, Jonson aims to amuse and instruct his audience by exposing human folly and vice. Jonson's comedies— *Volpone, Every Man in His Humor, The Alchemist,* and *Bartholomew Fair*—show us people we can laugh at because we see that their personalities are deformed by some characteristic defect: lust, greed, mulish stubbornness, or pride in their own cleverness. This kind of drama can be very funny, but it tends to be rather depressing. As Coleridge complained about Jonson's *Volpone,* it's hard to enjoy a play "in which there is no goodness of heart in any of the prominent characters."[23]

You can't love Jonson's characters, but you can hardly help loving Shakespeare's. Jonson's humor is all sharp satire, where Shakespeare's is generous and forgiving. But the central difference is that where Jonson, even more than most great comic dramatists, writes to amuse, to be funny and telling,

What They Don't Want You to Learn from Shakespeare's Comedies

Our human nature—including even the very limitations that define it—is a rich source of happiness.

Shakespeare writes to delight. Jonson aims at laughter; Shakespeare, at something very much like happiness.

Part of the secret to Shakespeare's success may be how much his comedies are like his tragedies. All of Shakespeare's plays, even the tragedies, have comic scenes. All of them, even the comedies, treat weighty matters. In the eighteenth century, Samuel Johnson argued that Shakespeare's plays were neither tragedies *nor* comedies "in the rigorous or critical sense," but rather:

> compositions of a distinct kind; exhibiting the real state of sublunary nature, which partakes of good and evil, joy and sorrow, mingled with endless variety of proportion and innumerable modes of combination; and expressing the course of the world, in which the loss of one is the gain of another; in which, at the same time, the reveler is hasting to his wine, and the mourner burying his friend; in which the malignity of one is sometimes defeated by the frolic of another; and many mischiefs and many benefits are done and hindered without design.[24]

So how *are* Shakespeare's comedies different from his tragedies? Well, the tragedies have sad endings, and the comedies end happily. But more specifically, the tragedies end in deaths and the comedies end with marriages. Shakespeare seems to consider marriage necessary to a happy ending as death is to sad one—at least for his kind of comedy.

And we know that Shakespeare's right. However much unhappiness marriage also causes—and however comically disappointed young lovers may always have been in even the best of real marriages—"young love satisfied"[25] is *the* image of happiness in this world. But like a lot of Shakespeare's insights into the fundamental structures of human nature, this is not something PC professors want to understand, much less let their students in on. Especially when you consider how "essentialist" Shakespeare's concept of marriage is. Marriage in Shakespeare is about the union of opposites: it depends on the complementary natures of the two lovers. In other words, Shakespeare's happy endings are all about the very aspect of reality that entire schools of feminist, "queer," and "gender" studies exist to deny: the natural differences between men and women.

Not only does Shakespeare show that men and women are different. He further offends the PC view of "gender" by showing marriage as an institution that takes those fundamental differences seriously— complete with husbandly authority, wifely obedience, the wickedness of fornication (and its disastrous effects), the special importance of pre-marital virginity for women, the shame of unfaithfulness, and so forth. The marriages that end Shakespeare's comedies are not like our modern secular marriage. Marriage in Shakespeare is not the decision of two consenting adults to confirm their love for one another and merge their lives, in the knowledge that either spouse can end the marriage at will,

Can You Believe the Professors?

"So I asked my students, what if Shakespeare is partly to blame for the danger that women have faced and continue to face in premarital sex?

"It has been compellingly argued, I explained, that Shakespeare has played and may continue to play a significant role in the establishment and maintenance of gender roles that subordinate women."

Robert I. Lublin, theater professor at the University of Massachusetts, Boston. "Feminist History, Theory, and Practice in the Shakespeare Classroom," *Theater Topics* 14, no. 2 (September 2004): 401.

and with important questions—such as when they begin living together, to what extent their property will be shared, and whether they will have children—decided separately. Marriage in Shakespeare's day was a package deal with its own definition. To marry in a Shakespeare comedy is to marry into an institution that's defined by religious authority, human nature, and the complementary natures of men and women, not by the decisions of the people getting married.

From the "gender studies" point of view, The *Taming of the Shrew* is Shakespeare's most offensive play. Katharina, the "shrew" of the title, is the older daughter of Baptista of Padua, who's having trouble finding her a husband. Katharina's younger sister, Bianca, is adept at the feminine art of pleasing by at least seeming to be gentle and compliant. Katharina is openly defiant towards her father and outrageously rude to Bianca's suitors. Baptista's solution to his problem: announce that he won't agree to any marriage for Bianca—and that she'll be at home studying, and unavailable to be courted by any of her suitors—until he's found a husband for Katharina. As luck would have it, Petruchio, a friend of one of Bianca's suitors, shows up in town looking to marry a rich wife. Petruchio has inherited his father's large estate (and improved it), but he's looking to add more. He also seems to be looking for an adventure away from home, "where," as he says, "small experience grows." He leaps at the challenge to woo, wed, and tame Katharina.

Their first meeting is not auspicious: Kate insults and even hits Petruchio, defying him to hit her back and show he's not a gentleman. But he manages to get the better of her, in the end. Petruchio's method combines language and behavior that's even more outrageous than Katharina's own with an elaborate attitude of chivalrous appreciation of her beauty and virtues.

After he's shown up to the wedding late and unsuitably dressed, and stomped and sworn his way through the ceremony, he insists that Katharina leave for his house without attending the wedding feast. His language is a disorienting combination of peremptory orders, outrageous insults, and solicitous defense of his cherished wife. Here's his response when Katharina announces that, whatever he says, she's staying for the feast:

> But for my bonny Kate, she must with me.
> Nay, look not big, nor stamp, nor stare, nor fret;
> I will be master of what is mine own:
> She is my goods, my chattels; she is my house,
> My household stuff, my field, my barn,
> My horse, my ox, my ass, my any thing;
> And here she stands, touch her whoever dare;
> I'll bring mine action on the proudest he
> That stops my way in Padua. Grumio,
> Draw forth thy weapon, we are beset with thieves;
> Rescue thy mistress, if thou be a man.
> Fear not, sweet wench, they shall not touch thee, Kate:
> I'll buckler thee against a million.

Their marriage continues in this vein. As long as she's stubborn, Petruchio makes life very uncomfortable for Kate—but always on the excuse that nothing is good enough for her. She can't sleep because, Petruchio discovers, the bed isn't made properly; she can't eat because the food isn't cooked right and wouldn't be good for her; he sends away the beautiful dress and cap that he has ordered to be made for her, on the pretense that they're no good, either.

And then, suddenly, Kate quits resisting, and decides that she'll be happier letting her husband run the show. Possibly she's worn down by having to live with the chaos Petruchio creates—which is very much like the chaos she used to create for her father and sister. Or perhaps she's come to respect the fact that her husband can outdo her at her own game.

Or it may be that she realizes that she doesn't, after all, need to behave like a spoiled brat to get the attention she's been craving.

In any case, the arrangement that Petruchio and Kate come to is the very essense of "essentialist" beliefs about men and women. In Kate's own words:

> Thy husband is thy lord, thy life, thy keeper,
> Thy head, thy sovereign; one that cares for thee,
> And for thy maintenance commits his body
> To painful labour both by sea and land,
> To watch the night in storms, the day in cold,
> Whilst thou liest warm at home, secure and safe;
> And craves no other tribute at thy hands
> But love, fair looks and true obedience;
> Too little payment for so great a debt.

The words about "painful labour both by sea and land" aren't literally true of Petruchio, who is heir to one fortune and has just married into another one.

But they get at some underlying truths about men and women that feminists don't want to hear: That men are typically more ambitious and willing to take risks, whereas women tend to care more about security. And that wives find being cherished and paid attention to the absolutely nonnegotiable thing in a marriage, whereas the one thing husbands can't do without is respect. And that even an intelligent and strong-willed woman—in fact, *especially* an intelligent and strong-willed woman, because she's likely to have despaired of finding such a husband—can be made very happy by the discovery that she's loved by a man who is in some sense her superior: "My mind hath been as big as one of yours," says Kate to two *not* so happy wives, "My heart as great, my reason haply more, / To bandy word for word and frown for frown; /But now I see our lances are but straws...." One thing that's very clear in *The Taming of the Shrew* is that men and women are so different that they're made happy by different things—or, to put it another way, that they can both look to marriage for happiness only because it's a complementary relationship that accommodates their differences.

The Taming of the Shrew is one of Shakespeare's earliest comedies. But Shakespeare doesn't leave behind what feminists and other PC professors think of as "gender stereotypes" (and the rest of us recognize as what men and women are really like) in his more mature work. *The Tempest,* from the very end of Shakespeare's career, is just as "essentialist" as any earlier comedy. Prospero takes what gender theorists call "the virginity fetish" quite seriously, and he knows that Ferdinand won't desire (and later appreciate) his daughter as intensely as Prospero wants him to, unless Ferdinand has to overcome some obstacles in pursuit of her. It's in the nature of a man to value a woman he wins only with difficulty. So Prospero creates artificial difficulties. He uses his knowledge of human nature, male and female, to arrange for his daughter's marriage to be a happy one, just as Shakespeare uses the same knowledge to create drama that touches the very wellsprings of human happiness.

Whatever the "gender studies" folks may think, Shakespeare isn't trying to "domesticate women"; he's not making any kind of case for how they ought to be treated, or what sort of rights they ought to have. He's just noticing what men and women are really like, and creating fascinating and delightful drama out of it. Shakespeare's celebration of the limits that define us—of our natures as men and women—upsets only those folks who find human nature itself upsetting. At the end of the line for the folks offended by gentle femininity and ambitious, competitive masculinity are the extreme positions that some feminists have suggested—that marriage is really just slavery, and that all sex is rape.[26] PC professors who find the obvious truths about men, women, and sex differences offensive in themselves are going to be offended by Shakespeare's comedy. But the rest of us might as well just relax and enjoy it.

The sonnets

Shakespeare's comedies are about happiness. They all end in marriages because marriage is the best picture of human happiness. It may be that "[t]he course of true love never did run smooth," but in the comedies Shakespeare finds a way for love to run, finally, to its natural consummation. Shakespeare's *Sonnets,* on the other hand, are about erotic experience that isn't satisfied (and contained) in marriage. The sonnets are about every *other* place that love can take you. They're about the possible off-label uses of *eros,* the love that admires and desires another human being. The *Sonnets* are Shakespeare's most up-close-and-personal poems, and they're about the wide range of erotic experience—both about a love that aims high above the level of ordinary erotic love and its satisfaction, and also about a love that falls far below it.

Shakespeare's *Sonnets* are the culmination of an Elizabethan fashion in sonnet sequences that began with Sir Philip Sidney's *Astrophel and Stella* (Star-lover and Star), written in the early 1580s under the inspiration of Sidney's sometime fiancée Penelope Devereaux. Usually ranked third, after Shakespeare's and Sidney's sonnets, are the *Amoretti* (little loves) of Edmund Spenser, the author of *The Faerie Queene.* The *Amoretti,* with a concluding *Epithalamion* (marriage song) were written to Spenser's second wife, Elizabeth Boyle, during their courtship.

The fourteen-line sonnet is—since Elizabethan times—*the* classic form for English lyric poetry. In the fourteenth century, the Italian poet Francis Petrarch wrote the "sonnet sequence" that was the model for the Elizabethan fashion: 366 poems about his love for a married woman named Laura. As in most ambitious English poetry, the lines of the sonnet are in iambic pentameter. The rhyme scheme of Shakespeare's *Sonnets* is looser than the scheme of the Petrarchan sonnet, which many English poets have also used. The "Shakespearean" sonnet consists of three quatrains followed by a couplet. In other words, Shakespeare's sonnets rhyme ABAB CDCD EFEF GG. That's in contrast to Petrarch's sonnets, and those of his more faithful English imitators. "Petrarchan" sonnets have an octave that rhymes ABBA ABBA and then a sestet that uses some combination of two or three different rhymes in its six lines: CDE CDE, or some variation thereof.

Here's the significance of the different rhyme schemes: In Italian sonnets, there's usually what's called a turn—a change in mood, a leap in the argument or the narration, or some new realization—between octave and the sestet. But in Shakespeare's sonnets, the significant shift in tone typically comes between the third (that is, the last) quatrain and the final couplet. The couplet can be a kind of summary or concentration of the ideas explored more expansively in the looser quatrains. The language of the couplet is then more pointed, or more elevated (or both) than the language in the rest of the poem. Shakespeare's Sonnet 87, for example, begins, "Farewell! thou art too dear for my possessing" and continues with an argument that that "possessing" was bound to be temporary, or even that it was illusory from the beginning. Then the sonnet ends with this couplet: "Thus have I had thee as a dream doth flatter / In sleep a king, but waking no such matter."

Or the final couplet can bring a new insight or a radical change of mood, in contrast to the sonnet's first twelve lines. In Sonnet 30, for example, the quatrains are all about the melancholy "remembrance of things past": "I sigh the lack of many a thing I sought.... And heavily from woe to woe tell o'er / The sad account...." But in the couplet there's a new thought and an entirely different mood: "But if the while I think on thee (dear friend) / All losses are restored, and sorrows end."

Sometimes the couplet is a real zinger, a sort of sting in the tail of the sonnet—as (quite appropriately) in Sonnet 129. The quatrains are a forceful and convincing, not to say angry and bitter, condemnation of lust: "The expense of spirit in a waste of shame / Is lust in action, and till action, lust / Is perjured, murderous, bloody, full of blame...." If you've ever done anything you're ashamed of under the influence of sexual desire, all the sonnet's descriptions ring true. In one sense it's a relaxation from the frenzied level of the quatrains' argument. But in another sense it's a new horror—very much like the self-disgust that follows the act of lust itself: "All this the world well knows yet none knows well, / To shun the heaven that leads men to this hell."

The Shakespearean sonnet fits the English language (in which rhymes are much more difficult to find than in Italian) more easily than the Petrarchan sonnet does. But the Shakespearean rhyme scheme also suits Shakespeare's genius exactly. The couplet provides ample opportunity for our greatest poet to do one of the things he does best: create those much-quoted lines that are somehow at the same time perfectly fresh, and yet as true as the oldest proverbs—as, for example, at the end of Sonnet 94: "For sweetest things turn sourest by their deeds, / Lilies that fester, smell far worse than weeds." And the three quatrains give Shakespeare three short and pretty much separate chances to attack his material, instead of one intertwined octave.

Shakespeare's sonnets are, in fact, the ultimate example of his habit of going at his material from every possible angle. It's not just that every sonnet has three separate quatrains, with as many fresh chances for attacking the subject of the poem from a different approach. The sonnets themselves are variations on the different themes that run through the sequence. The first fourteen, for example, are all arguments to a beautiful young man to have children, lest his beauty

What They Don't Want You to Learn from Shakespeare's *Sonnets*

Love and sex are serious things. If you treat them lightly, someone's going to get hurt.

die with him. With Sonnet 15, that theme begins to be combined with a related one: that Shakespeare will make the young man immortal by his poetry. And the sequence as a whole is a thoroughgoing exploration of love—looked at from every possible side, picked up and squeezed, turned upside down and shaken.

The great sonnet sequences before Shakespeare had, naturally, been addressed to women. Shakespeare's choice to address his sonnets (at least at the beginning of the sequence) to a young man has puzzled and disturbed readers for centuries now. It's a deliberately strange choice, and you can hardly blame our PC English professors, steeped in the politics of "sexual identity," for looking through Shakespeare's sonnets for evidence of his sexual orientation. But Shakespeare's sonnets aren't as simple as that. One clue to their complexity is that W. H. Auden, a twentieth-century Anglo-American poet and critic who indubitably *was* "gay" in our sense of the word, makes a very good case that the love expressed in the first 126 sonnets (which all seem to be about the poet's relationship with the young man) isn't primarily sexual.[27]

Precisely because homosexual experiences were out of the question for all but the most extreme Elizabethans, choosing to write about a man meant that Shakespeare could write poetry about love that transcends the natural appetites—if, that is, there is any such thing. Or, to put it another way, a passionate same-sex friendship is, at least since Plato, the obvious kind of relationship to explore, if you're interested in whether love between two human beings can rise above the biological imperative to couple and reproduce. Any poetry about the love of a man for a woman, no matter how rarefied, is going to be shaped, on some level, by sexual desire: "So while thy beauty draws the heart to love, / As fast thy virtue bends that love to good. / But, ah, Desire still cries, "Give me some food,"" as Sidney put it in *Astrophel and Stella*.

Romantic love between men and women may be a school of virtue, especially when the fulfillment of that love is postponed or denied. But that kind of love aims at a mutually satisfying consummation. Marriage is the arrangement according to which both the man and the woman get what they want, and what's good for them, each from the other.

By making the first object of his love poetry a young man, Shakespeare created a situation in which the good of the other was not something that would also satisfy the poet. The only way for the poet to desire the young man's fulfillment is for him to want something that the young man has to get somewhere else, outside of his friendship with the poet—or so it seems at first. Shakespeare admires the young man, and that admiration inspires a kind of desire that seems more disinterested than sexual passion. The poet's initial thought is that the beauty he admires should be reproduced, so he tries to persuade the young man to beget a son, who will still be beautiful when time and death have destroyed the young man's beauty. This love, however elevated above the ordinary boy-meets-girl sort of situation, still seems to partake in a familiar pattern: admiration fuels desire, a procreative impulse, an urge to use one's persuasive powers to influence the person one loves, and a passionate certainty that, somehow, love can conquer even death.

The poet's first generous impulse begins to be transformed into a desire to make the young man immortal through poetry—a project in which the poet is no longer just a disinterested admirer: "So long as men can breathe or eyes can see, / So long lives this, and this gives life to thee." This gift to the young man changes their relationship. The young man and the poet come to belong to one another in some way that is often defined but—partly because of the very number and variety of the definitions—continually shifting, impossible to pin down.

The course of the relationship between the poet and the young man provides an occasion for almost every kind of love poem there is—or, at least, for every possible kind of poem about love that aspires to the heights. Their friendship inures the poet to the failures and deficiencies of his own life; he seems to live through the young man, who is almost another self. But then, human nature being what it is, complications ensue. The young man's actions are not always as beautiful as his person. The poet is hurt by neglect, by a certain coldness, by the fact that the young man enjoys being flattered by other poets, and by a relationship that develops between the young man and a woman with whom the poet is sexually obsessed.

The "Dark Lady" allows Shakespeare to explore love from the other extreme. For her, the poet feels the kind of erotic love that falls below, rather than rising above, the common standard. The relationship between the poet and the lady is unequivocally physical, verging on a guilty sexual fetish. The relationships among the *Sonnets'* three main characters allow for a thorough exploration of the ugly side of erotic love, which has already begun to emerge from the breakdown of the poet's passionate friendship with the young man.

The situations in the sonnets are extreme. But the poetry hits right in the center of human experience. Shakespeare gives us the heights and depths of the human soul. And 154 sonnets that seem to say everything that it's possible to say about human love—and that every lover feels he can speak from his heart.

Chapter Four

THE SEVENTEENTH CENTURY
Religion as a Matter of Life and Death

> ...what in me is dark
> Illumine, what is low raise and support;
> That to the heighth of this great argument
> I may assert eternal providence.
> And justify the ways of God to men.
>
> —John Milton, *Paradise Lost*

The greatest seventeenth-century English literature is about the Christian religion, a subject that bores and irritates PC English professors. Many features of seventeenth-century Christianity are entirely alien to the culture of our intellectuals. But its most obnoxious aspect, from the point of view of political correctness, may be the idea that Christianity is not just "worthy of all our soul's devotion"[1] but worthy of what, in our culture wars, we now call "a place in the public square."

Reading the literature of seventeenth-century England puts you instantly in touch with a time and place in which Christianity was still acknowledged to be a matter of life and death. The 1600s saw the end of the Wars of Religion in Europe, and the establishment of religious tolerance as a characteristic feature of Western societies. Now that that very regime of tolerance is under unprecedented stress—from pressures as different as campaigns to force Christian pharmacists in the U.S. to prescribe abortion-inducing drugs, to proposals for incorporating Islamic *sharia*

The seventeenth-century literature you must not miss

John Donne, *Songs and Sonnets* and *Holy Sonnets*

George Herbert, *The Temple*

Thomas Browne, *Religio Medici*

John Bunyan, *Pilgrim's Progress*

John Milton, sonnets and *Paradise Lost*

Andrew Marvell, "To His Coy Mistress"

into the laws of Canada and Europe—it's an especially good time to take another look at what people wrote in the seventeenth century.

John Donne

Toward the end of the Elizabethan Renaissance a new elaborately self-conscious kind of poetry emerged. "Metaphysical" poetry has a lot in common with the "mannerist" painting that followed the art of the High Renaissance in Italy. Just as mannerism in painting is recognized by its lurid colors and exaggerated forms—think of El Greco—the metaphysical style in poetry is known by its far-fetched, highly intellectual, and deliberately difficult metaphors, or "conceits." As (an unsympathetic) Dr. Johnson explained in his *Lives of the Poets,* the thoughts of the metaphysical poets "are often new but seldom natural; they are not obvious, but neither are they just; and the reader, far from wondering that he missed them, wonders more frequently by what perverseness of industry they were ever found."

John Donne is the quintessential metaphysical poet. Donne's *Songs and Sonnets* is a collection of love poems written in his youth and circulated privately during his lifetime but not printed until after he died. It's brimful of ingeniously inventive—someone thinking along the lines of Dr. Johnson might call them *perverse*—comparisons, and of newly created verse forms (almost one for each poem).

In "A Valediction: Of Weeping," for example, Donne claims—among other conceits too numerous to mention—that his tears are valuable because they reflect his mistress's face, just as the face of the monarch is stamped on coins "For thy face coins them, and thy stamp they bear, / And by this mintage they are something worth." And next that each tear is a whole world because it's like a globe stamped with her image, and she's the whole world to him: "So doth each tear, / Which thee doth wear, / A globe, yea world, by that impression grow." And that, when she starts crying too, it's like Heaven dissolving into rain in Noah's Flood—since she's his Heaven. And that she will drown him because her influence is like the power of the moon on the ocean's tides: "O more than moon, / Draw not up seas to drown me in thy sphere." And, finally, that the two of them can kill each other by sighing: "Since thou and I sigh one another's breath, / Who'er sighs most is cruelest, and hastes the other's death."

"Far-fetched" is too mild a description for Donne's conceits. Over and over again, he starts with some cliché about love and reasons from it to a fantastic and outrageous conclusion, which, nevertheless, appears to be a genuine insight into the nature of love—if often a forced, awkward, or brittle insight.

Donne works technical and expert knowledge (both scientific and theological) into his poetry. He pushes hard on the inherent incongruities of erotic love—how it's both a rarefied spiritual experience and a shockingly physical one—and builds complex arguments about exactly how it all fits together. Donne's voice is often rough: "For God's sake hold your tongue, and let me love." His language is more direct and real than love poetry almost ever is: "Oh do not die, for I shall hate / All women so." And sometimes, in the intricate net he's woven, of lusts and loves and metaphysical complexities, he seems to catch hold, for a minute, of something

Can You Believe the Professors?

"…it was in spite of, not because of, Christianity that Milton, Donne and others wrote great poetry in the seventeenth century."

David Renaker, professor of English at San Francisco State. The Atheist Seventeenth Century Website, http://userwww.sfsu.edu/~draker/purpose.html, viewed 7/29/2006.

true, and beautiful: "For, nor in nothing, nor in things / Extreme, and scattering bright, can love inhere."

Donne's love poetry is endlessly fascinating, but his religious writings are even better. During his youth, Donne was living the irregular life that's celebrated in his erotic poetry, but he was also wrestling with religious questions. Donne was raised in a Catholic family when Catholics were considered traitors to the queen. (His own brother died in prison for harboring a Catholic priest.) "I had my first breeding and conversation with men of a suppressed and afflicted religion, accustomed to the despite of death, and hungry of an imagined martyrdom,"[2] John Donne wrote of his Catholic upbringing after he had abandoned the religion of his childhood for the Church of England. Donne did not succumb to pressure to be ordained into the clergy of the established Protestant church until after the age of forty—at the end of more than a decade of financial desperation. He had ruined his worldly prospects by entering into a secret marriage with the niece of his employer, the Lord High Keeper of the Privy Seal. The ensuing scandal landed Donne briefly in prison and set in motion the events that led (almost fifteen years later) to his agreement, under pressure from King James I himself, to be ordained in the Church of England.

What They Don't Want You to Learn from John Donne

God is even more exciting (and important) than sex.

Most of Donne's sacred poems were composed in the lean years between his marriage and ordination, though a few were written after he had become a Church of England clergyman. His sermons and "devotions" are among the finest religious prose in English: "No man is an island, entire of itself; every man is a piece of the continent, a part of the main...never send to know for whom the bell tolls; it tolls for thee."

Donne's religious works use some of the same elaborate metaphors and have some of the same roughness as his erotic poetry. Holy Sonnet XIX, for example, uses the kind of conceits familiar from his love poetry: "Inconstancy unnaturally hath begot / A constant habit; that when I would not / I change in vows, and in devotion." In other words, the unfaithfulness that Donne had practiced in his love affairs has made him unfaithful (paradoxically, *dependably* unfaithful) in his spiritual life. The practice he had breaking promises to women has created a habit that carries over to the promises he now makes to God.

Donne's repentance is just as changeable "[a]s my profane love, and as soon forgot." Yesterday he couldn't face Heaven; today he courts God "[i]n prayers and flattering speeches" as he used to court women. And tomorrow he feels real fear of God's justice, on account of his sins. Holy Sonnet XIX ends with another conceit—that Donne's devotion to God is like a chronic disease, with some days that are feverish and some that aren't. With this difference: "So my devout fits come and go away / Like a fantastic ague; save that here / Those are my best days, when I shake with fear."

"Goodfriday, 1613. Riding Westward" begins with an elaborate astronomical conceit of the sort Donne had used in his secular love poetry, now applied to his spiritual state: "Let man's soul be a sphere, and then, in this, / The intelligence that moves, devotion is." The "sphere" is the orbit of a planet around the Earth, according to the old Ptolemaic astronomy. The "intelligence" is the angel who was believed to pilot the planet in its path. But Donne's devotion to God is like a planet that has "grown / Subject to foreign motions"—his soul has been pulled out of his orbit around God by pleasure and business. This very day, on Good Friday, he ought to be in church contemplating the death of Christ on the Cross; but he's traveling on business. In church he would be facing east, toward Jerusalem and the place of the Crucifixion. On the business he's on, he's traveling westward.

The lines about the Crucifixion bristle with paradoxes. If, instead of facing west into the sunset, he were facing east, "There should I see a sun [Christ], by rising [on the Cross] set [die] / And by that setting endless day beget." He's afraid to look at "those hands, which span the poles / And turn all spheres at once, pierced with those holes." And at the poem's end comes another extended conceit:

> O, Saviour, as Thou hang'st upon the tree;
> I turn my back to Thee but to receive
> Corrections, till Thy mercies bid Thee leave
> Burn off my rusts and my deformity,
> Restore Thine image, so much, by Thy grace,
> That Thou may'st know me, and I'll turn my face.

Donne's religious poetry has enormous force—such great power, in fact, that it appeals to readers not at all in sympathy with the religious beliefs it expresses. Self-described atheist Camille Paglia, for example, took a phrase from Holy Sonnet XIV—the one that begins "Batter my heart, three-personed God; for You / As yet but knock, breathe, shine, and seek to mend"—for the title of her 2005 collection: *Break, Blow, Burn: Camille Paglia Reads Forty-Three of the World's Best Poems.*[3] Paglia has called herself "an atheist who passionately identifies with ancient Mediterranean paganism" and explained that "[s]ince I am not a Christian, I have little interest in the sacred sites of Jerusalem, aside from their archaeology."[4] But she's fascinated by Donne's religious poetry. Three of Paglia's "Forty-Three of the World's Best Poems" are by Donne, and, of those, two are from the *Holy Sonnets.* It's easy to see why. They're both truly great poems, and they're full of the *more*-than-life-or-death excitement of sin and death, Heaven and hell, and the knife's-edge drama of personal salvation—which Donne himself finally found to be more compelling than sexual love. It's a testimony to their power that Paglia, who has claimed that "Judeo-Christianity" "cannot deal with sex or aggression,"[5] can appreciate Donne's achievement.

The themes of Donne's religious poetry are themselves even larger and deeper than the mysteries of sexual love that he explored in his erotic poetry. In God, Donne found material that was big enough not to be overwhelmed by the elaborate intellectual machinery of his poetic technique. The Incarnation of God and the Redemption of mankind arguably can't be handled *without* the violent paradoxes and extreme incongruities Donne resorts to. In his devotional poetry, Donne still seems to be reaching. But he's reaching to comprehend and express something that, of itself, requires the human mind to stretch to the uttermost limits of its powers.

John Milton

Of the great English poets, John Milton is the one whose faith was the closest to what we call "evangelical" or "fundamentalist" Christianity. Milton's career—both literary and political—was deeply grounded in his Christianity. He was also, without a doubt, the most learned writer of literature in English. It's not just that he knew more; his poetry is the most ostentatiously educated of all great English poetry. Milton's seven years at Cambridge were only the prelude to six years of full-time independent study that he undertook to prepare himself for the literary career he believed was the proper use for the talents God had given him. Milton became fluent in Latin, Greek, Hebrew, and Italian, knew the great literature in them all, and also studied philosophy, theology, math, music, history, and science. He then spent most of his thirtieth year touring the Continent and meeting the great minds of his own day.

This monumental education was cut short by the impending Civil War in England. *Paradise Lost,* Milton's great English epic, wasn't published until he was fifty-seven years old. In the meantime, throughout the prime of his life, Milton was preoccupied with public affairs. The Civil War was the English edition of the Wars of Religion that had been raging in one European country after another since the beginning of the Protestant Reformation. The more radical Protestants in England—the ones we'd call "fundamentalist"—were proving to be anything but "easy to command" by government and church authorities. In the seventeenth century, these Protestants were called "Puritans" because they wanted to purify the church of the rituals (and the government by bishops) that they saw as Roman Catholic corruptions. Charles I and his Archbishop of Canterbury, William Laud, were attempting to move the Church of England—and, what was even more controversial, the Church of Scotland, the forerunner of our Presbyterian churches—back toward a style of worship and a form of church government closer to Catholicism. Laud's restoration of "popish" institutions outraged the hardcore Protestants. Resentment at Charles's highhanded style of governing combined with these religious grievances to pit Parliament against the king.

When the tug-of-war between them became a Civil War, Milton was firmly on the side of the "Roundheads"—as the Puritan troops fighting for the Parliament were nicknamed on account of their short haircuts. (The king's supporters came to be known as "Cavaliers.") After the Parliamentary army prevailed and King Charles was executed, Milton served as Secretary for Foreign Tongues (putting his elaborate education to practical use) under Oliver Cromwell, the victorious general who ruled England as Lord Protector. But after Cromwell's death, the traditional English government by "King, Lords, and Commons"[6] was restored.

The failure of the Puritan political project left Milton a despised and impoverished man, but it allowed him to fulfill his ambition to write a great epic poem. In *Paradise Lost* Milton bypassed the obvious subject matter for an English epic—the "Matter of Britain," those stories about

King Arthur that are the subject of Thomas Malory's *Morte d'Arthur,* and to which Edmund Spenser had turned to construct the elaborate world of *The Faerie Queene.* For Milton, the most important events of history were the events of the Bible, the central drama of human life was temptation, and the best kind of heroism was patient resistance to it.

Temptation is *the* theme of Milton's poetry. Take *Comus,* for example, which Milton wrote during the latter stages of his long education. It's a masque, a little play including music and dancing, with parts written for the children of the Earl of Bridgewater, at whose house the entertainment

What They Don't Want You to Learn from John Milton

"Fundamentalist" Christians aren't "poor, uneducated, and easy to command."

Michael Weisskopf, "Energized by Pulpit or Passion, the Public Is Calling: 'Gospel Grapevine' Displays Strength in Controversy over Military Gay Ban," *Washington Post,* February 1, 1993, A10; the *Post* issued a correction the next day.

was staged. The plot is the temptation of "The Lady," who was played by the Earl's fifteen-year-old daughter. The Lady's tempter is Comus, a wicked creature fathered by Bacchus, god of wine, on Circe, the witch who turned men into swine in *The Odyssey.* Comus lives in a dark wood and tempts travelers to drink his potion. If they succumb to the temptation—and, we're told, "most do taste through fond intemperate thirst"— their faces are transformed into the faces of wolves or hogs, tigers or goats. If the Lady fails the test, she'll join the beast-headed "rabble" of Comus' followers, who "roll with pleasure in a sensual sty."

Comus is about temperance, of course, and especially about that subset of temperance that's known as chastity (a very politically incorrect virtue, but one that's essential to the safety and happiness of fifteen-year-old girls). But the Lady's reward, if she passes the trial, isn't just to be safe in her present happiness and dignity. And it isn't the happy marriage that would reward the heroine of a Shakespeare play, either. The Attendant Spirit who comes down from the heavens to help the Lady (a "bright aerial" creature who might be a sort of theologically sophisticated cousin to Ariel, Prospero's errand-running spirit in Shakespeare's *Tempest*) explains what the stakes are. While most men live on this Earth like animals penned in a farmyard and do no better than "[s]trive to keep up a frail and feverish being," a few of them "by due steps aspire / To lay their just hands on that golden key / That opes the palace of Eternity." We can fall by temptation, but we can rise by it, too.

At the very end of the play, after the Lady has resisted Comus's wiles and been rescued by her brothers, the Spirit flies up to the heavens again, enticing the audience to follow him up into those delicious regions,

> ...those happy climes that lie
> Where day never shuts his eye
> Up in the broad fields of the sky....
> Mortals that would follow me,
> Love Virtue, she alone is free;
> She can teach you how to climb
> Higher than the sphery chime;
> Or if Virtue feeble were,
> Heaven itself would stoop to her.

Milton's best-known sonnet is also about temptation. In this case, the person being tempted is Milton. The sonnet is about his frustration with his blindness and his still unfulfilled literary ambitions. Milton's loss of vision was gradual, but he was blind by his mid-forties. The obvious temptation he's struggling with, in this poem, is to complain about the unfairness of it all, and to blame God. But the more subtle temptation behind the obvious one is the assumption that activity and accomplishment are what God demands of us.

When I consider how my light is spent

Ere half my days, in this dark world and wide,

And that one talent which is death to hide,

Lodged with me useless, though my soul more bent

To serve therewith my Maker, and present

My true account, lest He, returning, chide;

"Doth God exact day-labour, light denied?"

I fondly ask; but Patience, to prevent

That murmur, soon replies; "God doth not need

Either man's work, or His own gifts; who best

Bear His mild yoke, they serve Him best; His state

Is kingly—thousands at His bidding speed

And post o'er land and ocean without rest:

They also serve who only stand and wait."

Milton's heroic ideal is the patient obedience recommended by this sonnet, not deeds like the feats of arms that won glory for the knights of the Round Table. In all three of the great poems of Milton's maturity—*Paradise Lost, Paradise Regained,* and *Samson Agonistes*—the hero's trial is whether he will "stand and wait" on God's will, instead of giving in to the temptation to freelance in some way—to act out of his own impatience with God's plan.

The temptation of Adam and Eve is material ideally suited to Milton's genius, and it's the subject of his greatest work. Milton sets out the subject of *Paradise Lost* in the poem's famous opening lines:

Of Man's first disobedience, and the fruit

Of that forbidden tree, whose mortal taste

Brought death into the world, and all our woe,

With loss of Eden, till one greater Man

Restore us, and regain the blissful seat. . . .

Paradise Lost is a sort of anti-heroic heroic poem. In Milton's epic, all the heroic-seeming deeds are done by Satan, who starts a hopeless rebellion against God, and then daringly sneaks into Eden to engage in sabotage behind enemy lines. The Fall, the disaster that involves the whole human race in misery and death, happens because first Eve and then Adam start thinking they have to take heroic action, instead of obeying God's commandment. "Bold deed thou hast presumed, adventurous Eve," says Adam to his wife after she takes the forbidden fruit. "O glorious trial of exceeding love / Illustrious evidence, example high!" says Eve about Adam's decision to join her in her sin.

To make an epic about temptation work, Milton had to make the temptation actually tempting. He succeeded. At least since William Blake claimed in his *Marriage of Heaven and Hell* that Milton was "of the Devil's party without knowing it," quite a few readers of *Paradise Lost* have found Milton's Satan more attractive than his God. Some of our PC English professors are certainly among this number. David Renaker, for example, professor of English at San Francisco State University and creator of the "The Atheist Seventeenth Century Website" compares Milton's God to Stalin. (And, possibly more damning in the eyes of some English professors, to Richard Nixon.) He also enthuses about Adam's decision to follow Eve into disobedience.[7]

> ## What Else They Don't Want You to Learn from John Milton
>
> Obedience can be heroic (and, paradoxically, liberating).

To find Adam's self-immolation—which Renaker quite reasonably compares to the deaths of doomed lovers such as Tristram, Romeo, and Antony—attractive is one thing. (After all, it really is a beautiful thing for a man to love a woman more than his own life. Milton knows it is, and he expects us to be pulled in the direction of Adam's choice.) But not to be able to see the ultimate folly of Adam's fall is another. Adam's not just putting Eve before himself. He's preferring her to good sense, integrity, and God. It's a temptation men (and women, too) fall prey to in sexual relationships every day. Adam is abandoning what he knows is the right way, only so that he can keep a woman he understands is utterly corrupt. He may not know exactly how low Eve's already sunk, but he understands she's lost to everything good.

We, Milton's readers, do know the ugly details. As soon as Eve ate the fruit, she considered whether to offer it to Adam, too. Her first thought was to keep it to herself in order to make herself superior to her husband ("for, inferior, who is free?" she asked herself). But she changed her mind when she remembered that the fruit might kill her. Eve decided that she would rather make sure Adam died, too, than risk his surviving her, especially considering the possibility that God might create another woman. And then—as people who make their choices according to impulses like these inevitably do—she lied about what she was doing. Eve told Adam that if she believed the fruit would kill them "I would sustain alone / The worst, and not persuade thee; rather die / Deserted. . . . " As any advice columnist worth her salt would tell you, a woman like this isn't worth it.

Satan's kind of heroism—the Devil's energetic rebellion against God, and the apparently noble deeds Adam and Eve do under his influence— is meant to attract us, and it does. But Milton shows us that disobedience that begins by looking noble and doomed is ultimately just selfish, squalid, and cheap.

In *Paradise Regained,* he shows us the opposite: the perfect example of that patient obedience that Milton sees as the only true heroism. According to the New Testament, Christ is the new Adam. Christ's obedience unto death saved us from the original sin we inherited from Adam's disobedience. Any number of stories from the Gospels could be made to illustrate Christ's obedience. Milton, being Milton, chose Christ's temptation in the desert—the perfect counterpoint to the original temptation in the garden.

Satan tempts Christ with everything that motivates human beings—physical appetite, riches, ambition, learning—and He isn't moved by any of them. There's remarkably little action in *Paradise Regained.* It's all just Satan throwing everything he's got at Christ, and being repeatedly rebuffed. But Christ isn't just standing there; He's doing something. Or, rather, precisely by just standing there, He's doing the best thing He could possibly do. His perfect obedience is working to repair the sin of our first parents, and His victory will break the dominion of Satan, under which the whole human race has toiled since our expulsion from the Garden of Eden. The climax of the poem comes when Satan, who has set Christ on the pinnacle of the Temple in Jerusalem, tempts Him to throw Himself down, quoting the Scripture that promises that God's "angels... shall uplift Thee, lest at any time / Thou chance to dash Thy foot against a stone":

> To whom thus Jesus: Also it is written,
>
> Tempt not the Lord thy God, He said, and stood:
>
> But Satan, smitten with amazement, fell.

The premium Milton puts on obedience and the importance of temptation in his understanding of the Christian faith are essential to his argument for freedom of the press, which he made in a pamphlet entitled *Areopagitica: A Speech for the Liberty of Unlicensed Printing to the Parliament of England.* We tend to forget Milton when we think of the pioneers of free speech. Voltaire and John Stuart Mill are the historical figures regularly trotted out in support of the free-speech position: when, for example, cartoons of Mohammed spark deadly violence. We tend to assume that our rights to freedom of religion and speech originated in the Enlightenment criticism of religious faith, or else in the exhaustion that followed the Wars of Religion in the seventeenth century.

The popular myth about free speech is a history lesson in the dangers of taking religion too seriously. Protestants and Catholics, it's said, killed each other across Europe for more than a hundred years and then finally ralized that religion simply wasn't worth killing or dying for. In this telling of the story, we have freedom of religion because our ancestors figured out that religion is, on the one hand, impossible to know the truth about, and, on the other, not really important enough to warrant more bloodshed. This rationale for our intellectual freedoms is the position that sometime Milton scholar and celebrity "literary theory" guru Stanley Fish describes as "liberalism":

> In reaction to the apparent failure of mankind to identify the one truly meaningful thing around which life might be organized, liberalism sets out to identify the set of truly nonmeaningful things—things that no one will want to die for or kill for—around which life might be organized.[8]

The only safe place for religion, according to the liberal or Enlightenment way of thinking, is in private life. The government won't take sides in religious controversies, and religious people had better keep their arguments out of the public square. You can make any kind of claim for or against religion, as long as you don't attempt to "impose" your religious ideas on society at large.

But freedom of speech and the press were not invented by Enlightenment rationalists. In fact, during the Enlightenment itself, speech and the press were freer in conservative England, where Christianity was still taken seriously by the intelligentsia (though by no means all of them were believers), than in France, which was a hotbed of radical skepticism about religion. The history of the liberty to speak and publish in English law is long and complex and certainly doesn't begin with Milton.[9] But the publication of Milton's *Areopagitica* is an early high-water mark in that history. Milton doesn't argue for absolute freedom of speech: he takes it for granted that some opinions are outside the pale. But he does argue for a wide liberty to publish opinions, even erroneous ones.

What Else They Don't Want You to Learn from Milton

Our intellectual freedoms are Christian, not anti-Christian, in origin.

Now Milton certainly didn't argue for a free press out of indifference to religious truth—or out of exhaustion with religious violence, for that matter. Quite the opposite. Milton wrote the *Areopagitica* in 1644, between the two most important Parliamentary victories in the Civil War, at a time when the Puritan revolution seemed about to give birth, at last, to a truly, radically Protestant English society. The *Areopagitica* itself is suffused with this hope:

> Now once again by all concurrence of signs, and by the general instinct of holy and devout men. . . . God is decreeing to begin some new and great period in His Church, even to the reforming of Reformation itself: what does He then but reveal himself to His servants, and as His manner is, first to His Englishmen?

Milton was addressing himself to Parliament when Puritanism was in the ascendant, to urge the leaders of a religious revolution to decide for free speech "in the midst of your victories and successes"—not suing for peace with theological enemies who had fought his own side to a stalemate, just hoping to agree to live and let live.

Milton's argument for freedom of the press is the very opposite of the liberal or Enlightenment case. According to Milton, uncovering religious truth is *so important* that we can't afford to miss the opportunity to learn some piece of it that might never see the light of day under a regime of government censorship. The man who thinks the Reformation is complete, Milton argues, betrays that he is still very short of the whole truth. "Truth," he says, "indeed came once into the world with her divine Master, and was a perfect shape most glorious to look on. . . ." But since that time Truth has been hewn into a thousand pieces, and "scattered . . . to the four winds." Censorship might hinder the work of the truth-seekers who are trying to gather it up again.

Even "bad books" may be useful to the truth-seeker. The works of those in error are helpful to "a discreet and judicious reader" whom they may serve "to confute, to forewarn, and to illustrate." As Milton sees it, it's our job to sift through different opinions, to test them to find what's right: "all opinions, yea errors, known, read, and collated, are of main service and assistance toward the speedy attainment of what is truest."

But in addition to the actual discovery of truth, there is, in Milton's view, an independent value to our discernment and rejection of error. Milton's preoccupation with temptation is at the very heart of his defense of freedom of the press. We live in a world where good and evil "grow up together almost inseparably" because God wanted human beings to be free: Adam himself would have been "a mere artificial Adam," not a truly rational being, if God had not given him freedom to choose, and opportunity to fall:

> We ourselves esteem not of that obedience, or love, or gift,
> which is of force: God therefore left [Adam] free, set before him
> a provoking object, ever almost in his eyes; herein consisted
> his merit, herein the right of his reward, the praise of his absti-
> nence. Wherefore did He create passions within us, pleasures
> round about us, but that these rightly tempered are the very
> ingredients of virtue?

"For God," Milton argues, "sure esteems the growth and completing of one virtuous person more than the restraint of ten vicious."

Milton wanted freedom of the press for the sake of increasing the knowledge of religious truth and allowing God-given opportunities for the attainment of virtue. The liberal view is that religious truth is impossible to know, or dangerous to try to figure out, or both. The state should be neutral with regard to religion, any kind of speech or printing should be allowed—as long as religion is disqualified from influencing public policy.

But there's a problem with this arrangement. When nations exile religious truth from the public square, the number and scope of things that people can disagree about doesn't shrink. It grows. The issues that divided the Puritans and Royalists no longer seem to us to be matters for public debate. We don't want Congress to decide whether Christ's church should be governed by bishops or presbyters—or whether we should celebrate the Lord's Supper on a wooden table, or the Eucharistic sacrifice on a stone altar. These matters have been successfully banished from our political discourse. Those of us who still care about such questions are a tiny minority who would never think of attempting to impose our private religious beliefs on our fellow citizens.

Now we disagree, instead, about other issues: questions on which it would never have occurred to either Roundheads or Cavaliers that there could even *be* opposing opinions. We argue about abortion and euthanasia, about animal rights, about the nature of marriage. Beliefs and assumptions that were shared by virtually everyone in the West before the Enlightenment, and that the participants in the Wars of Religion may not even have realized depended on religious principles, are now matters of controversy.

In a backhanded sort of way, we've come around by experience to the realization that religion (or the lack of it) is a matter of life and death, after all. Peter Singer, the Princeton bioethicist, for example, argues that normal chimpanzees are more valuable than brain-dead human infants. It turns out that respect for human life really does depend on the belief that human beings are created in God's image.[10]

So Milton's epic about the Fall of Man—about Adam and Eve's decline from happiness and dignity into sordid selfishness—is not irrelevant to our own situation. Whether we still take temptation, obedience, and religious truth seriously, or if, to us, they seem like outmoded relics of our pre-Enlightenment past, Milton's works have implications for us all.

Chapter Five

RESTORATION AND EIGHTEENTH-CENTURY LITERATURE
THE AGE OF REASON

My dear friend, clear your mind of cant…you may *talk* in this manner; it is a mode of talking in society; but don't *think* foolishly.

—Samuel Johnson

Aphra Behn is the star attraction of the PC version of Restoration and eighteenth-century literature. Mrs. Behn, a playwright and the authoress of melodramatic (and mildly pornographic) "true stories," was justly ranked as a minor literary figure of the Restoration period until politically correct English professors started building a new curriculum around gender and race. Now Aphra Behn is widely touted as "the first professional woman writer" in English. And her works are pored over for insights into racism and sexism.

If you want to know what the "true history" of a girl sold into a bawdy house by her brother (to avoid paying her dowry) reveals about "the fantasy life and daydreams of women in late seventeenth-century England,"[1] then Aphra Behn is your cup of tea. And if you want your righteous indignation against the racism and sexism that, in your opinion, define Western culture, stoked, then Mrs. Behn's proto-novel *Oroonoko* (another true "history") is the book for you. It's the story of an African prince who is betrayed into slavery, leads a slave rebellion in Surinam, murders his

The Restoration and eighteenth-century literature you must not miss

John Dryden,
Absalom and Achitophel,
MacFlecknoe

Alexander Pope,
The Rape of the Lock,
The Dunciad

Jonathan Swift,
Gulliver's Travels

continued on p. 104

103

The Restoration and eighteenth-century literature you must not miss (continued)

Samuel Johnson,
    Preface to his
    Shakespeare edition

James Boswell,
    Life of Johnson

Samuel Richardson,
    Clarissa

Henry Fielding,
    Tom Jones

Thomas Gray,
    "Elegy Written in a
    Country Churchyard"

lady-love to prevent her from being raped after his death, and is finally tortured to death by dismemberment. *Oroonoko* is the ideal English literature to study—if the point of studying English literature is to sort out whether white women in slave societies were more colonized against than colonizing, or if race trumps gender in victim politics.

But if you *don't* think racism and sexism are the essential facts about Western culture, there's plenty of other literature from the same era to read. And if you suspect that Aphra Behn's writing appeals mainly to some of the least creditable aspects of our common human nature—maudlin sentimentality; a prurient interest in slavery, rape, prostitution, and torture; and cost-free self-righteousness about the sins of people long ago, far away, and very different form ourselves—then you may find more congenial company in the dead white males who used to make up the old Restoration and eighteenth-century literature curriculum.

John Dryden, Alexander Pope, Jonathan Swift, and Samuel Johnson are, in all of English literature, the four great deflators of every kind of pretense, hypocrisy, and self-deceiving folly. Of course, almost all great English and American literature was written by melanin-challenged men who are no longer with us. But the four writers whose works used to be the core of eighteenth-century reading lists are somehow even more Dead White Male than anybody else. They're hopelessly politically incorrect. These great no-holds-barred satirists shared an attitude that's the exact opposite of the euphemism-generating, affirmative action-demanding, victim-politics-breeding PC mindset. They were unapologetic champions of excellence and pitiless mockers of mediocrity. They didn't hesitate to use their talents to cut the competition down to size. Nothing was off limits—from the religion and politics of an intellectual enemy, to his obesity or venereal disease.

It's curious that three out of four of our Dead White Males were themselves seriously disabled. (Or should that be "differently abled"?) Alexander Pope was deformed by a disease contracted in childhood, which bent his body and stunted his growth. He was just four and a half feet tall, and often the butt of cruel jokes. Jonathan Swift suffered mysterious dizzy spells and spent years worried about his mental stability—before he finally became too ill to write or even speak coherently; he was put under the care of guardians three years before his death. And Samuel Johnson was afflicted with a wretched combination of physical and mental disorders that scarred his face, distorted his posture and gait, affected his eyesight, and kept him, his whole life, teetering on the edge of what we would call major depressive disorder.

What They Don't Want You to Learn from the English Literature of the Enlightenment

Realism, common sense, and good humor are more dignified equipment for life than victim politics, wishful thinking, and liberal guilt. (Plus, satire is a more effective weapon than emotional blackmail.)

But none of these men expected to be pitied, or even treated gently. Instead, they fought back. They didn't act like victims— or even survivors. Instead, they attacked with unexampled ferocity. And, what is most remarkable (from our PC-tinted perspective), they didn't try to bend or blur standards (of normality, or of excellence) to soften the reality of their disabilities; they didn't even steer clear of what must have felt like very sore subjects. Pope, writing to a lady who had belittled him because of his dwarf-like stature, doesn't deny she's right. He admits to having "little eyes / Little legs and little thighs" and even unspecified other "things of little size / You know where." Pope's defense (or rather, his full-barreled attack) is that she's the one who's really small, where it matters:

> You, 'tis true, have fine black eyes,
> Taper legs, and tempting thighs,
> Yet what more than all we prize

Is a thing of little size,

You know where.

Likewise Swift, worried about his own sanity, didn't avoid the subject of mental balance out of embarrassment. In fact, his greatest work is on that very subject. Swift gets some of his most remarkable effects by showing how even righteous anger at the injustice and stupidity of human society—which was his own stock in trade—can upset the precarious balance of the human mind. The literature of the Restoration and eighteenth century is characterized by clear-sighted realism. Reading these quintessential Dead White Males after dabbling in feminist and "post-colonial" literary criticism is delightfully bracing.

Dead white male #1: John Dryden

John Dryden is the genius of Restoration literature. His poetry set the pattern for the next century. Dryden established satire as the dominant genre of the English literature of the Enlightenment, and the heroic couplet as the dominant verse form. Dryden's couplets are inimitable (though often imitated). They're as smooth and clear as glass. Take, for example, the first few lines of Dryden's *Absalom and Achitophel.* Dryden is telling the story of Absalom, King David's son, whose rebellion against David ended in Absalom's death. But Dryden's version of this Old Testament history is really the story of King Charles II and his illegitimate son James Scott, the Duke of Monmouth. Because Charles had no son born in wedlock, the heir to the throne was his Catholic brother James Stuart (later James II), whom Protestants wanted to bar from the succession: some of them preferred James Scott as the next king. Dryden exploits the similarities between this situation and the Absalom story; he glosses Charles's philandering as the polygamy that was permitted to King David in Old Testament times:

> In pious times, ere priestcraft did begin,
>
> Before polygamy was made a sin. . . .
>
> Then Israel's monarch after Heaven's own heart,
>
> His vigorous warmth did variously impart. . . .
>
> To wives and slaves; and, wide as his command,
>
> Scattered his Maker's image through the land.

Dryden pulls off—apparently effortlessly—the ticklish feat of parodying the king's adultery and his son's dangerous ambition without causing offense.

Where Dryden *wanted* to offend, that same superb control made him devastating. Here he is in *MacFlecknoe,* suavely insulting an inferior poet named Thomas Shadwell. Dryden begins by supposing that Shadwell has been named as official successor to a wretchedly bad Irish poet named Richard Flecknoe. Here's Flecknoe, explaining how Shadwell beat out the competition:

> Shadwell alone my perfect image bears,
>
> Mature in dullness from his tender years:
>
> Shadwell alone, of all my sons, is he
>
> Who stands confirmed in full stupidity.
>
> The rest to some faint meaning make pretence,
>
> But Shadwell never deviates into sense.

Dryden and his eighteenth-century literary heirs did not suffer fools gladly. Satire dominates Enlightenment-era English literature as no genre dominates any other literary period.

By the late eighteenth century, we've reached the classicizing period of English letters. The critical impulse—to categorize and evaluate, to prune rather than to fertilize—is in the ascendant. The literature of this era is urbane, accomplished, and clever. It has lively and even powerful elements, but it's never characterized by naïve enthusiasm or careless abundance. "Wit" is the prized quality. Sophistication is the prevailing attitude. There's passion in Restoration and eighteenth-century literature. There's even violence. But the violence is about fending off the irrationality that threatens to overwhelm good sense. Our Dead White Males' most devastating weapons are the superior intelligence and the self-control of the man who looks down on laziness, stupidity, vain pretense, and intemperate passions, and exposes them for what they are.

Dead white male #2: Alexander Pope

Pope isn't as smooth as Dryden (nobody is). But he's an even more vigorous, not to say ferocious, defender of good sense and good taste. Alexander Pope was the premier literary figure of his day. As he himself bragged about the power of his satire (in one of the end-stopped couplets typical of eighteenth-century poetry—one concise and perfectly balanced thought in just two lines): "Yes, I am proud; I must be proud to see / Men not afraid of God afraid of me."

Pope's *Dunciad* is a more ambitious *MacFlecknoe*: Pope takes on not just one ridiculous pretender to poetic genius, but the entire intellectual scene in eighteenth-century Britain. Pope's satire is more circumstantial and savage than Dryden's. *The Dunciad* lampoons dishonest publishers, plagiarizing poets, politicians who live by bribery, flatterers and bawds, men who fritter their intellects away on coin- and butterfly-collecting, schoolmasters whose pedantry shrinks, rather than expands, their students' minds. Pope heaps scorn on the sloth, stupidity, and hypocrisy of the whole race of pretentious dunces who, he argues, are reducing British culture to ignorance and anarchy:

> Lo! thy dread empire, Chaos! is restored;
> Light dies before thy uncreating word:
> Thy hand, great anarch! lets the curtain fall;
> And universal darkness buries all.

There's never been such a perfect expression of the perennial conservative insight that everything is going to the dogs.

Pope's *Rape of the Lock* is satire of a gentler sort. *MacFlecknoe* and *The Dunciad* both use the conventions of epic (or *heroic*) poetry to make their targets look small by contrast. But *The Rape of the Lock* is a whole delightful mock-heroic world. The poem was originally an attempt to help patch up a feud between two families, arising from an incident that involved an eligible young man and a coquette. Robert Petre ("the Baron" in the poem) had insulted and enraged Arabella Fermour ("Belinda") by surreptitiously cutting off a lock of her hair. Pope tells the story with all the conventions of epic poetry.

Like the gods and goddesses whose intervention decides the battles of Homer's *Iliad,* Pope's fairy-like sylphs and gnomes exert their invisible influence over the world of flirting and coffee-drinking (coffee was trendier in the eighteenth century than it would be again until the Age of Starbucks). Homer sang of the arming of Achilles; Pope gives us Belinda's arrangement of her hair and face. He treats a card game between Belinda and the Baron as armed combat.

Pope ridiculously juxtaposes really important things with trivialities (that can seem earth-shatteringly significant to frivolous minds generally, and particularly to the young and inexperienced). Here's the chief of the sylphs speculating about the nature of the mysterious danger—"wrapt in Night" by the Fates—that threatens Belinda:

> Whether the Nymph shall break Diana's law [lose her virginity],
> Or some frail china jar receive a flaw,
> Or stain her honour, or her new brocade,
> Forget her prayers, or miss a masquerade....
> Or lose her heart, or necklace, at a ball;
> Or whether Heaven has doomed that Shock [her lapdog] must
>   fall.

The *Rape of the Lock* is about keeping things in perspective, about living with the limitations you can't change, and about the value of good humor.

These lessons are never out of date—though they may sound harsh to us, accustomed as we are to euphemisms and wishful thinking. All the more reason we can benefit from hearing them. Pope wrote about the "rage, resentment, and despair" of "ancient ladies when refused a kiss."

Sharon Stone vs. Alexander Pope: Who Talks Sense about Female Sexuality?

Here's Sharon Stone, promoting *Basic Instinct 2*:

> "In America we tend to erase women after 40, and it's a period when women become their most interesting. They are sexual in a different and alluring way," added the star, who recently became the face of Dior skincare. "This film expresses that sexual allure in an unabashed and provocative way—in a way that is gritty and dangerous and quite presumptive."

And here's the advice that Pope has Clarissa give Belinda in *The Rape of the Lock*:

> But since, alas! frail beauty must decay,
> Curled or uncurled, since locks will turn to grey;
> Since painted, or not painted, all shall fade,
> And she who scorns a man, must die a maid;
> What then remains but well our power to use,
> And keep good humour still, whate'er we lose?

Richard Simpson, "Sharon Stone Shows Instinct for Sex Appeal," *Daily Mail*, March 16, 2006.

We call old people "seniors" and pretend that the "sexism" that "erases" women over the age of forty can be cured by consciousness-raising. Pope knew that the balance of power between the sexes inevitably shifts with the progress of time. He warned young women to use their beauty well while they have it. Pope's clear-headed satire is an excellent antidote to the large amounts of *cant* (the eighteenth-century term for polite or ideology-driven nonsense) that we hear about men and women, whether from feminist English professors or from over-the-hill Hollywood actresses.

Dead white male #3: Jonathan Swift

The third of our quartet of Dead White Males, Jonathan Swift, wrote satire that's at once more savage than Pope's and more suave than Dryden's. Here's how he pulls it off: Rather than pouring scorn on the objects of his ridicule from a great height (as both Dryden and Pope do, each in his own way), Swift gets *inside* what he wants to ridicule and exposes its absurdity from within. He creates a bland surface for his satire by inventing an alter ego, an innocent or blindly enthusiastic persona. This character lets the cat out of the bag by talking so naively about things that everyone takes for granted that he lays bare the rapacity, dishonesty, and folly that underlie established institutions and generally accepted attitudes. Or else he enthusiastically proposes some horrific scheme that, Swift establishes, follows logically and inevitably from opinions that everyone accepts without question.

Swift wrote poetry, but his great satires are in prose. Probably the best known is his "Modest Proposal" for ending poverty in Ireland. Swift's persona on this occasion is an enthusiast with the perfect scheme for improving society, the kind of man who was called a "projector" in the eighteenth century. A projector was a sort of cross between a think-tank wonk and a man who writes long letters to the editor. This particular projector's recommendation for the betterment of the Irish is the introduction of cannibalism into Ireland: "I have been assured by a very knowing American [Indian] of my acquaintance in London," he advises blandly, "that a young healthy child well nursed is, at a year old, a most delicious, nourishing, and wholesome food...."

The starving Irish poor would be relieved of the expense of bringing up their children, and, what's more, could add substantially to their cash income by supplying human flesh to the tables of the well-do-to at ten shillings a child. The joke (if you can call it a joke) is in how close the enthusiastic projector's proposal is to the actual state of Irish affairs. Human flesh will be so expensive that, fittingly, only landlords can afford it: "who, as they have already devoured most of the parents, seem to have the best title to the children."

The most memorable of Swift's innocent narrators is the often shipwrecked Lemuel Gulliver. First Gulliver finds himself in the land of the six-inch-tall Lilliputians. Their petty court intrigues and ridiculous ancestral quarrels (Big-Endians quarrel with Little-Endians over how to eat boiled eggs) parody British politics and religious strife. On his next voyage, Gulliver ends up in Brobdingnag, among people so large that he can make a comb for himself from one of their nail clippings. Human society comes in for more exposure there, as the Brobdingnagian king learns enough about and wars and other horrors of the past European century from Gulliver to conclude that the human race is "the most pernicious race of little odious vermin that nature ever suffered to crawl upon the surface of the Earth." (The giant king recoils with horror from Gulliver's kind offer to show him how to make gunpowder.) Next Gulliver comes to the flying island of Laputa, where he meets a race of philosophers so abstracted from their surroundings by their various scientific speculations that they have to hire "Flappers" to whack them gently on the ears and mouths to remind them to listen and speak to each other.

Finally, Gulliver arrives in the land of the Houyhnhnms, intelligent horses whose civilization is free of promiscuity, lawsuits, warfare, and other human vices. Houyhnhnmland is also inhabited by the Yahoos, wild men like animals, who have no speech, but in whose dirty and improvident habits Gulliver comes to see the seeds of all the evils civilized human beings suffer.

Because Gulliver's previous adventures have encouraged us to look on human society with a jaundiced eye, we're ready to go along when Gulliver begins to see this society of talking horses as the apotheosis of all virtue. All of the vices that trouble human society—sexual infidelity, greed and laziness, violence and dishonesty—are unknown in this super-excellent equine civilization. The Yahoos, on the other hand, fight over their food and make themselves sick by gorging on it. Their sexual appetites are excessive. They dig useless colored rocks out of the ground and stubbornly hoard them. Faced with the contrast between the clean, moderate, rational Houyhnhnms and the vicious Yahoos, Gulliver conceives a visceral loathing of the wild men and a passionate admiration for his horse-like master.

But Gulliver's new mental outlook turns out to have problems, too. If we haven't already noticed something a little off in Gulliver's way of thinking before he's exiled from Houyhnhnmland, we're sure to be shocked by his attitude to the Portuguese sailors who subsequently rescue him. Gulliver is astonished by every sign of civilized behavior that his rescuers offer him, and he can barely stand the smell of the very kind Portuguese captain. But his behavior on his return to England is much worse. He spends four hours a day in the stable, conversing with two horses he's bought for this purpose. "They are strangers to bridle or saddle; they live in great amity with me and friendship to each other," Gulliver tells us. Even after five years at home, he can barely tolerate the sight of his wife and children. He prefers the company of the horses' groom because, "I feel my spirits revived by the smell he contracts in the stable." Gulliver is clearly insane.

The conclusion of Swift's masterpiece is a satirical tour de force. He turns the whole satire of Gulliver's *Travels* back on itself. The cause of his madness is his thoroughgoing awareness of the irrationality and viciousness of the human race, which is the very attitude we've been learning from his book. Gulliver's *Travels* is a clear-sighted view into human limitations—including the limitations of a clear-sighted view into human limitations. Swift's conservatism is even more conservative than Pope's. Human society is riddled with wickedness and stupidity. But, Swift suggests, indulging in righteous indignation about it *may only make things worse.*

Our own age is infested with a race of plaintiff's lawyers, crusading journalists, Chicken-Little-style safety advocates, and "fearless" Hollywood directors, all of whom live by exposing human imperfections. Unfortunately, all their works contain less real insight and entertainment than Swift's satire. And none of them seems to have a fraction of Swift's admirable awareness of the moral and psychological costs of making a career of pointing out other people's faults—a self-awareness movingly expressed in the Latin epitaph Swift wrote for his own tomb, which translates roughly: "Here lies the body of Jonathan Swift, doctor of sacred theology and dean of this cathedral, where savage indignation can lacerate his heart no more. Go, traveler, and imitate, if you can, this most vigorous champion of liberty."

Dead white male #4: Samuel Johnson

Samuel Johnson, our fourth and final Dead White Male, is the ultimate paleo's paleocon. Johnson thought Edmund Burke (the founder of modern conservatism, whom Johnson knew personally) a brilliant man but a dangerously radical politician. In eighteenth-century British politics, Tories were defenders of traditional religious and government authority, while Whigs championed the rights of the people. Johnson's Toryism was so thoroughgoing that he identified the Whigs' love of liberty with Lucifer's rebellion against God: "the first Whig," Johnson said, "was the Devil."

Johnson was a skeptic about many of the principles that we assume all educated opinion accepts: for instance, that truth will always triumph in open debate. He wouldn't enjoy, he argued, being put on trial for his life, even if he was innocent. The Whigs Johnson most despised were the American revolutionaries. His 1775 "Taxation No Tyranny: An Answer to the Resolutions and Address of the American Congress" capitalized on the fact (familiar to us from the well-publicized hypocrisies of the Hollywood Left) that people with the most liberal politics often have the most *illiberal* private lives: "how is it," he asked, "that we hear the loudest yelps for liberty among the drivers of negroes?" (The chief beneficiary of Samuel Johnson's will was Johnson's Jamaican servant, a former slave.)

In his own day, Johnson was known for his *Dictionary of the English Language,* for his keen and persuasive literary criticism, and for his *Rambler* and *Idler* essays. The *Dictionary* was the great achievement that established his reputation. Johnson's is the first serious attempt at a comprehensive English dictionary. He spent eight years compiling definitions for more than 40,000 words and demonstrated their usage with over 100,000 quotations from English authors. The *Dictionary* is a monument to the eighteenth-century impulse to systematize, standardize, and critique. But it was also shaped by counter-impulses. Johnson's dictionary is an individual and even eccentric document compared to the dictionary of the French language compiled over a period of decades by the forty members of the French Academy and published in 1694. Like Johnson's literary criticism, Johnson's lexicography benefits from his subtle understanding of the complex interplay between the abstract principles and the living language. As he wrote in another context, "there is always an appeal open from criticism to nature."

Fewer modern readers know Johnson from his own work than from James Boswell's famous biography. Boswell's *Life of Johnson* seems to bring us into the living presence of the man. It's also one of those books, like Samuel Pepys's diaries, that is perfect bedtime reading. It's broken up into bite-sized chunks, as Boswell reports this or that conversation, letter, or anecdote of Johnson's; and there's something worth reading on every single page.

The relationship between the great man and his great biographer is a curious one. Boswell was not a particularly admirable character. He was a sort of intellectual social climber who traveled Europe scraping acquaintance with well-known literary and political figures. He was also subject to all the vices that turn a man's life into an ugly and obvious mess: out-of-control drinking and gambling, promiscuity, and living beyond his means. And yet Boswell admired—and what's more remark-able, he *understood*—Johnson's totally opposite character enough to make Johnson live for us. Johnson's stubborn independence, his rectitude of mind, and his real, humble love of goodness, come through so clearly that we feel as if we ourselves knew and loved him.

"The proper study of mankind is man"—or is it?

Eighteenth-century English literature is refreshing and delightful—espe-cially to those of us fed up with twenty-first-century political correctness. But it's missing the rich texture of the literature of earlier eras (or of the Romantic literature to follow). Turning from Spenser and Shakespeare to Pope and Swift is like going from Technicolor to black-and-white TV— or more like going from a painting to a fine black-and-white line draw-ing. There's a new clarity, but eighteenth-century literature has a much more limited palette. It seems astringent, brittle.

There are two, interrelated reasons for the fact that reading Enlighten-ment-era English literature feels like stepping into a black-and-white world. First is the organic development of English literary culture. Any art tends to build to an era of exuberant success and then decline to a period of self-conscious carefulness. Where literary artists of an earlier time reached for greatness, artists of the eighteenth century aimed for correctness and polish. Too keen an awareness that you may be making a fool of yourself is incompatible with the freedom and range of action we see in the very greatest artists.

But this bleached or brittle effect is also the result of a truncated view of man. Consider Restoration comedy. The restoration of the monarchy meant the restoration of English drama, which had been abolished under Parliamentary rule. Restoration drama was much *more* risqué than the Renaissance drama that the Puritans had outlawed as a danger to morals. For the first time, actresses appeared on the English stage. Renaissance drama had still used boys for the women's parts, just as the medieval mystery plays had done. And (despite the postmodernists' attempts to pretend that Shakespeare's comedies were essentially drag shows), seventeenth-century audiences found the new co-ed drama quite a bit sexier than the old single-sex variety.

Restoration drama was influenced by the sexual morality—or, rather, the lack of it—in the court of Charles II. Restoration plays are cynical; their action takes place in a hard world where men and women use one another for their own profit and pleasure. In Congreve's *The Way of the World*, both hero and heroine have to pretend to be more callous than they really are, to avoid being hurt (here's where this era *does* have something in common with our own). The transition from Puritan earnestness to rakish comedy was liberating, obviously. But it was also a kind of settling for less. As an aspiration for a writer, 'to titillate and amuse' simply doesn't measure up to "To justify the ways of God to men."

A sense of scaling back, of horns drawn in, permeates eighteenth-century literature. The famous lines from Pope's *Essay on Man* capture this feeling of narrower limits: "Know then thyself, presume not God to span; / The proper study of mankind is man." The growth in knowledge—scientific, but also scholarly—seemed rather to shrink man's horizons than to broaden them: what had been mysterious was increasingly known to be mechanical. Skepticism was becoming ever more widespread: people now doubted (among other things) Christian revelation, the basis of government authority in divine law, the reliability of their senses, and even the existence of physical matter. Our Dead White Males were defenders of Christian faith, traditional authority, and the trustworthiness of human perception; but they were fighting a rearguard action. The projects of the Enlightenment—the attempts to master nature for the relief of man's estate and to clear away the old religion-based learning and build up the edifice of human knowledge on new scientific foundations—seemed large and ambitious at their beginnings. But as they developed, they seemed somehow to diminish man himself. Resistance to this diminishment fueled the Romantic Movement, which begins our next chapter.

Chapter Six

THE NINETEENTH CENTURY

REVOLUTION AND REACTION

I shall not cease from mental fight
Nor shall my sword sleep in my hand
Till we have built Jerusalem
In England's green and pleasant land.

—William Blake

Nineteenth-century English literature is fascinating on its own terms. In fact, the nineteenth century rivals the Renaissance as *the* great period for literature in English. But English Romantic literature also has a special you-can't-look-away-from-the-car-wreck quality to it for us. The great English Romantic poets lived through the beginning of a war—more precisely, a revolution—for the soul of Western civilization that's been raging ever since (sometimes breaking out into open conflict, even violence, sometimes simmering away beneath the surface). The English Romantics were among its earliest enthusiasts, victims, and veterans.

The revolution that continues to shape the modern world isn't only a political revolution, though it certainly has political aspects. As a matter of fact, one of its most revolutionary elements is the conviction that aspects of human experience previously assumed to be either beneath or above the notice of politicians are proper objects for political action: that a political program can remake society—even transform human nature. The French Revolution is the point at which this radical idea first took on flesh and blood.

The nineteenth-century literature you must not miss

William Blake,
  *Songs of Innocence
  and of Experience*

William Wordsworth,
  "Tintern Abbey,"
  Preface to *Lyrical
  Ballads,*
  "Ode: Intimations
  of Immortality,"
  The Prelude

Samuel Taylor Coleridge,
  *The Rime of the
  Ancient Mariner,*

continued on p. 120

The nineteenth-century literature you must not miss
(continued)

Kubla Khan,
Biographia Literaria

George Gordon Byron,
Don Juan

Percy Bysshe Shelley,
"Ode to the West
Wind,"
"To a Skylark"

John Keats,
"Ode on a Grecian
Urn,"
"Ode to a
Nightingale,"
"To Autumn"

Jane Austen,
Pride and Prejudice

Alfred Tennyson,
"Ulysses,"
In Memoriam

Robert Browning,
"My Last Duchess"

Charles Dickens,
David Copperfield

George Eliot,
Middlemarch

continued on p. 121

Lots of blood. The new age was midwived by that infamous revolutionary instrument the French referred to familiarly as "Madame Guillotine." The violence and chaos of the French Revolution inspired a reaction. Napoleon's rise to power marked the end of the most chaotic and experimental phase of the Revolution in France. But his conquests helped spread revolutionary ideas and institutions throughout Europe. Then England led the other powers to defeat Napoleon and reestablish something like the status quo before the storming of the Bastille. The monarchy in France was restored, for a while.

But that original revolution served as a precedent for many more. Some were bloody political events. The nineteenth century saw a series of attempts across Europe to revive and expand political freedoms by making revolution. And in the twentieth century—first in Russia, but afterwards in many other unfortunate parts of the world—came violent attempts to eradicate traditional culture and build human society up again from scratch on a scale that hadn't been seen since the French Jacobins declared that September 22, 1792, was really the first day of Year I of the Republic; introduced twelve newly invented months; abolished Sunday and replaced saints' days with days named after plants and farm animals; and imposed revolutionary time: ten hours to each day, a hundred minutes to each hour; a hundred seconds to each minute. But bloody revolutions were only the most obvious expressions of the radical impulse, continually breaking out in one form or another in the modern world, to uproot injustice once and for all by making everything new—at any cost.

Revolutionary repeat

The particular outbreak of the radical, revolutionary modern spirit that we're most familiar with—and that has done the most to shape English faculties on American college campuses—occurred in the 1960s. Many professors were themselves radicalized during that era. And younger lefty English professors look back to the '60s as a sort of golden age in which campus radicalism seemed capable of changing society.

Curiously, neither the aging veterans of the intoxicating '60s counter-culture nor the trendy young professors still trying to make names for themselves have much enthusiasm for studying the Romantic poets. The program for the 2005 convention of the Modern Language Association lists *794* different panels on subjects including "Redeeming Violence," "Marxism Now," "Film after *Brown v. Board of Education,*" and even "What Video Games Can Teach Us about Literature." And not *one* on William Wordsworth, Samuel Taylor Coleridge, or John Keats. Now, Wordsworth and Keats are certainly among the top ten English poets. Coleridge is also a very fine poet, and one of the greatest two or three literary critics who wrote in our language. Why have English professors lost interest in them?

It's no wonder, really, that a generation of "intellectuals" still clinging to the naive revolutionary fervor of their youth would be uninterested in the writings of men of real genius who were once caught up in exactly the same enthusiasm, but who thought longer and deeper about the underlying realities. Marx's observation that history repeats itself—the first time as tragedy, the second time as farce—seems particularly apropos to a comparison between the Romantic poets and the children of the 1960s.

The belief, dear to Baby Boomer hearts, that the anti-establishment, make-love-not war, don't-trust-anyone-over-thirty experience was something hitherto unknown in the history of the human race couldn't survive a thorough acquaintance with the great works of the Romantic era. It's all there: the intoxicating sense of infinite promise; the certainty that a single generation—the one fortunate enough to be young at just the right time—is special; the free love; the mind-altering drugs; the differences in temperament and character that make some people life-long

The nineteenth-century literature you must not miss (continued)

John Henry Newman, *Apologia pro Vita Sua*

Matthew Arnold, "Dover Beach"

Gerard Manley Hopkins, "Pied Beauty"

Oscar Wilde, *The Importance of Being Earnest*

Present at the Revolution

Writing about the Revolution "As It Appeared to Enthusiasts at Its Commencement," Wordsworth expressed themes quite familiar to anyone who lived through the '60s—or has had to listen to the Baby Boomers reliving their glory years:

> Bliss was it in that dawn to be alive,
> But to be young was very heaven!—Oh! times....
> Now was it that both found, the meek and lofty
> Did both find, helpers to their heart's desire,
> And stuff at hand, plastic as they could wish;
> Were called upon to exercise their skill,
> Not in Utopia....
> But in the very world, which is the world
> Of all of us,—the place where in the end
> We find our happiness, or not at all!

As Hillary Clinton put it, speaking for her generation at Wellesley in 1969, "We're searching for more immediate, ecstatic and penetrating modes of living.... If the experiment in human living doesn't work in this country, in this age, it's not going to work anywhere."

This is something of a sublime-to-the-ridiculous comparison, but there's no denying that Wordsworth understood perfectly well—more than 150 years before Hillary was born—exactly how she felt.

revolutionaries and others eventually "[s]adder and wiser" men; and the accusations of selling out against those who grew up.

Wordsworth wasn't just an enthusiast for the French Revolution. He actually went to France—for reasons very much like the ones that took

American Communists to Russia during the Revolution there; that led left-leaning young people from Europe and the United States (including Ernest Hemingway) to Spain during its Civil War; and that prompted "sandalistas" from the United States to Nicaragua to work in the Sandinista literacy campaign in 1980.

In France, Wordsworth formed a relationship, but not a legal marriage, with a French girl, Annette Vallon, and fathered a child (following another pattern that's become familiar to us: enthusiasm about overturning traditional authority in politics tends to go along with unconventional attitudes about sex). Wordsworth returned to England shortly before the bloodiest period of the Revolution. England and France were at war for the next nine years, during which he couldn't get back to see Annette and his daughter in France.

What They Don't Want You to Learn from the Romantic Poets

Intelligent radicals become conservatives when they grow up—make that, *if* they grow up.

Even the classic arraignment of a former counterculture hero as a sellout precedes the '60s by more than a century. Here's Robert Browning in "The Lost Leader" writing (in the early Victorian era) to accuse Wordsworth, who had recently accepted the post of Poet Laureate, of deserting the cause:

> Just for a handful of silver he left us,
> Just for a riband to stick in his coat—. . . .
> He alone breaks from the van and the freemen,
> He alone sinks to the rear and the slaves!

The style is miles above anything Abbie Hoffman ever had to say about Jerry Rubin, but you recognize the sentiment.

Thomas de Quincey's *Confessions of an Opium-Eater* also has obvious parallels in '60s counterculture experience. Like most prolonged attempts to use the human mind as a chemical laboratory, de Quincey's experience with opium begins in "pleasures" and progresses to "pains." Coleridge's use of the same drug played a role in the creation of some of the finest poems in the English language, including *Kubla Khan* and *Christabel.* But opium also had something to do with the fact that neither poem is finished—and with how few poems Coleridge wrote. Coleridge's opium addiction is a tragedy; the alcohol- and drug-induced haze that Beat poetry emerged out of (Allen Ginsberg's wretched *Howl,* for example, which is supposed to be the great Beat masterpiece) is only farce.

The Romantic poets experienced all the powerful feelings that have animated revolutionaries from France in 1789 to American university campuses in 1968—but they didn't stop there. The great Romantic poets went on *thinking* about those feelings. Sensitive and intelligent reflection on human emotion is the hallmark of English Romantic thought.

Wordsworth and Coleridge

The Romantic Era in English literature is often said to begin with the 1798 publication of *Lyrical Ballads,* a collection of poems written by Wordsworth and Coleridge. Certainly around the turn of the nineteenth century there was an explosion of truly great poetry, including lyric poems that are finer than any in English since the Renaissance—all in a radically new vein. The Preface Wordsworth wrote for the second edition of *Lyrical Ballads* in 1800 (seven years after his return from France) defends characteristics that made his new poems hardly seem like poetry to some readers: in particular, his use of "a selection of the language of real men," instead of the elevated and abstraction-laden poetic diction of the eighteenth century. The Preface to *Lyrical Ballads* also exemplifies something that the poems by Wordsworth and Coleridge share with the works of William Blake, George Gordon Byron, Percy Bysshe Shelley and

John Keats: a new self-consciousness, an interest in what we think of as human psychology.

Except that, for the Romantics, human consciousness was not a specialized subject for research scientists or doctors who treat mental illness. It was the business of mankind and, in a special sense, of the poet. Poetry, Wordsworth suggests in the Preface, might be able to help cure an increasingly widespread "craving for extraordinary incident," a kind of emotional addiction to "gross and violent stimulants." And what, according to Wordsworth, feeds this unhealthy habit? For one thing, political news: "the great national events which are daily taking place," and "the rapid communication of hourly intelligence." And, for another, corrupting forms of entertainment: "frantic novels, sickly and stupid German tragedies, and deluges of idle and extravagant stories in verse."

What They Don't Want You to Learn from Wordsworth and Coleridge

The difference between entertainment that degrades and entertainment that refreshes and ennobles.

Two hundred years later, we are the most relentlessly entertained and news-saturated population in the history of the world. But we ask very few—and very superficial—questions about the effects these stimuli have on us. We wonder whether television may cause attention-deficit disorder in some percentage of children, or if teenagers learn violence or sexual behavior from music or movies.

*But we don't ask, as Wordsworth did, what kind of people **we're** becoming:* what is happening to "the discriminating powers" of *our* minds, or what effect our choice of entertainment has on our own creative powers. Wordsworth suggests that poetry may be able to assist us in discovering healthy kinds of excitement—sources of pleasure (even intense pleasure) that would elevate rather than debase us. The "degrading thirst after outrageous stimulation" that Wordsworth complained about has not grown less in the intervening years; his suggestions about a cure are worth our attention.

But there's no point in expecting aging hippies and wannabe revolutionaries to appreciate the work of a man who gave up radical politics for poetry. (This is *not* the kind of turning on, tuning in, and dropping out they can relate to.) And the themes of Wordsworth's Preface to *Lyrical Ballads*—and the Romantics' ideas about poetry, generally—are unpopular with trendy English professors for another reason, as well. The whole thrust of the professors' "literary theory" is to direct our attention toward causes (whether political, sexual, or linguistic) that are supposed to be impersonal—and to distract us from the very things the Romantic poets are most interested in: "the human mind"; "the passions of men"; "the great and simple affections of our nature."

The Romantic poets are the great explorers of the mind of man, and especially of its power to create, for which they make very large claims. William Blake, for example, calls the imagination "the real man" and claims it "is not a state, it is human existence itself." Our English professors have gone to the other

Guess What?

→ If the Baby Boomers had been reading Romantic literature instead of the Beat poets, they might have grown up a lot faster—and done less damage along the way.

→ Jane Austen was a conservative Christian. Her novels are not "subversive": she was a fan (not a critic) of "the patriarchy."

→ Charles Dickens made wicked fun of liberals who put social reform, educational innovation, and ostentatious compassion ahead of their responsibilities to their own families.

extreme; they're reluctant to acknowledge that any such thing as the human imagination exists. "Imagination" isn't in their vocabulary. Instead, they've taken to writing about "the nineteenth-century imaginary," as if great literature were cobbled together out of some pre-existing stock of ideas that emerged spontaneously from the anonymous, mechanical processes of history.

But if you're still interested in the capacities of the human mind, the powers of the imagination, and the possibilities (and dangers) of man's creative ambitions, then you'll find Romantic literature very exciting. *Lyrical Ballads* itself is a good place to start. "Lines Composed a Few Miles above Tintern Abbey..." is probably the best known of the poems Wordsworth wrote for the original collection. In it, the poet revisits the banks of the Wye River after an absence of five years, during which the memory of the first visit has stayed with him, but he has changed. The relationship between the poet and "nature"—by which the Romantic poets meant more or less what we mean: the natural world out there (rather than the underlying structure of everything that exists, as speakers of English up to the eighteenth century meant by the same word)—is the explicit theme of "Tintern Abbey." And, in another sense, it's the theme of "Michael: A Pastoral Poem," which Wordsworth wrote for the 1800 edition of *Lyrical Ballads.*

"Michael" is a simple story ("unenriched with strange events"[1]) that explains a peculiar feature of the landscape: there's "a straggling heap of unhewn stones" lying in a dell beside a brook near the poet's home at Grasmere. The stones, we learn, are all that's left of an unfinished sheep-cote that an old man, a shepherd named Michael, began to build with his son. The son lays the cornerstone at his father's request, to be a kind of covenant between them, on the day before he leaves home for a job in the city, where he is going to earn money to clear the title to his father's land. At first the son does well. But then he stops working hard, falls into bad habits, and ends up fleeing England in disgrace. At almost the very end of the poem we see Michael at the sheep-cote, still struggling to build it, stone by stone, but failing, and leaving it unfinished at his death.

Devoid as this story is of "extraordinary incident," it's not lacking in emotional impact. As a matter of fact, it's almost too painful to read. But the psychic effect of the poem is very different from the effect of the "gross stimulants" we're used to being bombarded with. "Michael" communicates a kind of pain that it seems to do you good to think about. And there's plenty in the poem *to* think about, particularly on the question of what makes people (and things between people) go wrong. If you find yourself interested and moved by Wordsworth's poems of 1798 and 1800, you'll want to go on reading—"Resolution and Independence," "Ode: Intimations of Immortality," the great sonnets ("It Is a Beauteous Evening," "The World Is Too Much with Us," "Surprised by Joy," "Composed upon Westminster Bridge") and finally *The Prelude,* the great epic of human consciousness.

Though Wordsworth wrote most of the poems for *Lyrical Ballads*, the most famous single poem in the collection is Coleridge's *Rime of the Ancient Mariner.* Coleridge's great poem *is* chock full of "extraordinary incident": a voyage to the Antarctic; hardships at sea (among them, thirst so terrible that the Mariner bites his own flesh to drink blood so he can speak); a game of dice between Death and Life-in-Death for the Mariner's soul; and ghostly encounters with natural and heavenly spirits (the latter animate the bodies of dead sailors who, zombie-like, man the ship alongside the still-living Mariner for the last stage of the voyage). But there's an underlying structure—moral, psychological, and poetic—that makes the poem anything but an occasion for cheap thrills. Its events are iconic. We're strangely affected when the Mariner shoots the Albatross; when the other sailors curse it and incur the guilt of its death; when Life-in-Death shrieks that she's won the game of dice (and the Mariner's soul); and when the Mariner sees the water-snakes and "blesse[s] them unaware"— and then suddenly he's able to pray, and the Albatross falls from around his neck. We feel that somehow these events are representations of things we, ourselves, have done and suffered.

Byron and the Shelleys

Coleridge's *Rime of the Ancient Mariner* was an important influence on a work of "second-generation" Romantic literature published twenty years later: Mary Shelley's *Frankenstein; or the Modern Prometheus.* This short novel is a great place to start getting acquainted with Romantic literature if you're not yet in the habit of reading poetry. *Frankenstein* is the original source for all those horror movies about the tall monster with the square skull and the surgical scar across his forehead. But the book isn't just another horror story, or "Gothic novel." As Percy Shelley, the great Romantic poet (and Mary Shelley's husband) explained in the Preface he wrote for *Frankenstein*: "The event on which the interest of the story depends. . . . affords a point of view to the imagination for the delineating of human passions more comprehensive and commanding than any which the ordinary relations of existing events can yield."

"The event" he's referring to is Victor Frankenstein's creation and animation of a nearly human monster (of particular relevance to us in the age of cloning and stem-cell experimentation). As for the "human passions"—well, you have to read the book. To follow Frankenstein from his happy boyhood; through his scientific ambitions, their success, his remorse, his efforts to cope with his out-of-control creation, his sufferings at the hands of the monster, and his obsession with revenge; to his death at the end of the novel is an education in the mystery of the motives of human action. (And that's without even considering the passions of the monster, who is, in many ways, the more interesting character.)

One of the numerous fascinating questions about Victor's psychology is why he doesn't seem to pick up on obvious clues that the monster is threatening his friends and family, virtually all of whom fall prey to his creature while Victor himself is distracted by other aspects of the apparently insoluble dilemma he's created for himself. Another mystery is how Victor remains an attractive, even an especially admirable man—and he does—at the end of the novel, by which time it's clear that both his great talents and his appalling blind spots are responsible for so much mayhem, and grief.

There are some obvious similarities between Victor Frankenstein and Percy Shelley, whom his wife (at least, she was his wife by the time the novel was published) seems to have used as a model for her hero. The authoress of *Frankenstein* was, when she began writing the novel, living in close proximity to two men who were at once brilliantly creative and enormously destructive. In her introduction to the 1831 edition of *Frankenstein,* Mary Shelley explains when and how she came to write the novel. She, Percy Shelley, Byron, and Byron's doctor, John Polidori—all living in Switzerland in the summer of 1816—had been reading ghost stories, and they'd decided to try writing some of their own. But Mary couldn't think of a story. Until a night when she'd sat up listening to Shelley and Byron discussing experiments in galvanism: applying electrical currents to the bodies of dead animals had been discovered to make their lifeless muscles contract. Possibly, the poets speculated, "the component parts of a creature might be manufactured, brought together, and endued with vital warmth." That night, Mary couldn't sleep; she kept seeing images that would become the material for her book, beginning with "the pale student of unhallowed arts kneeling beside the thing he had put together."

What Mary Shelley's introduction doesn't explain is how the eighteen-year-old future authoress of *Frankenstein* came to be in Switzerland with Shelley and Byron in the first place. This back story sheds some light on the destructive capabilities of these two extraordinarily creative men. Shelley and Byron are among the greatest and most original poets in the

English language, and the chaos and misery they wrought in their personal lives is almost on a scale with their poetic achievements. Mary was the daughter of the well-known radical William Godwin and the early feminist Mary Wollstonecraft (of whom more below). She met Shelley at her father's house, which was a magnet for radical intellectuals and a natural stop for Shelley, who had been expelled from Oxford for writing an atheist pamphlet.

> ## What They Don't Want You to Learn from Second-Generation Romantics
>
> The human mind has enormous creative powers—which, if abused, can be terribly destructive.

When they met, Shelley was married, having eloped with Harriet Westbrook, the daughter of a London coffeehouse owner, after his expulsion from Oxford. Shelley's habit of falling in love easily and often had already made his wife miserable. But he and Harriet had become reconciled to the extent of conceiving a second child and solemnizing their marriage in a Church of England ceremony. By the time the baby was born, Shelley had abandoned his wife and was living with Mary Godwin, who was then also expecting his child (born, too premature to survive, three months after Harriet's).

Mary's step-sister Jane ("Claire") Clairmont, was also living with them. Claire's own involvement with Shelley may explain why Mary complained, years later, that Claire had "poisoned my life when young." But in the spring of 1816 Claire was obsessed with Lord Byron, who had slept with and abandoned her. Apparently this was an experience that literally hundreds of other human beings, including his own half-sister and a number of male lovers, eventually shared. Byron's approach to sexual relationships was half-heartedly guilty, increasingly disgusted, and wholly cynical, while Shelley's was passionately idealistic—and even principled, in its way. Shelley wasn't afraid of making commitments, of a sort. He contracted marriages pretty much as early and often as he had the opportunity to, given the strictures of nineteenth-century family law: he married Mary Godwin in December of 1816, less than three weeks after his first wife drowned herself. But his ideas about fidelity were unlikely to make any woman happy. As he explained in *Epipsychidion* in 1821—when he was still living with Mary but now infatuated with an Italian girl named Emilia Viviani:

> I never was attached to that great sect
> Whose doctrine is that each one should select
> Out of the world a mistress or a friend,
> And all the rest, though fair and wise, commend
> To cold oblivion,—though it is the code
> Of modern morals, and the beaten road
> Which those poor slaves with weary footsteps tread,
> Who travel to their home among the dead
> By the broad highway of the world—and so
> With one sad friend, perhaps a jealous foe,
> The dreariest and the longest journey go.

It's difficult to guess which man caused more misery. No doubt Byron made more people unhappy, but the ones Shelley hurt must have experienced emotional pain of an almost unexampled intensity. Shelley was so intoxicatingly attractive, and he was capable of such enthusiastic and all-consuming passion for a woman, that his love must have held out the prospect of almost otherworldly happiness. But he couldn't see why one woman he had been in love with should complain when he became just as passionately interested in the next one.

Each man's poetic style approximates his personality, not to say his seductive technique. Byron's poetry—especially *Don Juan,* his masterpiece—is rakishly attractive, negligently superior, carelessly cruel. Byron was (or posed as) a great admirer of Pope and Dryden, a great scorner of Wordsworth and Coleridge. He created a new kind of poetry that combines the satiric genius of the eighteenth century with the psychological sophistication and natural diction of Romantic poetry. Shelley's poems, on the other hand, are rhapsodic, exquisitely beautiful, supple, and intoxicating.

If *Frankenstein* is your introduction to the second-generation Romantics, it makes sense to begin reading their poetry with some works on the same Promethean theme (Prometheus being the titan who defied the gods to befriend mankind and was punished by being fixed eternally on a rock where Zeus's eagle daily devoured his regrown liver): Byron's *Manfred,* a three-act drama about a Promethean (or Byronic) figure who defies divine law and remains defiant to the end, and Shelley's typically rapturous *Prometheus Unbound.*

But to get the full flavor of their geniuses, you have to go on to Byron's *Don Juan* and the great poems Shelley wrote in the last years of his life: his "Ode to the West Wind," "To a Skylark," "The Sensitive Plant," and "Adonais," an elegy for John Keats, the youngest of the great Romantic poets, who died of tuberculosis in 1821. Shelley survived Keats by only a little more than a year, drowning on a sailing trip with a friend (with whose wife, as it happens, Shelley was in love at the time). He was twenty-nine years old. Byron died less than two years later, having fallen ill while with the rebels fighting for Greek independence from the Ottoman Empire.

Keats

John Keats, the most beloved of the Romantic poets, was a man who couldn't afford the aristocratic vices of Byron and Shelley. In fact, he was made deeply unhappy in the last year of his short life by the realization that he would never achieve even the modest portion of happiness he did aspire to—marriage to the girl he loved—because he was dying. Keats was training to be a surgeon (a lower-middle class profession in the early nineteenth century) when he realized he had extraordinary poetic abilities. "O for ten years," he wrote at the age of twenty-one, "that I may overwhelm / Myself in poesy; so I may do the deed / That my own soul has to itself decreed." Those lines aren't immortal verse, but within an amazingly short time Keats was writing poems in the very first rank of English poetry. It was a good thing he learned quickly, because he didn't have ten years; he had less than five.

Keats's first long poem, *Endymion*, written in 1816 and published in 1817, was not a success. He began again with *Hyperion*, an ambitious poem he was never able to finish, about the conflict between the Olympian gods and the titans (including Prometheus), in 1818. And then came Keats's annus mirabilis, the extraordinary year in which he became engaged to Fanny Brawne and wrote "The Eve of St. Agnes," "La Belle Dame Sans Merci," and his peerless odes: "Ode to Psyche," "Ode to a Nightingale," "Ode on a Grecian Urn," "Ode on Melancholy," and "To Autumn." It's fitting to end Keats's too-short story, which is a tale about love, death, and great art (and also to end the story of Romantic poetry) with the famous stanza from the "Ode on a Grecian Urn" about the lovers on the urn who, being painted, will never die:

> Heard melodies are sweet, but those unheard
> Are sweeter; therefore, ye soft pipes, play on,
> Not to the sensual ear, but, more endeared,
> Pipe to the spirit ditties of no tone:
> Fair youth, beneath the trees, thou canst not leave
> Thy song, nor ever can those trees be bare;
> Bold lover, never, never canst thou kiss,

Though winning near the goal—yet, do not grieve;

She cannot fade, though thou hast not thy bliss,

Forever wilt thou love, and she be fair!

Jane Austen: Without a room of her own

When we go from the great Romantic poets to Jane Austen, we're turning from truly great literary artists forgotten (or studiously ignored) by PC professors to a genius whose life and work have been not neglected, but distorted beyond recognition. Jane Austen is a real problem for the politically correct English establishment—and most especially for the feminists. She's obviously the greatest woman writer in English—possibly the greatest female literary artist, period. No other English writer, man or woman, is so often (and so justly) compared to Shakespeare. Feminist novelist and critic Virginia Woolf herself called Austen "the most perfect artist among women, the writer whose books are immortal."[2] But Jane Austen did it all without the "room of her own" and the money that Woolf's famous essay, "A Room of One's Own," explains women need in order to be able to succeed as writers of fiction.[3]

According to feminist theory, women have been robbed of opportunities by patriarchal oppression. Their real voices have been silenced by the subordinate roles—passive love object stuck up on a pedestal, submissive wife, doting mother, domestic drudge—that they've been forced into, in aid of male domination. What's necessary, if women are to come into their own as literary artists, is that they should throw off the shackles of the patriarchy and find their own independent voices.

But our greatest female writer somehow found her voice without having to be liberated from the patriarchy. Jane Austen spent her whole life financially dependent on her father and brothers, shared a room with her sister Cassandra, and, according to her nephew, must have written her novels—for want of that supposedly indispensable private room—"in the general sitting room, subject to all kinds of interruptions."[4] She was careful not to let visitors, including her own nieces and nephews, think that any project of her own took precedence over her duty to make them welcome, and her genuine interest in their concerns.

She managed men—from the Prince Regent's asinine librarian to her own beloved (but occasionally boorish, indiscrete, or ridiculous) brothers and nephews—in just the way a traditional woman used to handle a man: with a mixture of, on the one hand, flattering admiration for his splashier talents and respect for his superior position and, on the other, a serene confidence in her own mastery of the emotional aspects of the relationship. (If you're old enough, you may have observed this technique in a pre–women's liberation grandmother.) Somehow Jane Austen's genius was robust enough to survive and even flourish under conditions of "female subordination."

It's not as if feminism hadn't yet been invented in Jane Austen's day. Mary Wollstonecraft (Mary Shelley's mother and, like William Wordsworth, a sort of fellow traveler who lived in France during the Revolution), who was sixteen years Austen's senior, had a career that would do any feminist proud. Wollstonecraft started a girls' school, became a proponent of co-education, published a book[5] arguing that the "oppression" of women had produced a "gangrene" that pervaded society and comparing marriage with slavery and prostitution, took a lover who shared her radical politics and whose infidelities (commencing as soon as she became pregnant) drove her to attempt suicide.

Meanwhile Jane Austen was living a traditional woman's life—looking forward, as a little girl, to growing up and getting married, learning to play the piano, devouring novels (and writing hilarious spoofs of some of them), spending her youth as "the prettiest, silliest, most affected husband-hunting butterfly,"[6] and then, when it became clear she wasn't going to receive a proposal from any man she wanted to marry, settling into old-maidhood and the dignity of an aunt. And through it all she was cultivating attitudes—and, eventually, writing novels—incompatible with feminism of any stripe.

Nothing could be more alien to Jane Austen than the two attitudes that inevitably characterize feminists, whether of her day or of our own: humorless righteous indignation, on the one hand, and a kind of embittered peevishness, on the other.[7] (Mary Wollstonecraft is a good example of the angry or ranting school of feminism; Virginia Woolf, of the peevish or catty school.) The essence of feminism is the belief that life is horribly unfair—that the other half of the human race is in some kind of conspiracy (whether conscious or not) to keep women down. To the feminist, the structures of patriarchal society are links in the chain of female subordination. Every one of the thousand small distinctions that our society has traditionally made between men and women, and that haven't been completely eradicated even to this day, is another piece of evidence for the nefarious plot: naturally, for feminists, everyday life is full of occasions for outbursts of rage—or for harboring grudges and making sarcastic remarks, depending on your temperament. The one possibility that the feminists refuse on principle even to consider is that the traditional differences between male and female roles are necessitated by the real, natural, and ineradicable differences between men and women. Feminist literary critics call this idea "essentialism," and shrink from it in horror, as if it were the unforgivable sin against the Holy Ghost. And it's exactly what Jane Austen believed.

Celebrating "patriarchal values"

Miss Jane Austen found it quite natural that men and women should occupy roles defined by their sexes. Her religion, which she took very seriously indeed, taught her that wives should obey their husbands. Perhaps even more to the point, it taught her that human misery is caused not by traditional societal structures but by individual sin, and that every member of the human race, male or female, is capable of vice and folly and has a duty to struggle against them. This struggle—not the war between the sexes or a campaign of subversive resistance to the patriarchy—provides the drama in Jane Austen's novels.

The fact is, Jane Austen's novels show the failure of female self-control, on the one hand, and men's abdication of their proper responsibility, on the other, as among the chief causes of women's unhappiness. Far from being "subversive" of traditional gender roles, Jane Austen's novels celebrate them. This is one area where she's comparable to Shakespeare, and, arguably, outdoes him: her novels are masterful celebrations of marriage. Jane Austen paints what now has to be called old-fashioned marriage—the institution into which a woman entered expecting to be guided and protected by her husband, to look up to and to please him, and to be responsible for the management of a household and the nurture of children—as both the most usual and the most intense source of female happiness.

What They Don't Want You to Learn from Jane Austen

Gender is not "a construct." And "the patriarchy" isn't what makes women unhappy.

The feminists and other postmodernist critics have resorted to a variety of subterfuges to convince their readers—and possibly even themselves—that Jane Austen was in some sense in sympathy with their goals. Their wishful thinking is fairly obvious. Early feminist Virginia Woolf, for example, felt compelled to admit Jane Austen's greatness. But she was unhappy with Miss Austen's novels, whose confident femininity is quite at odds with Woolf's own rebellion against traditional female roles and her resentment of men. Woolf escaped from her dilemma by retreating into fantasy: she devoted her essay on Jane Austen to an exploration, not of the six novels she actually wrote, but instead of the six very different—but wholly imaginary—novels that Jane Austen "might have written had she lived to be sixty. We do not grudge it to him, but her brother the Admiral lived to be ninety-one."[8] (See what I mean about the peevish or catty school of feminism?)

Jane Austen critics in our own day also tend to argue from what's not there, though they don't go to the length of creating an entire alternative-reality oeuvre out of thin air. Instead, they argue from the "silences" in Jane Austen's novels. Or they find some slight similarity between a Jane Austen novel and another text, and then argue from the other text.[9] They grasp at every expression of discontent (from whatever cause) in Austen's letters and make it out to be a protest against the patriarchy. And they ignore and explain away the obviously anti-feminist ideas in the novels themselves. Everything Jane Austen says that's in line with "patriarchal values"—in other words, with the traditional wisdom of Western culture about men and women—is written off in one way or another. The standard feminist line, that Jane Austen is "subversive" of the patriarchy, can never be refuted by any amount of evidence. Every piece of counter-evidence either shows her slipping back into the false consciousness of a subordinated woman, or it's the camouflage of a secret feminist, or else it shows Jane Austen being only a part-time feminist, who at other times buys into patriarchal subordination so she can hang onto her membership in a dominant social class.[10] It's axiomatic for the feminists that there's nothing *to* see in the relations between the sexes but oppression by men and compliance or rebellion by women. Naturally, that's what they find in Jane Austen's novels.

But what if you take off your patriarchy-colored glasses? The postmodernists will laugh at your naïvety, but if you admit that there just possibly may be other things going on between men and women besides patriarchal oppression, you will pretty quickly notice that Jane Austen has her own ideas about "gender." And if you do Austen the courtesy of taking her ideas seriously—if you consider her insights about men and women as at least as worthy of your respect as feminist theory—you might (postmodernism forbid!) learn something.

Jane Austen is not "subversive." Jane Austen is _funny_. She happily pokes fun at every kind of superficiality and pretense—male selfishness, female hypocrisy, it was all fair game to her. She would have made hilarious hay with modern feminism. Jane Austen's complex and fascinating views on men and women can't be boiled down to a simple formula like the feminist slogans complaining that women have been silenced, or that men are afraid of female sexuality. But Austen's thinking does provide a pretty stark contrast with feminist theory. Take, for example, the "obscured female voice"[11] the feminists obsess over. Jane Austen suggests that women could generally benefit from more, not less, self-control and silence.

Women who are bossy (and talk too much)

Jane Austen's novels are full of women who are too free with their tongues. Some of them are just silly, or, at worst, embarrassingly vulgar—like Mrs. Bennet in _Pride and Prejudice,_ whose premature gossip about her eldest daughter's success with a rich young man determines the man's friend to get the young man out of the neighborhood, and nearly break her daughter's heart. Another one of her daughters complains, in one of many moments of excruciating embarrassment caused by her mother, that "years of happiness could not make Jane or herself amends for moments of such painful confusion." Other female characters' habits of selfish whining make their families miserable, and themselves ridiculous. And still others' loose talk betrays their lack of fastidiousness about sex. This kind of boldness does not—whatever the feminists may imagine about men's fear of the power of female sexuality—empower women in Jane Austen's novels. In _Mansfield Park,_ Mary Crawford loses Edmund by letting him see that she condemns a pair of adulterers not so much for their adultery as because they got caught. And the most brazen offender against delicacy in these matters, Lydia Bennet in *Pride and Prejudice*, ends up beholden to disgusted relatives and friends who have to bribe her seducer to marry her.

Then there are several women in the novels who combine a not very feminine insistence on being in control with a typically feminine eye for detail—a mixture that makes their bossy interference, especially in the lives of other female characters, a really painful persecution. Lady Catherine de Bourgh in *Pride and Prejudice* is one example: "Elizabeth found that nothing was beneath this great lady's attention, which could furnish her with an occasion for dictating to others." While the feminists tend to explain bad female behavior as the unfortunate outcome of the patriarchy's

What Else They Don't Want You to Learn from Jane Austen

If you're a woman, "finding your voice" probably isn't going to improve your life.

stunting and warping of women's lives,[12] Jane Austen shows this fault as the likely outcome of being spoiled by too much money. And—what would no doubt give the feminists fits if they could bring themselves to contemplate it—Jane Austen also suggests that the lack of a man in charge is a contributing factor to the cancerous growth of these women's egos. Lady Catherine and Mrs. Ferrars are rich widows; Mrs. Ferrars's daughter and Mrs. Elton both have their husbands wrapped around their little fingers.

Jane Austen is not a misogynist. It would be hard to find a writer whose attractive female characters are more attractive, and more truly admirable. But the women who let their "voices" just go or whose chief concern is how much power they have, are not her attractive characters.

Most of her heroines—and even her two most fascinating villainesses—engage in a high degree of self-censorship.

Emma Woodhouse, on the other hand, whom Jane Austen called "a heroine whom no one but myself will much like," is in some danger of ending up as an interfering, bossy old dragon in the Lady Catherine de Bourgh line. She's twenty-one years old, "handsome, clever, and rich." She's spoiled, not only because of her money and good looks, but also because her "affectionate, indulgent" father is a hypochondriac who

Are There Feminists in Jane Austen's Novels?

Not exactly. But there at least two characters who act a lot *like* feminists. Louisa Musgrove in *Persuasion* behaves like the ideal feminist heroine. She makes a huge production about her independence of mind. She's a girl who's determined to do what she wants, and who won't be turned from her decided course of action to please anyone else. Caroline Bingley in *Pride and Prejudice* stands up for women's accomplishments and condemns other women who won't join in solidarity with the sisterhood of women. And both of these characters come off looking uncommonly silly—not least because Louisa's apparent independence and Caroline's solidarity with the sisterhood *both have no other purpose than to impress some man.*

Louisa is naturally bold. But she's playing up her independence precisely because Captain Wentworth has praised her for being resolute. She's enjoying his attention, so she finds it natural to act in a way he approves of. When Louisa's stubbornness ends in a near fatal accident, Anne, the novel's real heroine, wonders "whether it ever occurred to [Wentworth] now, to question the justness of his own previous opinion as to the universal felicity and advantage of firmness of character.... She thought it could scarcely escape him to feel that a persuadable temper might doesn't have the energy to give her any guidance, and whose mind, in any case, would be no match for her own. Emma amuses herself with match-making, which the Woodhouses' family friend, Mr. Knightley (the only person who ever criticizes Emma to her face), points out is hardly a proper or delicate activity for a young lady.

Emma is an average or even archetypical young woman. She's freed up to be even more herself than most women because she's blessed with more than average of everything that a young woman could possibly want—

sometimes be as much in favor of happiness as a very resolute character." Later, when Louisa falls in love with a different man, she will cultivate different qualities—ones that suit him, instead: "…she would learn to be an enthusiast for Scott and Lord Byron.…Louisa Musgrove turned into a person of literary taste and sentimental reflection was amusing, but [Anne] had no doubt of its being so."

Caroline Bingley trumpets her solidarity with the sisterhood of women—standing up for women's accomplishments, and criticizing Elizabeth Bennet for acting as if women's abilities have any limits—precisely in order to make Mr. Darcy think better of her and worse of Elizabeth. But he sees right through her:

> "Eliza Bennet," said Miss Bingley, when the door had closed on her, "is one of those young ladies who seek to recommend themselves to the other sex by undervaluing their own; and with many men, I dare say, it succeeds. But in my opinion, it is a paltry device, and a very mean art."

> "Undoubtedly," replied Darcy, to whom this remark was chiefly addressed, "there is meanness in *all* the arts which ladies sometimes condescend to employ for captivation. Whatever bears affinity to cunning is despicable."

> Miss Bingley was not so entirely satisfied with this reply as to continue the subject.

money, good looks, intelligence, and freedom from the usual constraints parents impose. Her father's failure to be "patriarchal" is a necessary condition of the freedom that she abuses. Emma behaves the way she does because she's spoiled. Prosperity, admiration, and freedom from restraint spoil people, and large doses of all those things can spoil them completely—as anyone can deduce from the lives of Hollywood stars and Roman emperors.

Emma, as Jane Austen has Lady Catherine de Bourgh brag about herself, has "not been used to submit to any person's whims"; she has "not been in the habit of brooking disappointment." And the choices Emma makes—especially her choice of Harriet Smith, "the natural daughter of somebody" boarding at a local school, for a friend—show that always getting her own way is making Emma proud and selfish. Picking Harriet is partly about *not* choosing to be real friends with Jane Fairfax: a girl of Emma's own class, who's just as poor and just as beautiful as Harriet, but as intelligent as Emma

What Else They Don't Want You to Learn from Jane Austen

It's reasonable for a woman to look to marriage for happiness.

herself, and much more accomplished. But Jane reminds Emma of her own few faults and inferiorities, whereas Harriet gives Emma endless opportunities to indulge herself in condescension and advice, and to bask in Harriet's uncritical gratitude. Naturally Emma is determined not to marry. If she'd rather enjoy Harriet's blind flattery than make the effort to live up to a real friendship with a girl who's her equal, why on earth should she want a husband to look up to, and children (who are notoriously labor-intensive and ungrateful) to take care of?

But, luckily for her, Emma inhabits a world (part early-nineteenth-century England, part Jane Austen's peerless moral imagination), whose "patriarchal values" oppose her bad habits. In Emma's case it's only her own laziness and pride—not the women's magazines she buys, the self-help books she reads, and the professors she has in college—telling her to quit worrying about other people's feelings and say whatever she feels like saying, cheering her on when she puts herself first, arguing that it's beneath her dignity to follow a man's moral lead, and pointing out that she'd be a fool to look for happiness in marriage and motherhood. And, as a very ordinary young woman, Emma has some powerful impulses that undercut her resistance to "patriarchal values." Mr. Knightley's attention and approval have always been important to her. Fighting against her pride is her natural female desire to be guided—even corrected and improved—by the man she loves. And when she knows she loves him, and he loves her, she delights to remember, and to talk over with Mr. Knightley, the history of his influence on her. Emma, as an average sort of woman, is built in such a way that looking up to—and even promising to obey—a man she can truly respect doesn't seem like settling for being less than her solitary self; it seems like growing up into being something more.

Men who aren't patriarchal enough

There are plenty of spoiled men in Jane Austen's novels too, but men seem to spoil differently than women. Male human beings seem to have their own characteristic flaws—which definitely aren't the things feminists accuse men of. The feminists' villains insist on dominating women. Jane Austen's villains are more likely to shirk their responsibilities. Women in Jane Austen's novels cause pain by being bossy and interfering. But most of the damage men do is because they *don't* involve themselves and take charge. There aren't a lot of repressive patriarchs in Jane Austen's novels. What there are a lot of, are men who aren't patriarchal *enough*.

What Else They Don't Want You to Learn from Jane Austen

Most men would be improved if they were *more* patriarchal.

Jane Austen's novels are as full of men who ought to "find their voice," stand up for themselves, and take control as they are of women who won't shut up. There are the contemptible uxorious husbands who do mean and petty things under the influence of their awful wives. Mr. Elton humiliates Harriet Smith in public to please his vulgar new bride. John Dashwood lets his selfish wife persuade him to break the promise he gave to his dying father, to take care of his sisters. Underlining his self-imposed impotence, this sad excuse for a man explains—to the sister whose life he could transform at very little cost to himself, if he weren't a doormat for his selfish wife—"people have little, have very little in their power."

And then there are the men who fail to be effective fathers, allowing headstrong female relatives to come between themselves and their children. Mr. Bennet in *Pride and Prejudice* retreats into his library (and into his sardonic sense of humor) to escape his ridiculous wife and the daughters she lets run wild. Mr. Woodhouse, Emma's father, is so weak that it doesn't even occur to him that he has a duty to control Emma; he lets her take care of him. *Mansfield Park*'s Sir Thomas Bertram *looks* more like a real patriarch. He is a strict parent, and his strictness is a mistake—but not because he succeeds in controlling his daughters and teaching them to repress their desires. Quite the opposite. His mistake is *failing to interfere* to the extent of teaching his daughters "the necessity of self-denial and humility." Ironically, Sir Thomas's "severity"—in contrast to the "indulgence and flattery" of Mrs. Norris (their morally tone-deaf, interfering busybody aunt, to whom he's delegated too much of their upbringing)—has taught his daughters "to repress their spirits" only "in his presence." Sir Thomas doesn't really get to know his daughters until it's too late. The very worst thing he does—allow his daughter Maria to marry a worthless man he knows she doesn't love—he does because he's reluctant to scrutinize her motives too closely, and because he believes whatever is most convenient to him to believe about her temperament.

This same tendency not to take responsibility—to keep their options open, not to get involved—is what makes young men so dangerous. The villains in Jane Austen's novels are not rapists, wife-beaters, or even jealous husbands. They're men who don't stick around. It's not men's violent, "controlling" urges that make it necessary for parents to look out for their daughters; it's men's tendencies to avoid (or weasel out of) commitment that do. In each of the novels there's at least one man who pays a woman the kind of attention he knows (if he thinks it through) that he shouldn't pay her unless his intentions are serious—and they're not. In Jane Austen's view, this kind of behavior seems to be an occupational hazard of being male.

The benefits (to *women*) of "sexist" conventions

It's partly because Jane Austen saw that the "fault[s] of temper" and "evil habits in which we [indulge] to the discomfort of our fellow creatures, and the danger of our own souls"[13] were likely to be gender-specific that she was a fan of "patriarchal" conventions—rules for women that are different from the rules for men. To feminists, these rules seem to exist for the "subordination" of women and the "domination" of men. But Jane Austen could see good reason for them, even for the ones that look pretty silly to liberated twenty-first-century women. Here are some of the rules that Marianne Dashwood breaks in *Sense and Sensibility*. She makes no effort to hide from a young man who appears to be courting her that she's head over heels in love with him, even though he hasn't said he loves her.

She accepts an expensive present from him. She allows him to give her a tour of his aunt's house without having introduced her to his aunt. And—this is the really shocking breach of etiquette in the novel, the one that makes her own sister believe Marianne's partly to blame when the young man ends up jilting her to marry for money—*she writes letters to him, despite the fact that they're not engaged to be married.*

We can sympathize with Marianne's impatience with these rules. But surely we can also recognize that they had some basis in the stubborn realities of male and female psychology. Two generations after the triumph of "women's liberation," it's women, not men, writing letters to advice columnists to ask why their sex partners don't want to have real relationships. And it's women who have made bestsellers of *The Rules: Time-Tested Secrets of Capturing the Heart of Mr. Right* and *He's Just Not That Into You: The No Excuses Truth to Understanding Guys,* in the attempt to understand why, when they're the pursuers, their love lives don't work out the way they want.

> ## What Else They Don't Want You to Learn from Jane Austen
>
> Societal conventions exist for our protection; we discard them at our own risk.

Surely even feminist professors who study Jane Austen must know more men who are "afraid of commitment" than they know men who are jealous, abusing control freaks. But feminism teaches them that "the patriarchy" is always and everywhere the real problem. When Jane Austen expresses traditional beliefs—that men should be encouraged to take charge, that female self-control and even silence can be real blessings, or that the same virtues that prepare us for Heaven "will secure to us the best enjoyment of what this world can give"[14]—the feminists can't see what she's saying as a commentary on reality. But *you* can compare Jane Austen's ideas about what makes people happy or unhappy with the feminists' fantasies about subverting the patriarchy, and decide where you'll pin your hopes.

Victorian literature

The ending of Jane Austen's *Sense and Sensibility* is a lot like the end of the Romantic Era itself. Marianne Dashwood, badly burnt by her experiment with passionate Rousseauian naturalness, finds refuge in religious principle, conventional standards, and what we might call traditional family values. She marries—"with no sentiment superior to strong esteem and lively friendship"—the thirty-something bachelor whose conventionality she used to laugh at with the young man who went on to break her heart. Marianne settles for much less than she had once hoped. She's willing to settle because she's seen where her blindness to the cold, hard facts about human nature might have taken her. She had her heart broken, but it might have been even worse: her lover, it turns out, had already seduced, impregnated, and abandoned another girl who was in love with him.

The Victorian reaction to the excesses of Romanticism is a similar retreat from revolutionary hopes into tradition and convention. It didn't produce as spectacular a literature, but plenty of fine things very much worth reading were written in Victorian England. If the Romantic Era was a second golden age for English literature, the long reign of Queen Victoria is a silver age. There are a number of poets (beginning with Alfred Tennyson and Robert Browning, and including at least Matthew Arnold, George Meredith, and Gerard Manley Hopkins), essayists (Carlyle, Newman, and Ruskin, at least) and novelists (the Brontës, George Eliot, Thackeray, Trollope, and Hardy are the other big ones) that you absolutely shouldn't miss. But if you're going to try only one Victorian writer, it should be Charles Dickens.

Dickens

Dickens is known as a crusading social reformer. His novels expose a number of evils in Victorian society—the debtor's prison; the workhouse; the antiquated, irrational, and inhumane traditions of the legal profession and the court system—and he's looked on as a sort of literary patron saint of liberal reform. In some ways this idea of Dickens is fair. You have only to compare the children in his novels to the children in Jane Austen's to understand the Copernican revolution in attitudes that occurred in the intervening years.

In the novels of Jane Austen (a devoted and much-loved aunt who dropped everything to entertain and educate her beloved nieces and nephews), children are unruly barbarians in need of perpetual attention and firm discipline if they're to be molded into civilized adults; it's a sort of penance for an educated person to have to spend any significant amount of time in their company; and if they turn out badly it's very likely the children's own fault. In the novels of Dickens (who married and fathered ten children, then left his family for an affair with an actress), children are the victims—they're misunderstood and neglected, if not positively starved and abused. The selfishness and brutality of the grown-ups explains all their suffering, and if they go wrong it's probably the fault of their upbringing.

Dickens was, nevertheless, an astute observer of human nature. And he could not fail to notice (and pillory) faults that were typical of the new liberal thinking as well as those typical of the society it was reforming. *A Tale of Two Cities,* Dickens's novel about

What They Don't Want You to Learn from Dickens

Actions have unintended consequences. Reformers can do more harm than the injustices they set out to reform. And charity begins at home.

the French Revolution, was such a devastating criticism of revolutionary ideology that Margaret Thatcher presented Francois Mitterrand with a copy. *Hard Times,* the only Dickens novel to depict the conditions of factory workers, is as much an exposé of radical modern experiments in education as it is of the excesses of capitalism.

And Mrs. Jellyby, in *Bleak House,* is the ultimate picture of the evils of modern liberalism. Mrs. Jellyby loves the Africans so much that she not only neglects her family, but positively persecutes her own children in pursuit of her high, compassionate ideals. Her eldest daughter is an unpaid drudge working night and day for the African relief effort. Her younger children are deprived of her affection and forced to donate their own money to the cause she loves instead of them. Mrs. Jellyby is no revolutionary, leaving a trail of violent destruction in her wake. But her children are, nonetheless, casualties of the revolutionary era, in which large projects for the betterment of the human race crowd out both the individual's traditional responsibilities to his own and the absolute moral prohibitions of the pre-revolutionary morality.

Dickens's novels also illustrate the importance of unintended consequences—the great liberal blind spot—and make the case against the expedience that's the hallmark of the revolutionary mindset. The moral philosopher's answer to the revolutionary's you-can't-make-an-omelet-without-breaking-eggs point of view is that the end doesn't justify the means: it's never right to do evil that good may come of it. The novelist's answer is to show (as Dickens does, in dozens of fascinating plot twists) that it makes no kind of sense to do evil that good may come of it—simply because you don't know that good *will* come of it. You never know what results will actually follow from your actions.

Each of your choices sets in motion a complex chain of events that you can't hope to foresee, let alone control. Good and evil deeds have long shadows: the ultimate effects of your actions are determined more by the intrinsic character of the acts themselves than by your motivation at the time. Deeds of cruelty or greed have their own internal logic. You may do them to achieve some end that seems good to you, and you may succeed in your purpose. But the end you aim at is not the end of the effects of your action. You're likely to discover that your choice has some consequence that you never intended, even that you would have given anything to prevent, if only you'd seen it coming toward you. This discovery is the sad end—and the great lesson—of the Age of Revolution.

Chapter Seven

THE TWENTIETH CENTURY
THE AVANT-GARDE, AND BEYOND

'Tis true, the stuff I bring for sale
Is not so brisk a brew as ale:
Out of a stem that scored the hand
I wrung it in a weary land.
But take it: if the smack is sour,
The better for the embittered hour;
It should do good to heart and head
When your soul is in my soul's stead;
And I will friend you, if I may,
In the dark and cloudy day.

—A. E. Housman, *A Shropshire Lad*

Oscar Wilde died November 30, 1900, on the threshold of the twentieth century. The meteoric career of this enigmatic and paradoxical man is a fitting introduction to the literary history of the new century. Wilde achieved an almost unprecedented status as a public figure. He was a sort of symbol and evangelist for a new mental attitude—a little bit like a philosophy of life, and a little bit more like an outrageous and attention-getting pose—that became fashionable in England in the last decades of the nineteenth century.

The modern literature you must not miss

Thomas Hardy, "Channel Firing," *Far from the Madding Crowd*

Joseph Conrad, *Heart of Darkness*

continued on p. 154

The modern literature you
must not miss (continued)

A. E. Housman,
    A Shropshire Lad

William Butler Yeats,
    "Among School
    Children,"
    "The Second
    Coming"

T. S. Eliot,
    "The Love Song of J.
    Alfred Prufrock,"
    The Waste Land,

James Joyce,
    A Portrait of
    the Artist as a
    Young Man,
    Ulysses

Wilfred Owen,
    "Dulce et Decorum
    Est"

W. H. Auden,
    "Musée des Beaux
    Arts,"

Dylan Thomas,
    "Fern Hill,"
    "Do Not Go Gentle
    into That Good
    Night"

Evelyn Waugh,
    Brideshead
    Revisited

Decadents and aesthetes

The era for which Wilde is the icon is sometimes called "The Age of Decadence." "Aestheticism" is the name usually given to the philosophy that he expressed in his works (and brilliant conversation). Decadents and aesthetes—believers in "art for art's sake"—were reacting against Victorian moralism, but also against the confidence in progress that had characterized the Victorian era. Both decadence and aestheticism belong to a range of "avant-garde" movements that were sweeping through the arts in late nineteenth-century Europe.

The English aesthetes' revolt against moralism—their rejection of the idea that art has any moral purpose—was in a certain sense just a bubbling up again of the Romantic spirit that had been stifled by the Victorian reaction to Romantic excesses. Wilde studied at Oxford with Walter Pater, who was a sort of guru to the English aesthetes. "Art," according to Pater "comes to you proposing frankly to give nothing but the highest quality to your moments as they pass, and simply for those moments' sake." "To burn always with this hard, gem-like flame, to maintain this ecstasy, is success in life," he claimed.

It's obvious that aestheticism has Romantic roots. But, just as clearly, it's a less ambitious creed than the Romantic faith. The Romantics could still believe that their intense feelings were connected to important insights about man and the ordering of society—and that literature and the emotions associated with it had power to change human society for the better. The aesthetes denied that the experience of art had any significance beyond itself. In this sense, aestheticism, decadence, and other expressions of the new avant-garde spirit were *anti*-Romantic.

The folks writing avant-garde literature tended to live avant-garde lives. Paul Verlaine and Arthur Rimbaud, two French "symbolist" poets, probably took the thing as far as anybody: their relationship finally had to be sorted out by the criminal justice system when (some time after

Verlaine's obsession with Rimbaud had destroyed Verlaine's marriage and accelerated his substance abuse) Verlaine shot Rimbaud in a fit of possessive jealousy. Verlaine ended up serving time in prison—as did Wilde, as it happens. How Wilde ended up in prison is a fascinating story—one that sheds light on his work, and on the literature of the next century.

Wilde was a brilliant playwright. His masterpiece is *The Importance of Being Earnest.* It's a comedy of manners that's still hilarious today, a century after the manners it pokes fun at have vanished from the face of the earth. But Wilde began (and ended) his career more famous for his life than for his art. After a successful Oxford career, he set up in London as a sort of goodwill ambassador for aestheticism. The eccentric style of his dress, behavior, and conversation gained him notoriety, and imitators.

In his thirties Wilde began writing hit plays—*Lady Windermere's Fan, A Woman of No Importance, An Ideal Husband,* and finally *The Importance of Being Earnest.* Before Wilde's success in drama, he had written poetry, essays, some really lovely fairy tales ("The Selfish Giant," "The Happy Prince"), and one extraordinary novel. *The Picture of Dorian Gray* is interesting enough on its own terms; in juxtaposition to Wilde's life it becomes really riveting. It was an axiom of aestheticism that art should have no extrinsic purpose, that it couldn't be judged by standards of morality or truth outside itself. Epigrams Wilde wrote for *Dorian Gray* claim, "There is no such thing as a moral or an immoral book" and "All art is quite useless." Wilde's characters go even further. They talk as if life should be regarded as a form of art, so that human behavior can't be judged by moral standards, either—only by aesthetic ones. That's the doctrine Lord Henry Wotton teaches Dorian Gray.

Dorian meets Lord Henry in the studio of a painter who is completing Dorian's portrait. The painter's fascination with his model has already begun to make Dorian aware of his own beauty. The first thing Lord Henry teaches him is to fear what age will do to it. Under Lord Henry's influence, Dorian prays that his portrait will grow old while he remains always young and beautiful. And that's what happens: Dorian discovers that the picture, not he, suffers the ravages of time—and of his ugly deeds.

Emboldened by the knowledge that however debauched or cruel he becomes, only the portrait will betray his true character, Dorian goes on—under the influence of Lord Henry, and of a "poisonous book" Lord Henry gives him—to pursue the most exquisite and forbidden pleasures. It's a short step from Pater's equation of "success in life" with aesthetic ecstasy to Lord Henry's doctrine that "One could never pay too high a price for any sensation." But it's most definitely a step down.

Despite its aestheticist themes, *Dorian Gray* is really a moralistic Victorian novel. Dorian goes on looking so young and innocent that it's impossible for almost anyone to believe that he could be vicious. But everyone who gets close to him is corrupted and ruined. His friends and lovers end up as suicides, prostitutes, or opium-addicts. In the end, as you might expect, Dorian's own life ends very badly.

At the end of the novel, Dorian Gray misses a clear chance to get out of the trap he's in, though at a high cost. Dorian realizes that he can't repair his life (and so reverse the damage he's done to his picture) without publicly confessing a crime he has committed in secret.

Wilde seems to have decided that the same thing was true for himself. At least, Wilde's own secret crime *was* eventually exposed; and it came to light because of his own actions. He didn't confess, but he set in motion a chain of events that—as could have been predicted with reasonable confidence beforehand—led to his exposure, public disgrace, and financial ruin. (And he persisted in that course, even when it was almost certain what the consequences actually would be, and he had a clear escape route.) Wilde's claim that he put his genius into his life and only his talent into his books

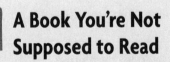

A Book You're Not Supposed to Read

The Unmasking of Oscar Wilde, by Joseph Pearce, Ignatius, 2005.

adds interest to the question of why he brought this disaster on himself.

His fall came at the height of his popularity, when both *An Ideal Husband* and *The Importance of Being Earnest* were playing on the London stage. Though he was married with two children, Wilde had become involved in a sexual relationship with a younger man, Lord Alfred Douglas. Douglas's father, the Marquess of Queensbury, publicly accused Wilde of "posing as a som-

What They Don't Want You to Learn from Avant-Garde and Modernist Literature

Christianity trumps the edgy art world.

domite" (he meant "sodomite"). And Wilde—egged on by Lord Alfred—decided to have him prosecuted for criminal libel. The defense was able to find a number of young male prostitutes (and also hotel employees) who could testify about Wilde's sexual habits. The prosecuting lawyer withdrew the case, and Wilde was arrested in his turn—for "gross indecency."

Wilde was tried twice: the jury at his first trial couldn't agree on a verdict. He was ultimately convicted—after passing up a chance to flee to the Continent and escape a prison term—and was sentenced to two years of hard labor. Wilde lived only three years after his release; he was received into the Roman Catholic Church on his deathbed.

Somehow, the pursuit of art for art's sake led Wilde full circle—back to a very black-and-white sort of moral universe in which there *are* such things as moral and immoral books (some of them are even "poisonous"); back to guilt, confession, and repentance; back to a very traditional kind of Christianity. ***It's remarkable, really, how many of the avant-garde artists who lit out bravely for the outer edges of human experience ended up turning around and fleeing from what they found there, back toward the heart of traditional Western culture and religion.***

A striking number of the actors in the morality play that Wilde made of his life found religion in their later years: besides Wilde himself, Alfred Douglas and even the Marquess of Queensbury (a very unpleasant character, and former proselytizer for atheism) eventually became Catholics. Joris-Karl Huysmans, the author of *à rebours* ("Against the Grain"), the novel on which Wilde modeled Dorian's "poisonous book," also converted to Roman Catholicism—though only after aestheticism and decadence had led him to explore Satanic rituals. Converting also—and even becoming a Catholic priest—was the poet John Gray (whose surname Wilde had appropriated for Dorian Gray). Wilde's Oxford tutor Walter Pater, who had lost his Christian faith in his youth, returned to the Anglican Church late in life. Aubrey Beardsley, the artist who made the illustrations for the famous English-language edition of *Salome,* Wilde's most risqué play (it was staged in France, having been forbidden to be performed in England), died a Catholic. And other decadents, aesthetes, and symbolists to follow the same path—through the avant-garde back to a conservative variety of Christianity.

Modernism

That same pattern held in the succeeding generations of avant-garde writers, whose artistic experiments were even more extreme than those of the aesthetes and the decadents. The "modernism" that followed aestheticism extended the Romantic revolution against tradition and convention to the traditions and conventions of the arts themselves. Artists threw away the basic tools of their own trades. Composers abandoned the octave to write twelve-tone music. Avant-garde painters abandoned first perspective, then representation of objects and human figures, and finally both draftsmanship and beauty. Architects, too, jettisoned the traditional canons of their art to create functional buildings modeled on machines.

Literary artists gave up rhyme and meter for "free verse" and storytelling for "stream of consciousness."

The results of these experiments were mixed. I don't think there's any need to feel like a philistine if you agree with the judgment of Cordelia and Charles in *Brideshead Revisited*—by Evelyn Waugh, another avant-garde convert to the Catholic Church—that "Modern Art is all bosh."[1] The visual arts, especially, seemed in the modernist era to become infested with something like contempt for beauty, for the artist's own skills, and for his audience.

As Waugh insisted, real art is first and foremost the art of pleasing. It's difficult to see why viewing the works of the Dadaists, for example—the copy of the *Mona Lisa* with a mustache painted on her upper lip, say, or the ordinary urinal set up in a museum as if it were a sculpture—is an *aesthetic* experience at all. These things attract attention for reasons that are very different from the qualities that draw people to earlier works of art, even ones as distant in time and as different from one another as the Parthenon and the paintings of Monet.

But some of the composers and writers did better. T. S. Eliot's 1922 poem *The Waste Land,* which perfectly captured the bleak post-World War I era, is beautiful in a painful modern way—despite (or paradoxically because of) the fact that the poem is full of ugliness

Eliot's masterpiece famously begins: "April is the cruellest month."[2] That insight is our introduction to a grim world in which every sign of life is sickeningly violent: "'That corpse you planted last year in your garden, / Has it begun to sprout?'"[3] Hope is painful because it's always false.

> ## What They Don't Want You to Learn from Evelyn Waugh
>
> "Art" the only aim of which is to annoy and upset its audience isn't really art.

What They Don't Want You to Learn from T. S. Eliot

Tradition is necessary for the creation of great art.

Resurrection is out of the question because even death is out of reach; there's no possible escape.

The Waste Land is in no recognizable genre. The poem doesn't tell a straightforward story. It isn't clear whose feelings are being expressed. The characters—an insomniac emigré Lithuanian aristocrat; a fortune-teller styling herself "Madame Sosostris, famous clairvoyante";[4] a London commuter (or at least someone who sees the crowds heading to work in the brown London fog, every man with his eyes "fixed...before his feet");[5] a mentally unbalanced woman brushing her hair and lashing her even more deeply depressed husband with savage words; a woman at a pub listening to ragtime music and talking about a friend's abortion; a "Smyrna merchant"[6] called Mr. Eugenides; Tiresias, the seer who in ancient Greek mythology was the only person to have been both male and female; and a drowned Phoenician sailor named Phlebas, among them—seem to merge continually in and out of one another.

Eliot's masterpiece is composed of various bits and pieces in disparate styles, from different points of view, in settings distant from one another in time and place, on apparently unrelated subjects. Parts of the poem are in German, French, Italian, and even Sanskrit. The reader has to guess how the fragments in this "heap of broken images"[7] (to quote from the poem itself) fit together. Eliot gets some heart-stopping effects simply by juxtaposing two quotations from different sources: where a quotation from the Buddha's *Fire Sermon* follows lines taken verbatim from the Elizabethan *Spanish Tragedy*, it almost seems as if Eliot's own poetry is somehow *between* the lines of his poem.

The bits and pieces quoted from earlier poetry seem, in contrast to the modern bits, to speak of a lost dignity and meaning, to point up the tawdriness of modern life. Andrew Marvell's "But at my back I always hear / Time's winged chariot hurrying near" becomes "But at my back from time to time I hear / The sounds of horns and motors, which shall bring / Sweeney to Mrs. Porter in the spring."[8] Oliver Goldsmith's

> When lovely woman stoops to folly,
> And finds too late that men betray,
> What charm can soothe her melancholy,
> What art can wash her guilt away?

becomes

> When lovely woman stoops to folly and
> Paces about her room again, alone,
> She smoothes her hair with automatic hand,
> And puts another record on the gramophone[9]

after a sordid scene in which a typist, "bored and tired," submits to the boorish attentions of "A small house agent's clerk, with one bold stare, / One of the low on whom assurance sits." *The Waste Land* expresses the sense that we often have—despite the progress that has created our unexampled prosperity—that the world is somehow less alive than it once was, that our lives are devoid of the significance human lives had in the past.

Eliot's poem was a huge success in all the most advanced circles. The scene from Waugh's *Brideshead Revisited* in which the eccentric Anthony Blanche reads a passage from *The Waste Land* through a megaphone for the edification of his less intellectual fellow-students at Oxford gives you a feel for the enormous impact of the poem. Eliot's voice seemed to be the voice of a prophet, speaking to the youth of the Jazz Age in a language they felt expressed their own experience. *The Waste Land* was a smash hit in the edgy art world of the 1920s.

Then Eliot converted to Christianity and shocked his readers by announcing his adherence to a conservative, not to say reactionary, world view. He

What Else They Don't Want You to Learn from Evelyn Waugh

Without religion, human beings are disgustingly selfish and shallow.

declared himself "anglo-catholic in religion, classicist in literature, and royalist in politics."[10] Eliot's conversion confirmed the pattern established in the avant-garde world of the 1890s.

Of course the conversions of a few avant-garde literary artists don't add up to a watertight argument for Christianity, or traditional Western culture. For one thing, there's plenty of great Modernist literature by people who kept moving in the other direction: James Joyce is the obvious counter-example. You can make an argument, though, that Joyce is the proverbial exception that proves the rule. Coming out of the warm heart of Irish Catholicism, Joyce had a starting point so much deeper inside traditional Western culture than the place where Waugh, Wilde, or Eliot began that he could run as hard and fast away from his roots as he wanted and still never get as far as they did. It's undeniable that even Joyce's later works—*Ulysses* and *Finnegans Wake*—are still suffused with a Catholic sensibility.

When we come to Evelyn Waugh, one of the last really first-rate British novelists, we've reached a literary artist whose major theme is the relationship between the modern sickness and the abandonment of the Christian faith. Waugh's later novels make a pretty explicit argument that Europe without the Faith is doomed. From the beginning (even before he had converted to Catholicism and come around to the belief that the Catholic Church was the ultimate source and guarantor of everything he prized) Waugh's fiction was about the collapse of civilization.

His first novel, in fact, is entitled *Decline and Fall.* It's the story of a hapless young man named Paul Pennyfather, the innocent victim of a bullying incident that gets him expelled from Oxford. Paul takes a teaching job (as the porter of his Oxford college predicts: "I expect you'll be becoming a schoolmaster, sir. That's what most of the gentlemen does, sir, that gets sent down for indecent behaviour."[11]) at a horribly incompetent and corrupt boys' school in Wales, gets swept into the orbit of an unimaginably glamorous woman, and is caught up into a glittering life that turns out to be financed by his lover's illegal activities as a procuress of English girls for prostitution in South America. It's the completely clueless Paul who ends up going to prison for her crimes, of course; she escapes unscathed.

In a Waugh novel you can assume that no one will get his just deserts. The innocent will suffer. The stupid and the selfish will flourish as the green bay tree. All of Waugh's pre-conversion fiction is about evil, which in Waugh is almost beyond banal. It has a stupid, unapologetic (even indignantly self-righteous) selfishness that beggars belief. The "bright young things" and other inhabitants of the upper class social set that Waugh wrote about were, in the 1920s, living through a revolution in sexual morality and family life that wouldn't reach most of America till the 1970s. In that environment, an adulterous wife's friends consider that her husband is behaving outrageously—"It's *too* monstrous that he should be allowed to get away with it"[12]—because he won't agree to a ruinous financial settlement so she can marry her gold-digging lover.

Waugh looks straight at prosperous wickedness and doesn't blink. He's the most unsentimental of writers. Waugh makes absolutely no concession to the reader's desire for poetic justice. Or for a happy ending, for that matter. Waugh offers a different kind of relief. His novels are all screamingly funny. He's got the iron nerve of an eighteenth-century satirist, in combination with a perfect ear for the absurdities of modern life.

Brideshead and *Sword of Honour,* Waugh's two great explicitly Catholic novels, make the case that without the Christian faith, Western civilization withers. Hooper in *Brideshead* is one character whose alienation from the roots of our culture makes him a stunted excuse for a man and a soldier:

Hooper had no illusions about the Army—or rather no special illusions distinguishable from the general, enveloping fog from which he observed the universe.... The history they taught him had had few battles in it but, instead, a profusion of detail about humane legislation and recent industrial change. Gallipoli, Balaclava, Quebec, Lepanto, Bannockburn, Roncevales, and Marathon—these, and the Battle in the West where Arthur fell, and a hundred such names whose trumpet-notes, even now in my sere and lawless state, called to me irresistibly across the intervening years with all the clarity and strength of boyhood, sounded in vain to Hooper.[13]

What Else They Don't Want You to Learn from Evelyn Waugh

The loss of the Christian faith means death for Western civilization.

"Trimmer," the hairdresser in *Sword of Honour* who is transformed into sort of pre-fab war hero by the War Office press officers to fill the propagandists' need for working-class heroes, is another such unfinished product.

The plot of Waugh's great war novel (the massive *Sword of Honour* was originally published in three novel-length installments: *Men at Arms*, *Officers and Gentlemen*, and *Unconditional Surrender*) turns on Trimmer's career. Guy Crouchback, Waugh's hero, begins *Sword of Honour* in a long funk. He's the heir of an ancient Catholic family, but his life has been blighted by the desertion of his wife Virginia, who went off with another man (and then another, and another), leaving Guy, who is bound by the Catholic Church's refusal to recognize divorce, unable to remarry—and unable to figure out what to do with the remainder of his life. The Hitler-Stalin pact is a moment of sudden clarity: "But now, splendidly, everything had become clear. The enemy at last was plain in view, huge and hateful, all disguise cast off. It was the Modern Age in arms. Whatever the outcome, there was a place for him in that battle."[14] Guy commits himself to the war as a modern crusader.

Complex events intervene. Guy misses, by the merest hair, a timely reconciliation with Virginia that might have restored his fortunes and those of his ancient family. The cause to which he devoted himself at the beginning of the war is tarnished by compromises with evil. And he comes to recognize that his own motives for joining in the war were criminally reckless. The spokeswoman for a band of starving Jewish refugees from the Nazis (whom Guy is endeavoring to save from the tender mercies of the Yugoslavian Communists) points out that the destruction caused by the war is, in part, the fault of men who wanted it because they believed "'their private honour could be satisfied by war. . . . They would accept hardships in recompense for having been selfish and lazy,'" and Guy recognizes himself: "'God forgive me,' said Guy, 'I was one of them.'"[15]

At the end of the novel the war is over and Guy is happy with a new wife, a daughter of the old English Catholic aristocracy. But the child that Trimmer fathered on Virginia, whom Guy remarried out of charity before her death, is Guy's heir. This cuckoo Guy's errant wife laid in his nest, this "Little Trimmer,"[16] this modern barbarian, is all the future to which the past of his illustrious family will give birth.

People call Waugh a snob, and they're right. He greatly treasured the highest achievements of Western civilization, and he utterly rejected socialist leveling as inimical to every human good. But the accomplishments of civilization—its art, grace, valor, and courtesy—aren't Waugh's ultimate goods. Even the simple decency that disappears in the absence of Christian morality isn't what he's after. All these things are impossible without the Faith, but they're not what the Faith is, finally, really *for*. The salvation of "the least of these"—the soul of Trimmer's baby—is the real point of the whole thing. The gospel teaches that whoever loses his life will save it; Waugh teaches the same thing about Western civilization. Only by rediscovering something else, something even more important than recapturing our civilization, will we have any chance of saving it.

In Waugh, we're back where English literature began: in the Dark Ages, where barbarian culture meets the Christian faith. Modern barbarian man is a very different animal from the noble savages who first sang about heroes like Beowulf, and it's impossible to tell what kind of culture, if any, will ultimately emerge from the clash between our old Christian civilization and our new barbarian selves. All our rich heritage may be destroyed. But, Waugh would argue, the heavy loss is worth it if even one soul is saved. And then, just as in the Dark Ages, there's no telling what might happen once souls begin to be saved. It's impossible to predict what glorious new things they will make—even in this world, in this little life we have on loan.

Chapter Eight

AMERICAN LITERATURE
Our Own Neglected Canon

Such as we were we gave ourselves outright
(The deed of gift was many deeds of war)
To the land vaguely realizing westward,
But still unstoried, artless, unenhanced,
Such as she was, such as she would become.

—Robert Frost, "The Gift Outright"[1]

American literature is not Allen Ginsberg, Toni Morrison, and Dan Brown.[2] PC English professors naturally gravitate toward American writers who share their disdain for America, Western civilization, and Christianity. But our best literature combines what's uniquely American with what's of universal value. While it has to be admitted that America has not produced a really world-class literature, there are American writers who have much more to offer than anti-Christian paranoia, victim ideology, and the clichéd incoherence of the Beats. A few of our writers have created really important literature—literature that's worth anyone's time and attention, and that we, as Americans, should know.

Big country, short attention spans

One notable thing about American literature is that, for such a big country, we've specialized in small literature. Two of our three greatest poets

The American literature you must not miss

Edgar Allan Poe,
Tales of the Grotesque and Arabesque

Nathaniel Hawthorne,
Mosses from the Old Manse

Herman Melville,
Moby-Dick

Frederick Douglass,
Narrative of the Life of Frederick Douglass: An American Slave

continued on p. 168

167

The American literature you
must not miss (continued)

Emily Dickinson, *Poems*

Walt Whitman
    Leaves of Grass

Mark Twain,
    Huckleberry Finn

Henry James,
    *The Portrait of a
    Lady*

F. Scott Fitzgerald,
    The Great Gatsby

William Faulkner
    *The Sound and the
    Fury*

Ernest Hemingway,
    *The Old Man and the
    Sea*

Ezra Pound,
    "The River
    Merchant's Wife: A
    Letter"

Robert Frost,
    "Stopping by Woods
    on a Snowy
    Evening,"
    "The Road Not
    Taken,"

Flannery O'Connor
    *Everything That
    Rises Must Converge*

(Robert Frost and, even more so, Emily Dickinson) are known for their fine short works. While twentieth-century American critics and writers developed a sort of obsession with "the great American novel," our best fiction is almost all short.

American writers have had big ambitions, but attempts to create monumental works often haven't turned out as well as projects of limited scope. In the nineteenth century Henry Wadsworth Longfellow and the other "fireside poets" turned out reams of workmanlike but mostly second-rate verse. And Walt Whitman wrote his sprawling *Leaves of Grass,* a collection of poems that add up to a kind of epic of the self-affirming ego. These include the well-known "Song of Myself," "I Sing the Body Electric," and "When Lilacs Last in the Dooryard Bloomed"—the elegy for President Lincoln that, in Joseph Bottum's telling phrase, "spreads Whitman like margarine across the nation."[3] There's wheat in Whitman's poetry, but there's plenty of chaff there, too.

Meanwhile, Emily Dickinson was writing her tiny jewel- (or dagger-) like lyrics. Ezra Pound's epic-length *Cantos* are impossible to follow; some of his shorter poems—especially "The River Merchant's Wife: A Letter"—are deeply moving. Edgar Allan Poe went so far as claim that there *was no such thing* as a *long* poem.

We've got a big country, but we've got short attention spans. If "the great American novel" has to be epic-sized (to match the wide open spaces of our country) then *Moby-Dick* is the obvious choice. But it's a sort of standing joke—Woody Allen built a feature-length film around it—that hardly anyone actually reads Melville's huge novel all the way through. Hawthorne's stories are wonderful, and his novels get longer and longer, but not better and better. *The Scarlet Letter,* early and short, is the best; *The Marble Faun,* the last and the longest, is the worst. Henry James's novels aren't American enough to qualify—he lived in Europe and England for most of his adult life. And Faulkner is so very regional that it's hard to think of his novels as embodying the American experience. All things considered, the top contenders for "the great American novel" have to be two very short books: Mark Twain's *Huckleberry Finn* and F. Scott Fitzgerald's *The Great Gatsby*. The short story, not the novel, is the quintessential American literary genre.

Maybe our attention spans are short because the American experience is less about perseverance than it is about fresh starts. Whatever the European discovery of America meant for the American natives, for Europeans it meant a chance to start over again. Landless younger sons and transported debtors, religious dissenters seeking to establish a society according to the dictates of their consciences, artisans looking for better compensation for their work—all these folks could get a second chance in America. And some of them got a third, and a fourth. America was a big, open place: it was much easier, here, to leave your mistakes behind you and start again.

A Mini-Course in American Literature

Because Americans excel in short forms, you can take a high-speed tour through our whole literature by reading bite-sized pieces of fine American writing from Edgar Allan Poe to Flannery O'Connor. Poems: Read just four tiny ones: Emily Dickinson's "The Soul Selects Her Own Society" (only 12 lines), Walt Whitman's "A Noiseless Patient Spider" (10 lines), Robert Frost's "Nothing Gold Can Stay" (8 lines), and Ezra Pound's "In a Station of the Metro" (only 2!). Stories: Read Poe's "The Cask of Amontillado," Hawthorne's "Young Goodman Brown," Faulkner's "Barn Burning," Hemingway's "Big Two-Hearted River," and Flannery O'Connor's "Everything That Rises Must Converge." Finish your whirlwind introduction to the American canon with two short novels: *Huckleberry Finn* and *The Great Gatsby*.

It's a fascinating question, what a fresh start can do for you, and what it can't. The awareness of the frontier always out there had some wonderful effects on the American character. It seems to have protected us from the cynicism that's the prevailing note in the modern European character. But you can't always solve your problems by getting away from them. As the psychologists point out, you can leave your job, or your hometown, or your marriage—but you always take yourself with you. Americans have continually had to realize that fact, and the best American literature explores that discovery.

The mystery of evil

The great theme of American literature is the mystery of evil. Here we are, on a brand new continent. We left our problems behind in our past, when we freed ourselves from the yoke of the despots of Europe. We established a truly righteous society of Christian saints. Or at least we escaped our troubles by leaving New York for Missouri, or Iowa for the Dakota Territory. Or if evil wasn't behind us, it was *out there* somewhere—in the wild woods with the Indians, in the forces of nature we had to contend against to cross the wide new continent, or in the vastness of the untamed ocean.

But the continually renewed insight of great American literature is that evil is not just "out there," and you don't leave it behind when you move on. Cruelty and suffering will keep reappearing, and their existence can't be forever blamed on the clinging corruption of the old things. One great work of American fiction after another dramatizes the (always late, always surprising) discovery that evil is really here, inside us, in the human heart. As William Faulkner explained in his Nobel Prize acceptance speech, the only things worth writing about are "the problems of the human heart in conflict with itself."

In *Moby-Dick* Captain Ahab pursues the great white whale, which cost him his leg, across the untracked ocean, as if one wild beast were the locus of evil in the world. But it becomes obvious that the real evil is in Ahab's own self-destructive obsession.

Edgar Allan Poe's stories plumb the extremities of sin and crime to which human beings will sink, and explore how their crimes transform them. "The Cask of Amontillado" focuses on the act of murder itself: we watch the narrator carry out a particularly exquisite act of revenge on his enemy. "The Tell-Tale Heart" concerns itself with the murderer's guilt, the only thing that keeps him from getting away with his crime.

Nathaniel Hawthorne's works are also about sin and guilt—*The Scarlet Letter*, of course, but also dozens of stories. "Young Goodman Brown" is one of the best. No murders are committed—in fact, Hawthorne leaves it unclear whether anything worse than a walk in the woods actually occurs. The story is set in early colonial Massachusetts, when Puritan rectitude was still the general standard.

As the story begins, Goodman Brown is bidding goodbye to his new wife, Faith, as he sets out on a journey. It's obvious that he's doing something he shouldn't: "What a wretch I am," he says to himself, "to leave her on such an errand...after this one night, I'll cling to her skirts and follow her to Heaven." He travels through the woods, wondering whether "a devilish Indian" may be "behind every tree," or "the devil himself" "at my very elbow." Pretty soon the Devil does show up, and it's clear that the young man has arranged to meet him in the woods.

What They Don't Want You to Learn from American Literature

Evil isn't "back there" or "out there"; it's in the human heart.

Goodman Brown almost turns back, but the Devil persuades him to talk things over. He has an answer for the argument Goodman Brown has fastened on for going home: "My father never went into the woods on such an errand, nor his father before him." But they did, the Devil assures him—and gives examples of actions he claims to have inspired in the young man's ancestors. Goodman Brown is further disconcerted by the appearances of several of his respected elders along the forest path, whose appearance helps wear down his powers of resistance.

The one last sure thing Goodman Brown clings to—the goodness of his wife—is torn from him when he hears her voice above the woods. "There is no good on earth;" he decides, "and sin is but a name." Maddened, Goodman Brown rushes toward the place of initiation, where he sees Faith, like himself, a convert waiting to be baptized into the satanic church. Once they're marked by the Devil, they'll be privy to each other's secret sins. "What polluted wretches would the next glance show them to each other," the young husband wonders, "shuddering alike at what they disclosed and what they saw!" Just before the deed can be done, Goodman Brown cries out to his wife to "look up to Heaven, and resist the wicked one."

He never knows whether she obeyed his warning. The instant Goodman Brown cries out, the Devil's church vanishes, and he finds himself alone in the woods. Goodman Brown's last-minute refusal can't save him entirely from the consequences of his experiment with evil. He can't know for sure whether the forms he saw in the forest were illusions of the Devil, an ugly dream of his own, or the real shapes of his teachers, neighbors, and wife. But the fact that he saw them changes the rest of his life. Goodman Brown sees hypocrisy and secret wickedness behind all the piety and humble happiness of his Puritan village. He's apparently avoided the Devil's baptism, but he's cursed with the belief in—if not the actual knowledge of—his fellow man's wickedness. His suspicions poison everything for him; he dies an embittered and hopeless old man.

There's good psychological insight in Hawthorne's story, which has special resonance today, when there's an online community for every perversion devised by the mind of man. The knowledge, or even the suspicion, that others share your secret sin undoubtedly weakens your own resistance to it, for exactly the reasons Hawthorne sets out in his story:

the community of co-conspirators is attractive, and its existence makes virtue and innocent happiness seem like illusions.

The possibility of escape

The mystery of evil continued to exercise the American imagination as the nineteenth century gave way to the twentieth. After the frontier experience came to an end, Americans found new places "back there" or "out there" in which to locate evil. The capitalist robber barons were the problem. Or the trouble was the bankers back East: Mankind was being crucified on a cross of gold. Or, on the other hand, our progress toward a well-ordered and healthy society was impeded by trashy riffraff who overburdened our new social services, and whose out-of-control breeding had to be gotten under control.

But increasingly, in the twentieth century, the locus of evil was thought to be culture itself—not just the European past, with its corrupt monarchies, but the very existence of a civilized tradition, felt as the dead hand of the past weighing on the present. The traditional conventions and expectations of society (whether of the old New York families in the Social Register, or of the neighbors in a small town in the Midwest) were felt as an intolerable burden. Americans would shake free of this stifling inheritance. We would shake off tradition and invent new, scientific ways of solving social problems and educating future generations.

All these different strains of thought left their marks in the American literature of the twentieth century. Happiness seems to be impossible without some kind of escape—whether from the neighbors or from the past. Edith Wharton's novels paint life among the old New York families as a stifling trap; Sinclair Lewis's *Babbit* and *Main Street* do the same thing for middle class life in Middle America.

Hemingway's heroes are always on the run from something (which might just turn out to be themselves). They're on their own, out in the wild, hunting or fishing. Or they're serving in foreign wars. Or they're Americans abroad, living in Europe—anywhere they might be able to hold together an integrity that's somehow impossible under the conditions of ordinary civilized life in their native America. F. Scott Fitzgerald's *The Great Gatsby* is about the emptiness at the heart of the American dream, the futility of the never-ending quest—"tomorrow we will run faster, stretch our arms farther"—for a happiness that is already lost in the past.[4]

Interestingly, the most successful regional American literature is the product of the part of our country with the *most* stifling, tradition-fraught culture. The South has always been the most backward-looking and Anglophilic part of America. It was for a long time the least progressive part of the nation. Southern culture was rural and agricultural while the North was urbanizing and mechanizing. The "Southern aristocracy"—which in some places made up pretty much the entire literate population—nurtured delusions of European grandeur. They[5] carefully reckoned their descent from the titled families of England and the Continent. Heredity had enormous meaning for Southerners, both for good and for ill.

The South was also the place it was *hardest* to pretend that evil was all somebody else's doing. It's ironic, really, that the Purtians' descendants in New England (Emerson, Thoreau, Whitman) were able to forget about our fallen human nature faster than the heirs of the gentlemen adventurers who brought a more relaxed version of Protestant Christianity to Virginia. After all, original sin was a bedrock belief of the Calvinist Puritans.

But Massachusetts Puritanism also included a powerful strain of what came to be called "American exceptionalism"—Alexis de Tocqueville's phrase for Americans' belief that we're special, that God has chosen America to be His in a particular way. This "exceptionalism" originated in the Puritans' Calvinist belief that they were among the elect whom God had chosen for salvation. But the facts on the ground were probably even more significant than the different religious histories of the different regions. White Southerners knew they were implicated in what's been called America's original sin, the great contradiction at the heart of America's foundation—chattel slavery, justified on the basis of race.

As slavery was outlawed in the states outside the South, the "peculiar institution" came to be *the* defining fact of Southern culture. Inequality and bondage were day-in, day-out realities for Southerners, who lived with slavery, and then through the war that ended it, and then in the long shadows of both. The best Southern literature *is* about race, in a way that no great English literature—not even *Othello*—really is.

Mark Twain, from Missouri, a border state, has a hybrid sensibility. He's part can-do, practical Yankee with no patience for medieval aristocratic pretensions—like the hero of his novel, *A Connecticut Yankee in King Arthur's Court.* But he's also the native son of a slave state.

Narrative of the Life of Frederick Douglass, American Slave

The greatest work of abolitionist literature is Frederick Douglass's *Narrative* of his life as a slave. The author was a man who had suffered the most outrageous wrongs, and the book undoubtedly had a rhetorical purpose. But it's nothing like the many sentimental, manipulative, and prurient books about American slavery that have been (and continue to be) written since the seventeenth century. It's a clear-headed, morally sophisticated, and deeply moving account by a greathearted man.

Why we should still read *Huckleberry Finn* (despite the ugly racial epithets)

Huckleberry Finn is a grand adventure about a journey down the great Mississippi River. It's also a psychologically realistic portrait of a boy running away from his brutal father and a man running away from the brutal institution of slavery. The Yankee in Twain delighted to poke fun at the absurdities and hypocrisy of Southern culture, infatuated with its delusions of nobility. "The King" and "the Duke" in *Huckleberry Finn,* sometime Shakespearian actors and full-time con men who trade on their supposed noble blood and their victims' cultural pretensions, are hilarious. But the Southerner in Twain could make the institution of slavery really live in his fiction.

In fact, in the character of Jim, the runaway slave, Twain reproduced some truths of a slave's existence—the way the slave's inferiority was taken for granted, and his real and horribly abused intimacy with the very people who denied his humanity—so vividly that *Huckleberry Finn* has fallen afoul of our modern censors. Jim's ignorance is felt to be an insult to the intelligence of modern-day descendents of slaves. The words the characters in the novel use about Jim's race seem to be violent offenses to human dignity, better not even mentioned in the classroom.

The problem that *Huckleberry Finn* poses to modern audiences is, in a particularly stark form, the same dilemma that all our culture sets for us. Which is the best way to handle the traces of human evil in the culture we've inherited from the past? "Multiculturalism" and political correctness suggest two conflicting answers.

There's the way of multiculturalist propaganda: the crimes of the past are continually brought to our attention so that we can remind ourselves of the wickedness of our culture, and be on guard against any recurrence. This self-flagellating blame-America-first attitude is a far cry from the robust self-confidence that's been typical of our American culture. And it inevitably leads away from American literature (whose hopelessly tainted authors can't be trusted) to the study of social history.

There is something recognizably American in the other PC approach—the notion that if only we can cut ourselves off from the hopeless guilt of Western civilization, if only we can scrub our language clean of masculine pronouns and eradicate every last Confederate memorial from our public parks—then we'll get beyond our hegemonic, African-enslaving, Indian-killing past into a bright new egalitarian future. From this point of view, it's best to forget all about *Huckleberry Finn*.

There's no question about what either attitude does to the study of literature—it kills it. And the death of our literary heritage might be worth it, if either perpetual self-flagellation or dropping the whole Western canon down the memory hole could ensure that no injustice on the scale of black slavery in America would ever occur again. But what if the ultimate source of that evil is not some special circumstance unique to the American South, or even to Western civilization? What if the real source of slavery and racism is in "the problems of the human heart in conflict with itself," which are always going to be with us, no matter how we try

Can You Believe the Professors?

Actually, in this case, it seems to be graduate students. But Jaudon, at least, is already teaching at Cornell. See the note below.

"This panel, proposed for the 2006 meeting of the Society for the Study of American Women Writers, will explore the ways in which the lens of "laundry" refracts literary and cultural practices into their component discourses. An analysis of laundry and its associated motifs (whiteness, washing, cleansing) not only foregrounds certain certain gendered and raced labor practices, but also draws together diverse discourses such as religious fundamentalism, psychoanalysis, and materialist accounts of labor history."—This "call for papers" asks for abstracts to be sent to Hilary Emmett and Toni Wall Jaudon, at Cornell University.

Posted at more than one website, including at http://www.unm.edu/~loboblog/mort/archives/cat_american_literatures_pre_1900.html, viewed 7/23/2006. For information about Toni Wall Jaudon's spring 2006 English 111.5 course on "How Normal Became the Norm: Disability in U.S. Culture and Policy," see http://instruct1.cit.cornell.edu/courses/engl111-05/, viewed 7/23/2006.

to escape them? Then neither perpetual self-recrimination nor historical amnesia is our cure.

"Never again" is, by itself, never good enough—because there's always an argument, the next time, about whether the new evil is the same thing we've sworn never to tolerate again. The injustice always reappears in a different form. The very parade of self-condemnation or the elaborate distancing of ourselves from the injustice of the past—by which we think we guarantee our innocence—can itself become the occasion, or even the excuse, for the next injustice.

But enforced ignorance is an even worse choice. Attempts to cut ourselves off from the knowledge of human nature that's available in the history and literature of our culture are bound to be counter-productive. People did the appalling things that our most painful literature portrays not primarily because they were Southerners, or Americans, or colonial imperialists tarnished by the hegemonic culture of the West. They did them because they were *human beings.* Human culture is the record of the long struggle to understand the human condition, and human nature—which will always be with us no matter how many fresh starts we get. Knowledge of that culture is a necessary weapon (*not* a liability) in the never-ending struggle for human dignity.

Literature from the Deep South

William Faulkner, the best-known Southern (and possibly the greatest American) writer, was born and bred and lived for most of his life in Mississippi: the poorest, most backward, least egalitarian state in the United States. Faulkner's ancestors were early settlers and landowners in the Deep South; his grandfather was a colonel in the Confederate Army. Faulkner wrote a series of interconnected novels spanning more than a hundred years of fictional time, about the inhabitants of the mythical Yoknapatawpha County, Mississippi.

Faulkner's characters, like real Southerners, are defined partly by the histories of their families. The Sartorises and Compsons are shabby Mississippi gentility like Faulkner's own family. The Snopses are sleazy white trash—early on, barn burners who resort to vandalism and animal cruelty to cover up their flight from their sharecropping debts; later on, up-and-comers who flourish in the New South economy in which the Compsons and Sartorises can't make it.

Like the French novelist Balzac, Faulkner lets the same characters show up in different novels—in one as the hero, then in a kind of cameo appearance in another. But unlike Balzac, Faulkner uses modern narrative techniques to tell his stories. His fiction marries the experimental narrative techniques of James Joyce to the native storytelling tradition of the American South.

The Sound and the Fury and *Absalom, Absalom* are often said to be Faulkner's two best novels. Parts of both books are narrated by Quentin Compson, who's a Harvard freshman in 1909-10; he commits suicide in the spring of 1910. *Absalom, Absalom* is largely a story that Quentin Compson tells his Harvard roommate, a Canadian named Shrevlin McCannon. The pretensions of Southern culture are an explicit theme of the book. Quentin's Harvard education is one of those luxuries that shabby genteel Southerners cling to, to reassure themselves that they're really the artistocrats they believe themselves to be.

The story Quentin tells Shreve is about Thomas Sutpen and his children. The hardbitten Thomas Sutpen appears mysteriously in Jefferson, Mississippi, in 1833, acquires 100 square miles of land by tricking or coercing an Indian chief, marries the daughter of a Methodist storekeeper, and has a son, Henry, and a daughter, Judith. In 1859, Henry brings a friend, Charles Bon, home from the University of Mississippi to visit his family for Christmas. Judith falls in love with Charles.

The next year Thomas Sutpen forbids Judith to marry Charles. Henry, siding with his friend, leaves home. Henry Sutpen and Charles Bon serve together in the Confederate Army for four years. In 1865, they return to Sutpen's Hundred, Charles still intending to marry Henry's sister. But Henry shoots and kills Charles in front of Sutpen's house.

Elements of Greek tragedy, Biblical history, and Southern Gothic are freely blended in *Absalom, Absalom.* But at its heart the novel is a mystery—not a whodunnit, but a why-he-dunnit kind of story. Why did Henry Sutpen, who defied his own father for Charles's sake, in the end shoot Charles rather than let him marry Henry's sister? Quentin tells Shreve several possible versions of the story. They speculate on why Henry had to stop the marriage.

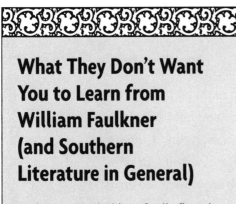

What They Don't Want You to Learn from William Faulkner (and Southern Literature in General)

Civilization is valuable. A fatally flawed culture beats no culture at all.

Quentin and Shreve imagine Henry, living through the War with Charles, discovering the truth about the man his sister loves. That truth has several layers. First, that Charles has a relationship—even a quasi-marriage—with an "octoroon" (a woman of one eighth African descent) in New Orleans. Then, more shockingly, that Charles is Thomas Sutpen's own first son, by a woman he married in Haiti. Quentin and Shreve imagine Henry, trying to accommodate himself to an incestuous marriage between his sister and his half-brother by telling himself

stories about a French duke who married his sister and was excommunicated by the pope.

But the real answer to the mystery is none of these. Henry is determined to let Charles Bon marry Judith, even incestuously, until he meets his father in the final retreat of the Confederate Army. What his father tells him changes Henry's mind: "*it was not until after he was born that I found out that his mother was part negro.*"[6] It's the miscegenation, not the incest, that Henry won't stomach.

But Charles is determined to force his way into his father's family, even if he dies in the attempt. As he explains to Henry, he would have abandoned his claim on Judith if at any time their father had sent him word—not even to ask him to leave her alone, but simply to acknowledge his paternity.

Thomas Sutpen is equally determined: He can't acknowlege Charles Bon in any way. His ambition for his family depends on the color bar that's the fundamental law of Southern culture: one drop of "negro blood" is an absolute disqualification from any kind of social status. Sutpen has to reject his own son to satisfy the craving for acceptance that's been driving him since he was rejected as a boy—sent away from the door of the plantation house where his trashy family were sharecropping in Virginia.

Henry sees things the same way. When Bon says Henry will have to kill him to keep him from marrying Judith, Henry says he can't, because Bon is his brother. *"No I'm not,"* answers Charles, *"I'm the nigger that's going to sleep with your sister."*[7] That's why Henry shoots him.

After the murder, Sutpen tries again (and then again) for yet another fresh start. Sutpen's final try ends in his own death, when Wash Jones, odd-job man living on the Sutpen place, kills him because he rejects Jones's trashy granddaughter (after Sutpen lashes out in disappointment that she's given birth to a girl, instead of the son he needs to establish a Sutpen dynasty and forever erase the image of himself as the rejected boy of his Virginia childhood).

At the end of the book, Shreve asks Quentin a final question: "Why do you hate the South?" And Quentin answers ("quickly, at once, immediately"): "I dont hate it."[8] But of course he does. Southern literature is great for the same reason that Southerners feel more trapped than people from other places in America. It's awful to have to live with your mistakes, instead of moving on and forgetting them. But there's something attractively *real* about Southern culture and Southern literature. What Quentin has, and feels as a burden, is a heritage that a Yankee (or a Canadian like Shreve) is naturally fascinated by—even, in some sense, envies.

Southerners have had to live with each other, in a way that a lot of other Americans haven't even tried doing. Instead of making a fresh start, Southerners lived with their sins, and with the people they hurt and were hurt by, for generation after generation—sometimes stewing in resentment and prejudice, sometimes taking revenge—but actually living with the descendents of the people their ancestors knew: descendents of slaves lived cheek by jowl with the descendents of slavemasters. The result is, at least Southern writers are aware that fresh starts, like the one Thomas Sutpen was trying for, cost something. You can't just erase everything you (or your ancestors) did before you decided to start again. Old sins have long shadows: in the Bible, in Greek tragedy, in Southern Gothic. Pretending you can simply move on is another rejection—of the responsibilities you carry from the past, and of the people that past binds you to—which pulls you back into the cycle of tragedy again.

"A hillbilly Thomist"

If the theme of Faulkner's fiction is that you can never really get a fresh start, the theme of Flannery O'Connor's is that you can—but only at an enormous price. Faulkner's religion, insofar as he had one, was the stoicism that Walker Percy, another Southern writer, claimed was the real religion of the South.[9] O'Connor was a Catholic—she called herself a "hillbilly Thomist"[10]—who found in her native Bible Belt the perfect setting for stories in which God's grace pierces through human defenses to offer self-satisfied, stiff-necked human beings one last chance to repent.

If Faulkner's fiction is Southern Gothic, O'Connor's is Southern grotesque. The grace O'Connor wrote about was not a comfortable thing. The New Testament passage from which she took the title of her second novel could be the motto for the whole body of her work: "From the days of John the Baptist until now, the kingdom of God suffereth violence, and the violent bear it away." O'Connor was brought up in the narrow American Catholicism of the mid-twentieth century, but her religious education took her in an odd way. Having been taught, for example, that her guardian angel accompanied her everywhere, she used, as a child, to lock herself in a room and whirl around wildly in a circle trying to hit him.[11] The Divine grace that O'Connor's characters encounter is the furthest thing possible from a pious platitude; its ultimate source is something that's more grotesque even than the events of an Edgar Allan Poe story, but that was present in one form or another in every Catholic home and every Catholic school in the 1950s: a Man nailed to a cross, dying in bitter agony.

Flannery O'Connor's stories typically end with a gruesome act of violence. In "A Good Man Is Hard to Find" a serial murderer shoots a grandmother. In "Greenleaf" a woman is gored by a bull. In *Wise Blood* a man blinds himself with lime. In "The Lame Shall Enter First" a man finds the body of his son who has hanged himself; he makes this discovery at the very moment when he's realized that he loves the boy, and that he's been neglecting him in a vain attempt to reform a thankless juvenile delinquent. If there's no physical violence in a story, there's a heart-rending loss or some other horrifying revelation.

In "Everything That Rises Must Converge," a young white man, Julian, is riding the bus with his mother when a black woman gets on with her little boy. Julian's mother is mortified to discover that the black woman is wearing the very same hat she is. And Julian is mortally embarrassed by his mother's attempts to condescend to the black family: she offers the black child a penny; the black woman responds with

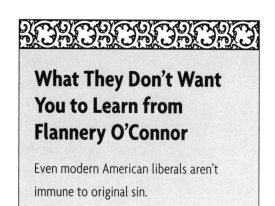

What They Don't Want You to Learn from Flannery O'Connor

Even modern American liberals aren't immune to original sin.

violent resentment. Julian is humiliated by his association with his embarrassingly out-of-date mother. She's sacrificed for her son—"her teeth had gone unfilled so that his could be straightened"[12]—but the education she's given him has only turned him into a resentful small-time intellectual snob who despises her all the more because he needs her so much. He wishes he could make the black people on the bus understand where his real sympathies lie, that he, unlike his mother, has solidarity with the just aspirations of the black race. To prove the point, he makes a production of asking a black man on the bus for a light, only to realize that he doesn't have any cigarettes. It's only when his mother has a stroke in the midst of Julian's self-righteous harangue that he suddenly remembers how much he needs and even really loves her.

Unhappy young intellectuals who are miserably uncomfortable in their parents' world (some of them suspiciously like Flannery O'Connor herself) are staple characters in O'Connor's fiction. O'Connor wrote to a friend that "Everything That Rises Must Converge" amounted to saying "a plague on everybody's house."[13] In other words, she was criticizing both traditional Southern racism, in which Southern whites feel comfortably superior to blacks, and the new Southern liberalism, in which Southern liberals feel comfortably superior to their parents and their less enlightened neighbors. Both states of mind are just different versions of the tendency to locate evil *somewhere else*—or, as O'Connor saw it, different ways of being satisfied to live without repentance, closed off to grace.

In *The Violent Bear It Away* O'Connor gives us another modern liberal Southerner—a schoolteacher named Rayber who's eager to cure his young nephew, Tarwater, of the religious fanaticism he's been trained up in by their ancient uncle, who believed himself to be a prophet and was raising Tarwater to be a prophet, too.

The boy Tarwater has a strong revulsion to this vocation. It absolutely makes him sick to think about the Heaven the old man used to tell him about. He imagines himself sitting on a green hill stuffed full of loaves and fishes—to the point of nausea. After the old man dies, Tarwater runs away from the cabin where they lived, setting it on fire rather than bury the old man's body. He goes to the schoolteacher uncle, hoping to find a life more to his liking in the city.

But the sociology that his schoolteacher uncle lives by isn't strong enough to compete with the Divine grace that's seeking a foothold in Tarwater's life. Some of the novel's funniest scenes show the schoolteacher's sanitized modern worldview clashing with the old prophet's uncompromising vision. For instance, the old man says just what he thinks (in Old Testament language) about the schoolteacher's finding his sister a boyfriend. And the teacher writes the old man up in a magazine as a case study in self-deluded religious fanaticism, and gives him the article to read. The teacher's up-to-date mental hygiene is really just a retreat from realities he can't face—including his overwhelming irrational love for his retarded son. The novel ends with several appalling acts of violence, as is only to be expected in a Flannery O'Connor novel. O'Connor is bent on showing us the cost of salvation, which is the only real fresh start available to us. The further we get from understanding original sin, that most essential truth about human nature, the more violent the intervention of grace—and the literature, for that matter—has to be, to get our attention.

Part II

WHY THEY DON'T WANT YOU TO LEARN ABOUT ENGLISH AND AMERICAN LITERATURE

Chapter Nine

HOW THE PC ENGLISH PROFESSORS ARE SUPPRESSING ENGLISH LITERATURE
(Not Teaching It)

Hey, hey, ho, ho, Western Culture's got to go.

—Stanford student protesters, marching with Jesse Jackson in 1987

It might take a violent supernatural intervention—a lightning bolt, perhaps—to persuade the modern barbarians who teach "English" in college to take any notice of English literature. The marvels that we've glimpsed in the first eight chapters of this *Guide* leave them cold. Everybody knows that our universities are full of PC professors who can be trusted to say outrageous (or unintentionally hilarious) things about everything from "the domestication of women" to the war in Iraq. What isn't so well known is the extent to which these folks have succeeded in preventing English and American literature from being taught at all.

The suppression of English Literature matters enormously. We can't afford to let it disappear. The problem isn't just that individuals will miss out on the profit and pleasure they could derive from Shakespeare and Jane Austen. Western civilization isn't in our genes, it's in our culture. Our great literature was an essential part of the education that used to make Americans and citizens of the West. If we quit teaching it, can we be sure we'll transmit Western civilization to future generations?

Guess what?

→ English departments are advertising more positions for experts in "multicultural" literature than in Shakespeare

→ Even when literature is the ostensible subject of a college English course, students often learn feminism, Marxism, or Freud instead

→ PC English professors' ugly jargon is a barrier to (not a tool for) understanding the literature

English professors teach anything and everything...except English literature

Just look at the course offerings in our English departments. Consider how many classes are devoted to material that isn't "English" by any definition: Marxism, "deconstruction," Afro-Caribbean writings in French, the cinema of Weimer Germany, and the Jewish literature of Latin America.[1] Another large proportion of what's being taught is dubiously, if at all, literature: pornography, the history of the blues, film noir or Westerns, "Chicano/a Intellectual Thought," pop music, detective fiction, comic books, or Stephen King.[2]

And it only looks to get worse. The folks doing the hiring for university departments of English seem to feel that they're already fully stocked with professors whose expertise is in Milton and Wordsworth, Emily Dickinson and Robert Frost. What they need, in their view, is more experts in "multi-cultural literature"; "literary theory"; "[p]ost-colonial literatures; [l]iteratures from countries other than America or Great Britain," "Hispanic—or Asian-American literatures"; or "multiethnic/ multicultural literatures." Judging by the job listings, if you want to become an English professor you'd be much better off specializing in multiculturalism than in Shakespeare.[3]

The real trouble isn't the occasional well-publicized outrage—a professor teaching contemporary British literature leads her graduate students in vandalizing an anti-abortion display,[4] or an instructor of freshman composition emails a student to suggest that our soldiers in Iraq should be shooting their

Three Books You're Not Supposed to Read

Tenured Radicals: How Politics Has Corrupted Higher Education, by Roger Kimball, Ivan R. Dee, 1998.

The Professors: The 101 Most Dangerous Academics in America, by David Horowitz, Regnery, 2006.

Illiberal Education: The Politics of Race and Sex on Campus, by Dinesh D'Souza, Free Press, 1998.

officers.[5] The deeper problem is the degree to which English professors in general are alienated from English and American literature. Consider the depressing proportion of the "English" curriculum dedicated to the dregs and rejects of other disciplines, which have somehow found a home in departments formerly devoted to the study of English.

Modern economics has disproved the "labor theory of value" that Marx's entire economic theory depends on, and Marxism as a political ideology has failed (and caused immeasurable suffering) everywhere it's been tried. But Marxism is still going strong in departments of English. Mainstream psychotherapists don't use Freudian analysis any more, but English professors do. *I, Rigoberta Menchu,* the supposed true story of a Guatemalan peasant woman's life, was exposed as a fraud in 1999, but it's still taught in English departments.[6] The men and women whose job title is "professor of English" give the very strong impression that they would rather profess *anything* but the English language and the great literature that's written in it.

Why they don't want you to read English and American literature

Imagine yourself, for just one minute, inside the world view of a PC English professor. If your project in life were—in the immortal words of those Stanford students in 1987—"Hey, hey, ho, ho, Western Culture's got to go," then of course it would never do to expose another class full of

---

Can You Believe the Professors?

"'In fact, the department paid for my copies of Deep Throat,' he said."

Ellis Hanson, professor of English at Cornell, telling Columbia News Service how the Cornell Department of English responded to his decision to teach pornography to undergraduates. Ariel Brewster, "Porn 101," Columbia News Service, March 14, 2006. http://jscms.jrn.columbia.edu/cns/2006-03-14/brewster-porn viewed 6/12/2006.

---

impressionable young people to the riches of that very culture every semester. Because, you never know—*they might like it.*

From the "Western Culture's got to go" point of view, the great works of English literature make up *the* most dangerous body of knowledge that the average college student is likely to encounter. They're enormously entertaining, they're dangerously informative about the real past of Western culture (not the horror story that the Left wishes we would all believe about our racist, sexist, and homophobic history), and they're in our own native language.[7]

Everybody loves a good story. And the teenaged college freshman who is assigned a tale by Chaucer or a Jane Austen novel and reads with attention because he's enjoying the story is learning a thousand things that contradict the "progressive" theory of human history, according to which our forebears were the brutish oppressors of women and minorities, over whom we enjoy an unquestioned moral superiority. Students with direct knowledge of how the "dead white males" (and their surprisingly lively womenfolk) actually thought and wrote are a lot less likely to fall for the line that life was a hell of unenlightened stupidity and oppression back in the bad old days, before feminists and leftist politics set us free.

But as much as the PC professors may wish it would go away, English literature can't be entirely hushed up. Chaucer, Shakespeare, and the rest first became part of the old literary "canon" because of their universal appeal. Students can't be forever distracted from literature by movies, "graphic novels," or the history of jazz. Here's where "literary theory" comes in.

"Theory"—Marxism, feminism, deconstruction, and bashing dead white males

Deconstructionist guru Paul de Mann wrote about "resistance to theory." But "theory" itself could be accurately described as "resistance to literature." Students are now taught to read in a way that not only keeps them from learning anything from the literature they read for their "English" classes—it inoculates them against ever learning anything from literature in the future.

At least, if you've never read Shakespeare, you can always read him later. But if you've taken a "theory"-driven Shakespeare course, you've been given a kind of anti-Shakespeare vaccination. You already know that the plays are full of racist and patriarchal structures—that's what you've been taught to look for when you read. You'll never take Shakespeare seriously as a source of insights into human nature, or the meaning of love.

"Literary theory" boosts your immunity to education. We all have a natural resistance to ideas (and standards of beauty) outside the current fashion. None of us eagerly questions our own insular ways of seeing things. "Theory" erects a barrier of "postmodern" thought between students and the literature from which they might otherwise learn.

"Theory" comes in a variety of poisonous flavors. Try studying English Literature in college, and your professor may be a Marxist—still pushing the ideology that justified murders in the tens of millions and caused untold misery over the course of the twentieth century. (Our universities are the only places in the world, outside the North Korean and Cuban prison-states—and a few bloodthirsty insurgencies in places like Nepal—where Marxism is still taken seriously.)

Or you might be taught by a proponent of radical feminism, "gender studies," or "queer theory." Or by a deconstructionist, who uses literature to demonstrate the impossibility of

Can You Believe the Professors?

(PIG)

"This article outlines Joseph Stalin's attempts, from the 1930s until his death, to democratize the government of the Soviet Union."

Grover Furr, professor of English at Montclair State University in New Jersey, introducing his article on the history of Soviet Communism. Stalin and the Struggle for Democratic Reform, Part One" published online in *Cultural Logic: An Electronic Journal of Marxist Theory and Practice* 2005, volume 8, http://eserver.org/clogic/2005/furr.html viewed 6/20/2006.

A Book You're Not Supposed to Read

Theory's Empire: An Anthology of Dissent, edited by Daphne Patai and Wilfrido Corral, Columbia University Press, 2005.

meaning. Or by some kind of multiculturalist—an expert in "postcolonial studies," "global literature," or any one of an ever-multiplying variety of "[fill-in-the-blank] studies" that are less about the genuine achievements of non-Western cultures—or about "minority" or "marginal" writers within the Western tradition—than they are about using the writing and experiences of non-Western and "marginalized" minorities as a stick to beat Western culture with.

Postmodernist jargon: hideously ugly, mentally crippling

And at the same time you're learning to slice Chaucer or Shakespeare half a dozen postmodern ways, you'll also be picking up a new vocabulary. The special vocabulary that PC English professors and graduate students use is remarkable for its *exclusion* of certain concepts and whole ways of thinking.

Graduate students in English quickly learn, for example, not to talk about poets in terms of their individual genius, and not to refer to poems as having been "created"—rarely even as having been "composed" or "written." The sophisticated postmodern way to talk about the writing of literature is as "production." Calling a sonnet by Shakespeare or Wordsworth a "literary production" makes it seem as if that work of art resulted from more or less the same kind of impersonal and automatic process as the assembly of a car or refrigerator.

IF YOU WANT TO SOUND LIKE A PC ENGLISH PROFESSOR . . .

Don't Say: *"work of literature"*

Say: *"literary production"*

Because:[8]	What's the difference between writing poetry and cranking out manufactured goods?
Don't Say:	*"the book," "the poem," "the novel", or "the play"*
Say:	*"the text"*
Because:	How dare we claim that great literature is any different from beach reading—or from the telephone directory, for that matter?
Don't Say:	*"human being"* or *"person"*
Say:	*"the subject"*
Because:	For PC English professors, the fathomless complexity of the human person is reduced to "the question of subjectivity." In other words, these overeducated barbarians sit around scratching their heads about *whether there are any such things* as human beings capable of real knowledge and freedom of action—or if all our thoughts and behavior are determined by class, race, gender, the "hegemonic culture," the "power structures" in texts, and so forth.
Don't Say:	*"intellectual history"*
Say:	*"reception history"*
Because:	Why acknowledge the possibility that human beings discover, judge, communicate, accept, or reject ideas for good reasons if, instead, you can talk about intellectual history as if it were something like holding a cup while somebody pours milk into it?
Don't Say:	that a poet, novelist, or critic *"emphasizes"* something or *"brings it to our attention"*
Say:	that he *"foregrounds"* it
Because:	Again, these folks' default position is always to make the creative or rational activities of the human mind sound as much as possible like mere physical events.

Don't Say:	*"opposites,"* and in particular:
	"truth" and *"falsehood,"* or
	"good" and *"evil,"* or
	"right" and *"wrong,"* or
	"beauty" and *"ugliness,"* or
	"happiness" and *"misery"*
Say:	*"binaries,"* or *"presence and absence"*
Because:	Why acknowledge that any of these things really exist when you can pretend that "binary opposites" are generated from some kind of irrational compulsion human beings have to compare and contrast and divide things into twos, rather than from the nature of reality?
Don't Say:	*"Communist"*
Say:	*"Marxist"*
Because:	That way, you won't have to defend Communism, which for some mysterious reason has acquired a bad reputation.

Can You Believe the Professors?

"I asked some teacher friends if they have withdrawn their sympathies from certain books because of the racism, sexism, homophobia, or ableism of the texts. One person told me she had stopped teaching Hemingway, Ovid, and Boccaccio because their works disgusted her with their overt misogyny."

Lennard J. Davis, professor of English, disability and human development, and medical education at the University of Illinois at Chicago, explaining why he's considering giving up teaching Joseph Conrad's *Heart of Darkness*. Lennard J. Davis. "The Value of Teaching from a Racist Classic (*Heart of Darkness*)," *The Chronicle of Higher Education* 52, no. 37 (May 19, 2006): B10.

Don't Say:	*"Marxist"*
Say:	*"New Historicist"*
Because:	That way, you won't have to defend Marxism, which for some mysterious reason has acquired a bad reputation.
Don't Say:	*"New Historicist"*
Say:	*"Cultural Studies Professor"*
Because:	That way, you won't have to defend New Historicism, which for some mysterious reason—well, you get the picture.
Don't Say:	that you're going to *"criticize," "analyze,"* or *"disagree with"* a piece of literature or criticism
Say:	that you're going to *"interrogate"* it
Because:	Could it be that, to the kind of person who finds Marxism appealing, *torturer* sounds like a more exciting and valuable job than *literary critic?*
Don't Say:	*"the imagination"* (of a poet or novelist—or of his readers)
Say:	*"the imaginary,"* meaning the ideas and images current during a particular era or among a certain set of people—"the eighteenth-century *imaginary,*" for example
Because:	The *imagination* is the name for a creative capacity of the human mind, and postmodernists would rather ignore our power to create, and even the existence of the mind itself.
Don't Say:	*"benefits"*
Say:	*"privileges"*
Because:	If something *"benefits"* someone, it supplies him with some real, objective good that human beings can enjoy; if it *"privileges"* him, it merely makes him superior to someone else—it gives him status and power,

197

Can You Believe the Professors?

Some course offerings in "English" at American colleges and universities:

English 276.401 Comparative Cross-Dressing (Cary Mazer) University of Pennsylvania, Spring 2006

English 279.401 Images of Childhood in Israeli Film and Literature (Nili Gold), University of Pennsylvania, Spring 2006

English 290.402 Gender Relations in 19th Century Romantic Ballet: Sex, Drugs and Crime (Marion Kant) University of Pennsylvania, Fall 2005

English 448b Globalization & Postcolonial Writing (Shameem Black), Yale University, Spring 2007

English S3024D Topics in literary theory: reading Freud (D. Moses) Columbia University, Summer 2006

English 22807 32852 Race and Ethnicity in the Caribbean, University of Chicago (Rosamond King), Fall 2005

English 32300 Marxism and Modern Culture (Loren Kruger), University of Chicago, Spring 2006

English 30201 Intro Theories of Sex/Gender (Lauren Berlant) University of Chicago, Winter 2006

English 398 Latino/a Popular Culture (Brady, M.), Cornell University, Spring 2007

English 597 Sex Outside the City (Scott Herring), Pennsylvania State University, Spring 2007 "This seminar explores how the urban/rural divide haunts queer studies."

English 363 The Bourgeois (Franco Moretti), Stanford, Fall 2006 "An interdisciplinary attempt to define the ruling class of modern times."

All course titles and other information, including language excerpted from course descriptions, are taken from the course offerings advertised by university English departments at the urls below: http://www.english.upenn.edu/Courses/Undergraduate/2006/Spring/English-276.401, http://www.english.upenn.edu/Courses/index.php?level=Undergraduate&year=2006&semester=Spring&course=English-279.401, http://www.english.upenn.edu/Courses/Undergraduate/2005/Fall/English-290.402, http://www.yale.edu/english/courses-spring07.htm, http://www.ce.columbia.edu/summer/english.cfm, http://english.uchicago.edu/courses/grad_autumn05.shtml#3, http://english.uchicago.edu/courses/grad_spring06.shtml#3, http://english.uchicago.edu/courses/grad_winter06.shtml#1, http://www.arts.cornell.edu/english/sp07u.html, http://english.la.psu.edu/graduate/Coursedescriptions.htm, http://english.stanford.edu/courseDetail.php?course_id=1031, viewed 6/12-13/06.

the only goods the postmodernists are willing to admit actually exist.

Don't Say:	*"male"* and *"female"*
Say:	*"masculinities"* and *"femininities"*
Because:	"Gender" is "a construct."

Don't Say:	*"belief in nature" (or even in objective reality)*
Say:	*"essentialism"*
Because:	That way, acknowledging certain inconvenient realities—differences between men and women, say—can be made out to be another nasty "ism" like racism, colonialism, and so forth.

Talking like a postmodernist English professor makes it harder, not easier, to understand Wordsworth's or Shakespeare's poetry. Or, at least, it makes it harder to understand how those poets (and all their readers before the past half century or so) thought about their poetry. To Shakespeare and Wordsworth, writing poetry did not seem like an impersonal manufacturing process. If we want to understand how they thought about their poems, we can't talk this way.

Reality-denial as a critical stance

Of course, if the PC English professors are right, it's no great loss. Why should we *want* to be able to think like Shakespeare and Wordsworth (or the *Beowulf* poet, or John Donne, or Milton, or Keats)? All their ideas—that old way of thinking about individual genius, beauty, poetic creation, free will, the salvation of the soul, truth, and virtue—were just so much "ideology" masking the oppression of women, the "privileging" of white males, the perpetuation of the exploitive capitalist system, the inchoate workings of our unconscious sexual desires, and so forth. To take the ideas of the writers of English literature seriously is to be pathetically naïve—or, worse, to participate in the oppressive mindset of the past.

So the postmodernist English professor sets out to understand literature (and life) from a stance wholly alien to those old ideas. In the process, he demonstrates (by reducing his own position to absurdity) how very useful those traditional concepts were for understanding literature, and reality.

The trick in "theory"-influenced academic work is to assume that some obvious feature of reality is only an artificial "construct," and then to theorize about how and why it got constructed. Take, for example, Dympna Callaghan's feminist analysis, in the introduction to *A Feminist Companion to Shakespeare,*[9] of the power of the word "whore." Drawing on Judith Butler's *Excitable Speech: A Politics of the Performative,*[10] Callaghan develops an ingenious feminist explanation for the undoubted fact that this word is a painful insult. Neither Callaghan nor the author of the article she's introducing[11] even acknowledges the existence of the explanation that immediately occurs to the rest of us: Sleeping around is in fact a rotten way for a woman to behave (especially if she's promised to be faithful: in her wedding vows, say). Women are normally ashamed of sexual infidelity and sexual indiscretion. And it very naturally causes them pain to have other people accuse them of it, whether truthfully or not—just as it hurts any of us to be charged with dishonesty, greed, or gross selfishness.

This explanation (which these feminists would sneer at as "essentialist" if anyone were so gauche as to suggest it) is not even considered and rejected. It's simply ignored out of existence. Here's Callaghan's quite different account of why women find it upsetting

---

Two Books You're Not Supposed to Read

At War with the Word: Literary Theory and Liberal Education, by R. V. Young, Intercollegiate Studies Institute, 1999.

Literature Lost: Social Agendas and the Corruption of the Humanities, by John M. Ellis, Yale University Press, 1999.

Can You Believe the Professors?

"Historians of sexual difference have argued that 'sex as we know it' was invented some time 'in the eighteenth century,' but the modern conception of sexual difference that Thomas Lacqueur identifies as 'the two-sex model' seems clearly anticipated in Shakespeare's representation of Lady Macbeth."

Phyllis Rackin, professor emerita of English at the University of Pennsylvania and former president of the Shakespeare Association of America, announces a groundbreaking discovery. Phyllis Rackin, *Shakespeare and Women* (Oxford: Oxford University Press, 2005), 125. For Lacqueur's "two-sex model," Rackin cites Thomas Lacqueur, *Making Sex: Body and Gender from the Greeks to Freud* (Cambridge, Massachusetts: Harvard University Press, 1990), 149.

to be called whores: "the word is injurious because in the long history of its usage it has become freighted with systemic patriarchal violence."[12] It's not just that a man who calls a woman a whore may be likely to hit her; in fact, the "patriarchal violence" inherent in the insult is effective even if the insult is made by another woman (after all "women, no less than men, inhabit and implement the social and conceptual structures of the patriarchal order"[13]—presumably we're helping prop up the patriarchy out of some kind of false consciousness). It's that the insult has the potential "to deprive women (who might be disowned by their kin as the result of allegations of unchastity) of all means of social and economic support."[14]

Call me "naïve," but I have trouble believing that women—either in Elizabethan England or in America today—usually object to being called "whores" for *economic* reasons. The feminist explanation makes any kind of sense only if all the other possible explanations (from religion, from morality, from nature, from ordinary experience) are ruled out of court from the beginning. Which is exactly how "theory" works. All those powerful impersonal forces the different stripes of postmodernists believe in—

An English Professor You *Can* Believe

"The essays that the graduating B.A.s would submit with their applications were often brilliant. After five or six years of Ph.D. work, the same people would write incomprehensible crap. Where did they learn it? They learned it from us."

Frederick Crews, professor emeritus of English, the University of California at Berkeley. Sandy Starr, "Pooh-poohing Postmodernism: Frederick Crews, Author of the Long-Awaited Sequel to *The Pooh Perplex*, Discusses the Transformation of Academic Disciplines into 'Incomprehensible Crap,'" Spiked-Online.com, November 5, 2002, http://www.spiked-online.com/Articles/00000006DB0F.htm viewed 6/14/06.

"Western hegemony," "late capitalism," "repressed" sexuality, "the patriarchy," and so forth—fit beautifully into the vacuum created by their refusal to acknowledge obvious realities.

Of course it wouldn't make sense for literary critics and scholars to swallow wholesale "what everyone knows"—or even the beliefs of the writers they study. It's part of their job to look critically at everything about their subject. But it's unmitigated arrogance, not critical appraisal, to assume from the start that all the activities and beliefs of our ancestors were determined by impersonal forces they were too stupid to understand. Western culture (to a greater degree than any culture we know) has fostered the capacity for criticism, including self-criticism—for which the postmodernists' attempt to stand outside that culture, and even outside human experience, is a very poor substitute.

Our English departments are desperately in need of reform—or replacement. There are signs of hope in a handful of newly founded colleges, and of returning sanity in some established universities. But we can't afford to wait for the folks running most of our universities to come to their senses before we learn about our great literature, and teach it to our children.

Do you, dear reader, want the kind of education that civilized generations of Americans before the postmodernists gutted the curriculum? You can frustrate the PC professors' plans to disrupt the transmission of our civilization to the next generation. If you want to thwart the revolutionaries and the nihilists, and put a spanner in their plans for the future of the human race, you need to teach yourself English Lit. To find out how, keep reading.

Chapter Ten

WHAT LITERATURE IS *FOR*: "TO TEACH AND DELIGHT"

> I believe that man will not merely endure: he will prevail. He is immortal, not because he alone among creatures has an inexhaustible voice, but because he has a soul, a spirit capable of compassion and sacrifice and endurance. The poet's, the writer's, duty is to write about these things. It is his privilege to help man endure by lifting his heart, by reminding him of the courage and honor and hope and pride and compassion and pity and sacrifice which have been the glory of his past.
>
> —William Faulkner, 1950 Nobel Prize acceptance speech

Before you can study the great English and American literature on your own, you need to know the answers to two questions: First, what are you studying *for*? (What are you trying to achieve in studying literature?) And second, how do you know which literature really is great? (You can begin with the lists in this *Guide*, but you want to become a judge of literary merit in your own right.)

What literature is really for

So why—before the PC professors gutted the curriculum—was literature the cornerstone of a liberal education? Because it propped up the patriarchy? Because it's a source of those intense feelings the "art for art's sake" folks pursue? Because literature makes a good substitute for religion (after all, we have to get meaning from somewhere)? Because we

Guess what?

→ Art isn't just for art's sake

→ Great works of literary art teach us to love what's noble and spurn what's base; they civilize us

→ It *is* possible to know which works of literature are truly great

A Book You're Not Supposed to Read

The Abolition of Man by C. S. Lewis, HarperSanFrancisco, 2001.

need "transgressive" writers to serve the vital function of upsetting conventions?

The answer? None of the above.

Literature was at the heart of the old-style education because of its unique ability to *civilize.* The classic statement of this idea is Sir Philip Sidney's *Defense of Poesy.* Sidney wrote during the English Renaissance to defend "poesy" (not just poetry, but any kind of fiction) against the Puritan belief that it was corrupting. But Sidney doesn't just argue that "poesy" is harmless entertainment. He calls poets "the first bringers in of all civility" and claims "no philosopher's precepts can sooner make you an honest man than the reading of Virgil."

Why exactly is poesy necessary for individual virtue, and for civilization itself? Because in achieving its end—"to teach and delight"—poesy does what no other art or science can do.

The poet, says Sidney, "painteth the outward beauty" of virtue. *Poetry shapes your character by teaching you to love what's noble and aspire to it, and to despise what's base and avoid it.* The philosopher can teach you the abstract principles about right and wrong. But he can't make you love what's good and recoil from what's evil. Poesy *shows* you honesty and courage and loyalty in all their inherent nobility, and makes you *want* them for yourself. Poesy can "strike," "pierce," and "possess the sight of the soul." Great literature doesn't just add to what we know. It changes how we feel and see. Poesy civilizes and ennobles us.

This civilizing power is not the only reason people read literature, but it's the chief reason that literature has always (until recently) played such a large role in education. More than 2,300 years ago, Aristotle explained that young men should learn music (including poetry sung to instrumental accompaniment) because of how the pleasure it gives affects the character. As he explains, "... since virtue is about delighting and loving and hating aright, clearly nothing is more necessary to learn and to make a habit than to judge rightly, and to delight in good characters and noble acts."

Which literature is truly great?

Assuming we want to be delighted and taught, civilized and ennobled, how do we know *which* literature is truly great? The good news is, it isn't as hard to figure out as the postmodernists pretend. The dismantling of "the canon"—the great works of literature that used to be the backbone of the English curriculum in our universities—was a chief aim of the "deconstruction" of our English departments. Today even a severe critic of what now goes on in those departments feels she has to soften her criticism with this assurance: "No one's arguing here that we return to a very narrow canon, to uncritical piety in regard to the literature of our culture...."[1]

In fact, the canon in those days of yore was anything but narrow. It was continually revised in a perpetual free-for-all among readers across the

Just a Spoonful of Sugar?

Virtue in the abstract is hard to swallow. But the medicine only *seems* bitter—because the philosophers set down the "bare" moral rule with "thorny argument." Fleshed out in all the particulars of song and story, goodness is naturally delightful. Virtue, as Sidney conceives it, isn't obedience to some abstract moral rule. It's the embodiment of all that's noble and attractive in human life. It's *being* a greathearted ruler like Xenophon's Cyrus, a straight arrow like Aeneas, a fountain of ingenuity like Ulysses.

generations, in which the "uncritical piety" of some was inevitably answered by the energetic denigration of others.[2] The only reason to concede that the traditional canon can't come back is that you buy into the reasons the postmodernists got rid of it in the first place.

What were those arguments? Essentially, that "the canon" must have been established to "privilege" white males because 1) there were so few women writers and authors "of color" in it, and anyway 2) there's no such thing as an objective standard of judgment about literature. After all, who are we to say that *Hamlet* is more valuable reading than *The Boy Scout Handbook*? It was high time, the agitators for the various schools of "theory" argued, to even things up by moving members of "excluded" groups up to the top of the reading lists—and to stop presuming to judge literature by traditional standards of aesthetic value, tainted as they were with the various oppressive "ism"s.

That leveling impulse was no more productive of justice, equality, and prosperity for all in literary judgments than it has been in any other area. (The one sure way to destroy any institution—a nation's economy, for example—is to insist that nothing can be done until everyone is included on a 100% equal basis.) There's no real mystery about why the great works of English and American literature in "the canon" were almost all written by dead white males. The prerequisites for literary achievement were, to put it mildly, unevenly distributed during the period of time when great literature was being written in English.

In earlier, less prosperous times, education was necessarily the privilege of a fortunate few. Naturally, few members of the breastfeeding, baby-rocking, diaper-changing, household-managing half of the human race could afford to avail themselves of that privilege.

The case of race is more grievous. There's nothing natural about the state laws that *forbade the teaching of reading* to American slaves. "People of color" were a tiny minority of English-speakers worldwide through the early centuries of English literature. By the time significant numbers

What Do You Mean "*our* literature," Kemosabe?

The great literature in English is *ours* if we're Americans—whether we're descended from Puritans who settled Massachusetts, Indians forced westward by the European settlers, gentlemen adventurers who laid claim to Virginia, Africans sold into bondage and brought to America in chains, Chinese who built the railroads, those "huddled masses yearning to be free" who left Europe for a better life in the nineteenth century, or laborers who came across the border from Mexico in the twentieth century for the same reason—as long as we claim the history and culture of this great country as our own. It's only by the infamous "one-drop rule"—the same color bar that justified chattel slavery—that an American whose ancestors were slaves in this country somehow has less reason to consider *Paradise Lost* and the rest of the canon of great literature in English as his own literary heritage than any other American—say, the grandchild of Italian or Polish immigrants whose skin tone is a few shades closer to Milton's.

The men who wrote and ratified our Bill of Rights harked back to Milton's *Areopagitica* for their ideas about freedom of speech. Abraham Lincoln acquired his mastery of the English language (and his extraordinary knowledge of human nature) reading Shakespeare. At the height of the Cold War, William Faulkner used his Nobel Prize speech to do the essential job that poets since Homer (in English since *Beowulf*) have done: He reminded his hearers that the things that ennoble man are more important than mere physical survival, and that the preservation of those things depends on our willingness to face death with courage. We Americans have a splendid heritage, and the great literature in English is an indispensable part of it.

There's no racial or geographic qualification for membership in what Winston Churchill called "the English-speaking peoples." In fact, Anglo-American culture (which ended the slave trade and defeated Nazism and Communism), English and American literature, and the English language itself are all great partly by virtue of the contributions of many different ethnic groups and languages.

of people of African descent did speak English, they were, through no fault of their own, in no position to write literature.

Modern prosperity has made it possible for more women to afford education. And racial injustices have been rectified. Black Americans have enrolled in our universities in greatly increased numbers over the past few decades.[3] Unfortunately, that's the very period of time during which "the canon" has been dismantled. Trying to correct for the "imbalance" in the canon by denying the descendents of slaves an education in our great literature—the very literary culture that enabled a descendent of slave-holders such as William Faulkner to become a great novelist—is "affirmative action" of the most self-defeating kind.

Truth, beauty, and goodness

Judgments about literary merit aren't absolute. But they're not entirely subjective, either. People make rational arguments about what literature is great, and why. And those arguments inevitably appeal to certain capacities we all share. In one way (and to one degree) or another, we all appreciate and desire beauty, admire what's good, and recognize truths—and also feel compelled to seek them out, and take pleasure in recognizing them. Literature, like music and the visual arts, shows us what's good and beautiful. And literature, even more than the other arts, appeals especially to our ability to recognize and love truth: after all, it conveys *meaning* in *words.*

You can't identify great literature by trying to weigh the total amount of truth, beauty, and goodness there is in any given work of literary art. We come upon the truths and beauties we find in great literature as "things / Extreme and scattering bright,"[4] glimpses that shine out from the particular incidents or words—a turn in the plot of a play, an arresting image in a poem. But any argument that a work of literary art is great inevitably appeals to one or another of these three qualities: to the work's superior truth, or its moral value, or its piercing beauty—or to some combination thereof.

The participants in the old free market in literary valuations all appealed to those criteria. T. S. Eliot's detractors, for example, thought his poetry deliberately ugly and unrealistic; admirers thought Eliot was artfully expressing painful, and strangely beautiful, realities other kinds of poetry couldn't capture. To a certain (rather depressed) sort of man in a certain (rather modern) kind of mood, a sunset really can seem somehow like a body prepped for surgery.

Unfortunately, the free market in opinions about which literature is great has been effectively shut down now for about twenty years. College professors evaluate literature by largely political standards. (Which texts can help us understand the plight of medieval women? Which work best exposes the atrocities of colonialism and racism in seventeenth-century America?) But—at least until that conversation about which literature is really great picks up again somewhere—we'll do very well if we go back to reading the same old works of literature college students were reading before "theory" hit.

The first eight chapters of this *Guide* provide only a sampling of what you can learn from the great literature in the English language. The study of literature is ideally a life-long project, begun in youth, aided by the best teachers, and continuing to exercise your mind and enrich your experience far beyond your formal education. Studying the great works of "the canon" can help you develop powerful skills: look what Shakespeare did for Winston Churchill. As Lady Susan, Jane Austen's wickedest and most fascinating villainess, says, "Consideration and esteem as surely follow command of language as admiration waits on beauty. . . . " But a literary education isn't just for profit—or pleasure, for that matter.

Or rather, the greatest literature will open your mind to powers and pleasures beyond the everyday pleasure-seeking and jockeying for power that take up too much of our mental energy "Getting and spending we lay

The Greatest Body of Literature in the Modern West—Maybe in the History of the World—Is in Our Own Mother Tongue:

We're in luck: Michelangelo's *Pieta* and Beethoven's Fifth Symphony don't need any translation, and we can read Shakespeare in the original. Nobody can touch the English when in comes to literature, just as nobody beats the Germans in music or the Italians in the visual arts. (Some wit has pointed out that the French are second-best at everything.) The English take first place in drama (Shakespeare). They win in lyric poetry, too (Shakespeare again, plus the other Elizabethans, the seventeenth-century poets including Milton, and the Romantic poets). They place or show in the novel (the Russians win that category). And they've got competitive entries in all the other categories, too—from the epic (*The Faerie Queene, Paradise Lost*) and the romance (Malory's *Morte d'Arthur*) to the essay (Bacon, Addison and Steele, Dr. Johnson).

waste our powers," as Wordsworth put it. The best literary art is concerned with those "great and permanent objects" (Wordsworth again) that are of lasting importance to the human mind. Great works of literature are touchstones by which you can test the ephemeral interests and ever-shifting desires of your day-to-day existence.

Once you begin to know really good literature, you'll want to fill your mind with it. You'll find yourself measuring the objects you pursue, the satisfactions you achieve, and the kind of person your actions are making you against the standards you find in our classic novels and plays. You'll want to store poetry up for your old age, so you'll have something of real value to turn over in your mind in the nursing home: you'll be able to close your eyes, put your head back during the perpetually running soap operas and quiz shows (or whatever fresh humiliation they've dreamed up for "seniors" by then), and see Shakespeare's sonnets, or Jane Austen's marvelous characters, instead.

You need to get to know the literary classics in English. If you do, here's what you'll find: First, beauty—undying loveliness, breathtaking intensity, heartbreaking pathos. And truth—every kind of human experience, distilled into meaning. Finally, goodness—drama that purges your mind, poetry that that makes you hunger and thirst after noble acts, novels that teach happiness.

Part III

HOW YOU CAN TEACH YOURSELF ENGLISH AND AMERICAN LITERATURE

Because Nobody Is Going to Do It for You

Chapter Eleven

HOW TO GET STARTED
(Once You Realize You're Going to Have to Read the Literature on Your Own)

> …nothing can permanently please, which does not contain in itself the reason why it is so, and not otherwise.
>
> —Samuel Taylor Coleridge, *Biographia Literaria*

The good news is, you can teach yourself the great literature in English. You can learn the skills that English professors used to teach before political correctness took over the English departments—beginning with the structural analysis of literature, as recommended by literary giants themselves. Great writers are also great readers; you can't do better than take their advice.[1]

"Close reading"

"Close reading" and "structural analysis" are two names for the first thing that ought to be taught in every introductory English Literature class—but that you can also teach yourself, if you have to. The first principle behind analyzing literature is that any great work of art *is* great (is beautiful, has a profound effect on many readers, is permanently interesting to the human race) *by virtue of how it's put together.* A work of literature is a particular arrangement of language chosen for certain effects: any poem, for example, conveys meaning, makes its own kind of verbal

Guess what?

→ Authors of great literature are also great teachers of careful reading

→ In truly great literature, there's a good reason for the selection and placement of every word

music, and gives rise to certain feelings, as well as thoughts. The power of a truly great work of literary art will always be something of a mystery. But you can get closer to the heart of that mystery (understand it more clearly, feel it more keenly) by analyzing its structure.

Close reading has a bad reputation in some circles, partly on account of the excesses of English professors—from "the New Critics" who dominated literary criticism in American universities in the middle of the last century to the "deconstructionists" of today. But close reading was not invented by the New Critics, and it needn't lead down the blind alley of deconstruction. In a certain sense, of course, close reading is simply what the most interested, intelligent, and disciplined readers have been doing since there was any literature to read. But in another important sense, close reading as it was taught in our universities before the advent of "theory" is an invention of the Romantic era. You can see its origins in the literary criticism of the Romantic period, some of it by men who were themselves creators of great literature. The Romantics' way of reading was both more psychologically sophisticated and more minute and careful than earlier criticism.

Thomas de Quincey's "On the Knocking at the Gate in *Macbeth*" is a good example of the Romantics' critical approach. De Quincey fastens onto the effect that one particular event in Shakespeare's tragedy has on him. After Macbeth has murdered Duncan, a knocking is heard at the castle gate. De Quincey couldn't figure out why that knocking affected him so powerfully. "In fact," he explains, "my understanding positively said that it could not cause any effect." But he wouldn't let the problem go. He refused to be talked out of his feeling; he "waited and clung to the problem" until he could work out a reason for those emotions: an explanation grounded in the instincts, passions, and natural sympathies of the human mind, and a new insight into how *Macbeth* affects us as powerfully as it does.

The Romantic critics reckoned that if a work of literature was truly great—if, for example, it was written by Shakespeare—then no part of that work would fail to repay investigation. De Quincey claims that Shakespeare's works

> are to be studied with entire submission of our own faculties, and in the perfect faith that in them there can be not too much or too little, nothing useless or inert—but that, the farther we press in our discoveries, the more we shall see proofs of design and self-supporting arrangement where the careless eye had seen nothing but accident.

Coleridge's observations about poetry in general are along the same lines as de Quincey's observations about the "design and self-supporting arrangement" of Shakespeare's works. Poetry is written in meter, and meter is "calculated to excite" a "perpetual and distinct attention to each part" of the poem, Coleridge explains in his *Biographia Literaria.* Because "nothing can permanently please, which does not contain in itself the reason why it is so, and not otherwise," each part of a *good* poem has to justify that minute attention.

Coleridge explains how a schoolmaster taught him that: "In the truly great poets . . . there is a reason assignable, not only for every word, but for the position of every word. . . . " Coleridge's teacher required his students to compare individual words in Homer's poetry with synonyms, and "attempt to show, with regard to each why it would not have answered the same purpose; and wherein consisted the peculiar fitness of the word in the original text."

Reed's Rule

During the final decades of the last century, fortunate students at Chapel Hill, North Carolina, learned from Mark L. Reed (Wordsworth scholar and now professor emeritus at U.N.C.) a formula, distilled from the Romantics, for reading literature. Let's call it "Reed's Rule."

Professor Reed taught his students to ask about each piece of literature they read, *Why is this word, and no other word, in this place, and no other place?* This question is what the structural analysis of any piece of literary art has to boil down to: if you want to know how a poem or a play works, you need to ask yourself why each of its parts was selected for inclusion, and how it fits into the structure of the whole.

If you ask this question systematically of any great work of literature, you discover amazing things. In fact, if you teach literary analysis to college freshmen, you find out that your students are soon able to uncover what look like "proofs of design and self-supporting arrangement where the careless eye had seen nothing but accident." The only snag is that they often have trouble *believing* that poets *really* "put all that into" a piece of literature "on purpose." What you have to remember is that a certain level of skill means the effortless, even the unconscious, application of rules that at a lower level of skill requires careful consideration. (Just compare the different amounts of attention that experienced and novice drivers have to pay to keeping the car in the lane.)

What seems like an ordinary line of poetry

"All those things" that you begin to notice when you read literature closely *are* "really there." Take, for example, a line from Milton: "And thus the Filial Godhead answering spake." This particular line, from Book VI of *Paradise Lost,* doesn't seem like a particularly interesting line, as lines by Milton go.[2] In fact, it has the look and feel of the transitional formula ("Thus he spoke . . .") that Homer uses between speeches. All the information it conveys is that the Son of God is going to be the next speaker, and that what He says is going to be a response to the last speaker. But you could easily spend significant time teasing out precisely how this particular line adds to the impression of monumental solidity and ponderous significance that's characteristic of Milton's verse.

One of the facts you'd eventually fasten on is that the line is full of elements balanced against each other. Take the first two words, for example: "And thus." "And" points back to the previous line, telling the reader that what comes next is an addition connected to what came before. But "thus" points in the opposite direction, forward to what's going to be said in the next line. The line also ends with two words poised against each other in a similar way: "answering spake"—"answering" refers back to the previous speech, and "spake" gestures forward to the speech that's to come.

But the most interesting balanced pair of words is right in the middle of the line: "Filial Godhead." These two words contrast with each other in several interesting ways. First, on the level of sound. Both "Filial" and "Godhead" are built of two syllables, and in each case both syllables end with a single sound—"L" in "Filial" and "D" in "Godhead." But "Filial" is all continuously pronounced consonants (in other words, you can go on saying "F" and "L" steadily until your breath runs out) and (relatively) "high vowels"—that is, vowels pronounced at the front of the mouth, with the teeth almost closed. To say the vowels in "Godhead," on the other hand, you have to open your mouth wider. And the "G" and "D" sounds are

Which Editions Are the Best?

The short answer: Whichever ones you're going to *read*. The weight and size of the book is probably more important than any other consideration, at first. Better a lightweight paperback of *The Taming of the Shrew* that you'll actually take to the beach, or read while you eat lunch at work, than *The Complete Works of Shakespeare* in the finest scholarly edition, which is too bulky to carry with you anywhere, and which you won't want to get peanut butter or sunscreen on. You'll be interested in disputed readings later. First, you need to get into the habit of reading the literature.

"stops"—that is, saying either one of them is a single event in your mouth, you can say them over and over again, but not continuously.

Next, consider the different histories of the two words (which partly explain why they sound so different). "Godhead" is a noun of Anglo-Saxon origin, while "Filial" is an adjective derived from the Latin. In English, Latinate words tend to have more abstract and ethereal connotations, while words of Anglo-Saxon origin tend to feel comparatively earthy and concrete—compare the different mental pictures suggested by the Latin-derived "aureate" to those aroused by the Anglo-Saxon-derived "golden." And yet in Milton's line the Anglo-Saxon word "Godhead" has the "head" suffix (as in "maidenhead"—later "maidenhood"—the native English term equivalent to the Latinate "virginity") that makes it an abstract

Literature Online

The resources now available online for the study of English and American literature are amazing—and new ones are being added every day. You can get complete editions of a large number of out-of-copyright works at http://www.gutenberg.org/ (including, for example, the First Folio of Shakespeare's plays, so that you can read the same 1623 text as readers for whom the Bard was a living memory). And many universities support sites that make wonderful literary resources available—a *much* better use of professors' and graduate students' time than churning out more postmodernist criticism. The University of Victoria, for example, hosts an Internet Shakespeare Editions site at http://ise.uvic.ca/index.html where you can see, among other fascinating things, close-up photos of each page of the U.C.-Los Angeles Library's copy of the first (1609) edition of Shakespeare's *Sonnets*.

noun. In Milton's phrase, it's the Latin-derived (and therefore naturally more abstract-seeming) adjective "Filial" that paradoxically makes the abstract noun "Godhead" refer to a particular individual, turning it from the abstract quality of divinity into a name of the Son of God.

And on the level of meaning, too, there's plenty to compare and contrast. "Filial," the adjective for *son,* which is a dependent and junior sort of concept, here modifies a noun that names the most absolutely independent and senior reality in the universe: God Himself. That's a paradox for you. Yet it's no more paradoxical than the fact that God, Who is one and perfect, should have a Son at all. That paradoxical relationship is, as it happens, an important theme of the passage of *Paradise Lost* in which this particular line appears, and of the poem as a whole. When you further consider that the speaker here is also the Word Who was with God and Who was God in the beginning, you begin to see that Milton's apparently simple, functional line is fraught with meaning and majestic balance sustained by the two perfectly balanced words—which almost seem to be weights poised against each other—at its center.

To get that effect, Milton didn't have to think, "How can I get a sort of feeling of large masses balanced against one another into this line?—Oh, I know, I'll put two words that make an interesting contrast right in the middle." He didn't have to bite the end of his feather quill pen and ask himself, "Now, what's an adjective for 'son' that's derived from Latin, instead of Old English?"—much less to try out the vowels and consonants in the various possible word choices to see what his tongue and teeth were doing when he said them. He didn't need to consult his dictionary to see which words were derived from Latin—he wrote Latin poetry himself, and effortlessly coined his own Latinate English words.[3] He knew as much about the sounds of the different vowels as Bach knew about the timbre of each instrument he wrote for. Milton's mastery of his art was such that he could write great verse as easily as you or I can write comprehensible English prose. Persistent attention plus knowledge yields insight into that art.

Attention boils down to persistence in following Reed's Rule: Read word by word, and keep asking, *Why is this word, and no other word, in this place, and no other place?* Then go on to ask yourself the same question about *this phrase, this line, this incident, this character, this chapter,* and so forth.

But how can you acquire the *knowledge* you need? Every single thing you know or can learn about the English language and about other pieces of literature makes you a better-equipped reader. However basic your knowledge of English, you've got enough know-how to start with. But there's always plenty more to learn.

The nuts and bolts of literary analysis

What follows is brief guide to some kinds of expertise you can work on accumulating, in order to be a better reader of great literature. Being a serious student of literature means understanding these things and knowing the technical terms for them. "Iambic pentameter," "omniscient narrator," "epic simile," and "Spenserian stanza" and the like—NOT "binaries," "reception history," "masculinities and femininities," "literary production," "presence and absence," "imaginary" (as a noun), and "foreground" (as a verb)—are the genuine terms of art that students of literature need to know. I've begun with examples of how what you already know (or can find in any dictionary) can be quite useful for the close reading of literature.

The words themselves (what they mean, what they sound like, where they come from)

Your first resource is a dictionary. Step #1 in reading any piece of literature is to know what every word in it means. If you're not 100% sure of a word, look it up. Don't make the mistake of letting the language just wash over you like so much undifferentiated experience. And don't figure that you can guess what unfamiliar words mean from their context. Really good writers do things with words that you won't understand unless you already know what they mean. Look at how Robert Frost uses "subsides" in "Nothing Gold Can Stay." Frost writes about the "early leaf" that's "a flower / But only so an hour." He continues, "Then leaf subsides to leaf."[4] If you don't know (or take the trouble to find out) that *subside* means *sink* or *settle* or *go down,* then you'll miss what Frost is doing: He's describing growth—which we think of as hopeful, fertile, and prosperous, a coming into maturity—as a falling away from perfection, a settling back into some lesser state.

And there's much more you can know about words than what they mean. From a good dictionary (*The Oxford English Dictionary* is the best) you can learn about the history of a word: what it used to mean in the past, what other words it's related to, and what particular strain of the English vocabulary it belongs to. Was it part of Old English? Was it Norman French? Is it derived from Latin, or Greek? Each of the languages that contributed to modern English had its own typical way of combining sounds—general characteristics of the sort that make French sound different from German. Plus, the history of the English language means that French and Latin words aren't just mixed randomly into the Old English ones. The Norman Conquest means that there are different layers of vocabulary, one on top of another.

The Anglo-Saxon-derived word for a thing—*cow,* for example—is typically down-to-earth, simple, ordinary; it makes you think of an actual, individual animal. It's from the same stratum of our vocabulary as all those short, rude "four-letter" words. Norman-French-derived words tend to seem more abstract, less individual: *beef,* for example, which we more often use for the food than for the animal itself. Then on top of this

Digging into English

*The **cow**, the old **cow**, she is dead;*
It sleeps well, the horned head.

— A. E. Housman, *A Shropshire Lad*

*John Lockwood laughed with the folks below stairs at the manner in which my lord, after five years abroad, sometimes forgot his own tongue, and spoke it like a Frenchman. "I warrant, says he, that with the English **beef** and beer, his lordship will soon get back the proper use of his mouth."*

— William Makepeace Thackeray, *Henry Esmond*

In a low hamlet, by a narrow stream,
*Where **bovine** rustics used to doze and dream,*
She filled young William's fiery fancy full,
While old John Shakespeare talked of beeves and wool!

— Oliver Wendell Holmes, *A Rhymed Lesson*

French-derived vocabulary sits yet another stratum of Latin-derived vocabulary that is still *more* abstract: *bovine,* for example—which we use either in scientific descriptions ("bovine spongiform encephalopathy"), for abstract cow-like qualities, or in elevated, consciously poetic descriptions. These different strata of vocabulary are available to any writer in English, and the fact that he can choose among them means that he has an enormous range of different effects available to him.

A use for English grammar, after all

Grammar, too, will help you read poetry better—beginning with grammar as easy as the difference between present and past tense. Consider, for example, "The Lady of Shalott" by Alfred Tennyson. The beginning of the poem describes the Lady as she sits on an island in the middle of a river on the road to Camelot, weaving pictures of the reflections she sees in a mirror. There are hints that the Lady may be dissatisfied with her lot: "She hath no loyal knight and true." "But," the poem says, "in her web she still delights. . . ." Until, that is, the mood of the poem suddenly changes in the middle of the eighth stanza. If you're used to thinking and talking about even the most basic facts of English grammar, you will be able to put your finger on just how it happens: the narrative changes without warning from present to past tense:

> A funeral, with plumes and lights
> And music, went to Camelot;
> Or when the moon was overhead,
> Came two young lovers lately wed.
> "I am half sick of shadows," said
> The Lady of Shalott.

The switch from present to past creates a feeling of moving from a living, moving world into one in which everything is suddenly pale and lifeless.

T. S. Eliot uses the same device in "Sweeney among the Nightingales," for an even more dramatic effect. There the shift from present to past tense carries us from an uninspiring scene of twentieth-century social life into an ancient tragedy:

> The host with someone indistinct
> Converses at the door apart,
> The nightingales are singing near
> The Convent of the Sacred Heart,
>
> And sang within the bloody wood
> When Agamemnon cried aloud,
> And let their liquid siftings fall
> To stain the stiff dishonoured shroud.[5]

Meter, verse forms, genres, and beyond

Vocabulary and basic grammar will take you far in reading literature, and they're only the beginning. You'll also want to know about meter and rhyme in poetry and the histories of different literary genres.

Compare, for example, Milton's "Tempt not the Lord thy God, He said, and stood" to these lines from Tennyson's *Maud*:

> She is coming, my own, my sweet,
>
> Were it never so airy a tread,
>
> My heart would hear her and beat,
>
> Were it earth in an earthy bed.

The ten monosyllables in Milton's line are like marble blocks, while Tennyson's lines trip off the tongue. There's more than one reason for the difference. But one important one is that Milton and Tennyson used different kinds of "feet," as the rhythmic units in our verse are called. Milton was writing in "iambs"—five of them per line, in fact, to make "iambic pentameter" lines, whose rhythm is da DUM da DUM da DUM da DUM da DUM. Tennyson's lines are a little irregular, but they're mostly anapests: da da DUM da da DUM da da DUM.

Our poets play with the intrinsic rhythms of the different meters. But they also play off the expectations that go with particular verse and stanza forms. There's blank verse, the unrhymed iambic pentameter used by Marlowe and Shakespeare for drama, and by Milton for epic. There's the heroic couplet (two rhyming lines of iambic pentameter) that was used for eighteenth-century satire. And there are a wealth of different stanza forms, each with its own unique character. Take "Spenserian stanza," invented for *The Faerie Queene*: eight lines of iambic pentameter and a final line of iambic hexameter (an "Alexandrine"), with a rhyme scheme of ABABBCBCC. The final Alexandrine gives the Spenserian stanza a sort of extra-full-stop at the end. And the fact

Two Books You're Not Supposed to Read

A Student's Guide to Literature, by R. V. Young, Intercollegiate Studies Institute, 2000.

The Trivium: The Liberal Arts of Logic, Grammar, and Rhetoric: Understanding the Nature and Function of Language by Miriam Joseph Rauh, Paul Dry, 2002.

that the stanza uses just three rhymes in nine lines gives it a tightly woven texture. But a new poet can tap previously unused potential in a stanza form, even give it a wholly new flavor, as Wordsworth does by writing in "rhyme royal"—previously used by Chaucer—but using a different sort of diction ("a selection of the language really used by men") in his "Resolution and Independence."

Literary genres work in a similar way. Anyone who sits down to write an epic is trying to do the same kind of thing as Milton, and before him Homer and Virgil. He won't be able to forget *Paradise Lost*—and neither will his readers.

You could spend a lifetime learning everything you could possibly use to read great literature better. But as you can see from the "vocabulary" and "grammar" examples above, you already know (or can easily find out) enough to get started. And this kind of knowledge snowballs. Once you begin, it's hard to stop learning. The literature itself will teach you, if you just keep at it.

LEARN THE POETRY BY HEART— SEE THE PLAYS— GOSSIP ABOUT THE NOVELS
(THAT'S JUST WHAT JANE AUSTEN DID)

> Some books are undeservedly forgotten; none are undeservedly remembered.
>
> —W. H. Auden[1]

Guess what?

→ Great works of literature are benchmarks against which you can measure your life

→ Poetry is meant to be memorized

→ Great plays should be seen (or acted in) not just read

→ It's not "naïve" to talk about fictional characters "as if they were real people"

→ Reading Jane Austen will boost your moral intelligence

As fascinating as close reading can be, sitting down to analyze literature is hardly the normal way of getting to know it. Novels and poetry weren't typically written to be read by professionals (even by experts in dramatic structure, poetic technique, or the painstaking business of editing texts, much less by PC specialists in colonialism and homophobia). And most plays aren't meant to be read at all—they're meant to be performed.

Close reading takes undivided attention, large quantities of time, and an unusual level of personal discipline. Great literature richly repays that time and attention. But many of us simply can't afford the investment. There's just one short period in most people's lives when intensive literary study is practical: during their undergraduate education. If you got through college without devoting significant energy to this project (Thank a PC English professor!) you probably don't have the time now.

But there are other methods, less time- and energy-intensive, for getting to know great English and American literature. Some of these techniques are ideal for the little bits of time in the interstices of even the busiest life: on the commuter train, while you're at the park with a toddler, in the waiting room at the doctor's office. Other literary activities provide opportunities for entertaining yourself and making connections with other people on a more satisfying level than club-hopping or cocktail party chitchat.

Besides what literary culture can do for your mind and your social life, it can add something like intensity or weight, on one side, and something like steadiness and comfort, on the other, to the events of your life. The Army lieutenant whose words inspire the men he leads in battle because he knows Henry V's St. Crispin's Day speech; the lover who loves with greater passion, and attention, because he's read John Donne; the believer who prays in Milton's words, or T. S. Eliot's; the widower who has Shakespeare's "Men must endure their going hence" carved on his wife's tombstone; the woman who manages her relationships with greater integrity because of Jane Austen—all these have added something at once inspiring and steadying to their own lives.

The "gross and violent stimulants" that Wordsworth was already complaining about in 1800 promise very little beyond a transient intensity of feeling. Great literature offers something better. It shows you things that are—intensely—desirable. And then it serves as a kind of benchmark against which you can measure your life. There's no point in trying to measure up to, for example, the version of love you learn in our popular music, which makes any extreme experience—the most saccharine fidelity, the ugliest betrayal, the most painful loss—seem equally intense and equally attractive.

But you can be true (or false) to the standard of love you find in Shakespeare's *Sonnets.* Or to the very different, but also attractive, ideal for marriage in Chaucer's "Franklin's Tale." You can learn humble piety from

George Herbert, and try to live it. Or courage from *The Battle of Maldon.* You can learn, in a thousand different ways, to distinguish what's truly desirable from what's shoddy and false. You can let the great novels teach you to see how a human life makes a certain kind of shape that's either admirable or despicable. You can try for something like Shakespeare's (or Keats's) generosity, Johnson's intellectual integrity, or the spare honesty of Anglo-Saxon poetry.

But you won't have these standards to live up to, if you don't know the literature. To be civilized by it, you have to get to know it. So you need to learn great poetry by heart. And see the classic plays as often as you can. And make the great novels your bedtime reading, and their characters the people you gossip about with your friends. It's time to get started.

Learn the poetry by heart

You should be learning poems by heart (even if you have the time for intensive structural analysis, but especially if you don't). Poetry is meant to be memorized—*meant* not so much by the people who write it as by its very nature. All the formal features that distinguish poetry from prose—rhyme, meter, and so forth—are also devices that assist the memory. Originally (before writing was invented), poetry was simply language arranged so that it could be remembered and recited again.

Each poetic tradition had its own mnemonic device. The classical poetry of ancient Greece and Rome used quantitative meters: different patterns of (literally) long and short syllables. Ancient Hebrew poetry used parallelism, as in Psalm 19: "More to be desired are they than gold, yea, than much fine gold, sweeter also than honey and the honeycomb." Old English poetry, like verse in the other Germanic languages, used stress and alliteration as its mnemonic devices. And English poetry since Chaucer uses counted syllables in repeating rhythmic patterns, and often rhyme, as well.

Try learning a poem by heart, and you'll see how its formal features help your memory. Start with a Shakespeare sonnet. You're sure you've got something of real quality, there. And it's short and relatively simple to manage. Sonnet 18 is a good choice, or 94, or 116. First read it out loud. Poetry isn't properly appreciated with the eye alone. Language is meaning, but it's sound, too; and poems make many different kinds of music. Read the sonnet over to yourself a few times, and write it on a piece of paper you can keep in your pocket or purse. Close the book, fold your paper, and see how much you can remember. Take it in parts—one quatrain at a time. The metrical pattern and the rhyme scheme will serve as crutches for your memory. Because of the meter, you know how long each line has to be—so you know how much of what you do remember fits in that line, and how much in the next, and you know the rough shape of what else you have to look for in your memory. And because of the rhyme, you often know how the next line has to end.

Take the paper with the poem written on it with you wherever you go, and try again the next time you're bored and have a few minutes—in line at the grocery store or the bank, say. You'll discover it's easier to remember more of your sonnet this time. And when you have time and pen and paper, try writing as much of it as you can from memory. Keep working away at it like this till you can say and write your poem perfectly.

You'll find out all sorts of things about the sonnet in the process of memorizing it. People think of "rote memorization" as the opposite of truly understanding things. But memorizing and analyzing a poem are really two avenues of approach to the same state of knowledge about a piece of poetry. Anyone who's written an essay analyzing a short poem—or who's taught the close reading of poetry to students—will tell you that if you analyze a piece of poetry carefully enough, you come away knowing it by heart, without ever having tried to learn it. The fact is, once you know why (or at least some of many reasons why) each word, and no other word, is in its place, and no other place, then you know that each

What's Wrong with the "Poems" You See in Magazines?

A lot of modern poems, of course, are written in "free verse"—poetry that's distinguished from prose only by divisions between the lines. A metrical genius like T. S. Eliot could use what he knew about traditional meters and the natural rhythms of speech to write memorable poetry that isn't in any particular meter. But novices who try writing poetry without submitting themselves to any formal requirements inevitably produce results that simply aren't memorable. Amateur poets (especially schoolchildren) would be much better off trying a sonnet—they might learn something about structure and rhythm.

word in the poem has to be exactly where it is, which is just another way of saying that you have the whole poem in your memory.

Now, memorizing a poem doesn't put you instantly in the position of the careful student who's studied it first and can recite it perfectly because he knows how it's put together. But you're on your way there. To begin with, it's literally impossible to memorize things without, in some sense, understanding them. Memory and meaning are intimately connected in many mysterious ways. When people need to learn material that they don't understand, they have to give it artificial meaning. Medical students, for example, learn the names and positions of the bones in the human body using silly mnemonics, while orthopedic surgeons really know them, from working with them every day. But nobody becomes an orthopedic surgeon without being a medical student first

Something similar happens in the study of literature. Rote memorization and understanding go hand in hand. Your sonnet will be almost impossible to memorize until you arrive at a basic understanding of what it says. And learning the poem by heart, and carrying it around in your head afterwards, is bound to make you notice things about it—some of the very same things that you would notice if you were engaged in close reading. For example, consider what happens when you're first getting the poem by heart: You're perpetually reading it, then turning away from it, trying to remember what it says, and *guessing* what the next word must be, when you're not sure. When you look back at the poem and see that you've guessed wrong, you're surprised by the right answer, and you wonder why the poet chose the word he did, instead of the one you guessed.

Suppose you're learning Sonnet 94—the one that begins, "They that have power to hurt and will do none"—and you're working on the third quatrain. You've memorized up through "The summer's flower is to the

Learning to Evaluate Literature

Appreciating literature is even more politically incorrect than understanding it. The PC attitude toward English and American literature is one of condescension and indictment, not humble amazement. The guess-and-be-surprised phenomenon makes memorizing poetry an excellent first step toward learning to evaluate literature. If you guess wrong about the next word or phrase in a Shakespeare sonnet, what he wrote *always* turns out to be an improvement over what you guessed. But the same thing isn't true about everyone who writes verse. Noticing what's better about the great poets' choices than yours—even noticing that they *are* better choices—is the beginning of literary appreciation.

summer sweet, / Though to itself it only live and die, / But if that flower with base infection meet" and you're groping for the next line. "The *something* weed outbraves his dignity," you think. And then you look back at the poem, where you see that it's "the *basest* weed." But surely, you think, that *can't* be right. Shakespeare's just used "base" in the line before: "with base infection meet." The repetition makes the line sound a little flat; there's a sense of being let down. Why, you wonder, would Shakespeare write such a disappointing line? And then, before you know it, you're asking yourself, "Why this word and no other word in this place and no other place?" You notice that the staleness of the line is a kind of reflection of what the poet is saying about the kind of people "that have power to hurt and will do none"—and you've suddenly understood something about how Sonnet 94 works.

It's not just individual words that perpetually surprise you as you memorize poetry. Over and over again, you remember the gist (or what you think is the gist) of the next line, and you formulate something like it. But the real line is structured differently—or it even turns out not to mean quite what you thought it meant. Running your eyes over a page of poetry and thinking you've read it is one thing. Correcting your initial impression about what it said, and getting the actual words fixed in your memory, is something much better.

You're not finished learning your sonnet the first time you can repeat it perfectly: it will take many repetitions before it's permanently fixed in your memory. But once it is, think what you've got. Literature is the one kind of art you can take with you wherever you go. Once you know a Shakespeare sonnet by heart, you *own* it—the real thing, not a copy—as surely as the Louvre owns the *Mona Lisa.* So don't stop with one sonnet. Try another. And once you've built up some muscles in your memory, try something longer. Pick a medium-length poem of undisputed excellence: Milton's *Lycidas,* Keats's "Ode to a Nightingale," or T. S. Eliot's *Ash Wednesday.* Even if you never know it by heart, you'll learn amazing things in the process of trying. And if you do learn it thoroughly, you'll have added something astonishing to your collection. Instead of being bored out of your mind when you're waiting in line to renew your driver's license, you've got a collection of museum-quality art in your own head, and you can look at it at your leisure.[2]

See the plays as often as you can—
or, better yet, *act* in them

Reading Shakespeare's plays is no substitute for seeing them on the stage. (Preferably, if you have a choice, not in one of those performances where the whole play has been re-imagined as having taken place in Nazi Germany or JFK-era Washington, D.C.—though even productions like those can't completely kill the power of Shakespeare). Shakespeare isn't just a lot of quotations strung together end to end; the drama isn't there simply to provide occasions for beautiful poetry (in the way that the librettos of most operas exist only for the music). A play is, as Aristotle explained, primarily an *action.* Seeing one performed brings out elements you miss if you just read it.

But it's even better to act in it yourself. If you want to *really* get to know a play, nothing beats going through the whole thing every night for three solid weeks on the stage of your local community theater. Even if you have to volunteer to help with the scenery or the lighting (this works beautifully for those of us with no acting ability), simply being there for performance after performance lets you get to know a play inside out.

Or can spice up your social life with the great drama in English. Get a group of friends together for a dramatic evening. Aspects of your friends' personalities that might otherwise have never emerged will be revealed, and you'll have something new and different to talk about over dessert afterwards. You don't need to learn the parts, put on costumes, or even do any real acting—except with your voice. Just pick a good play that has enough parts for everyone you want to invite, sit down together with books and drinks, and read the thing through together, with everyone taking a part.

Casting is always interesting. Once you've read a couple of plays together, you'll have an idea of who's got natural acting talent; you can give those folks the bigger parts. But typecasting is fun, too. In any group of friends, there's bound to be someone who's just a little bit more like Lady Macbeth than anyone else. Shakespeare's insight into human character is unparalleled—it's great fun to watch your friends giving free rein (in the play, where nobody really gets hurt) to those characteristic tendencies in their personalities that are usually kept in check.

Shakespeare is the richest read, but comedies of manners are fun, too. And they can be better for smaller groups because there's usually a small number of parts. Any Oscar Wilde comedy is fun to read. Congreve and Sheridan are also good choices. Great drama can provide you and your friends with truly memorable evenings.

Read the great novels, lend them to your friends, and gossip about the characters

The really good novels in English were mostly popular books in their own day. There's no reason we can't make them our entertainment, too. Coleridge says more devastating things about the idleness and stupidity of novels than conservative critics say about television—with some justification. But the best novels are books nobody needs to apologize for reading, books "in which the greatest powers of the mind are displayed, in which the most thorough knowledge of human nature, the happiest delineation of its varieties, the liveliest effusions and wit and humour, are conveyed the world in the best-chosen language."[3]

Almost the first thing you learn when you study novels in an American university today is that it's hopelessly naïve to talk about the characters "as if they were real people"—human beings you can like or dislike, approve or disapprove of. Natalie Tyler, the author of *The Friendly Jane Austen,* describes how graduate study in English made her almost forget why she loved Jane Austen:

> I was still wondering why Elinor Dashwood found Edward Ferrars so appealing and whether or not Jane Austen was endorsing the decision of Charlotte Lucas to marry Mr. Collins. The novel is a *text,* I was reminded, and it was naïve to treat the characters, those verbal constructs, as though they were real people with whom I could interest myself.[4]

And of course there is value in remembering the presence of a human creator behind all the persons and events in a novel. In some novels—*Frankenstein* and *Wuthering Heights,* for example—the main characters are characters not just of the author, but of a narrator who's also a character that the author has invented. The question of how reliable a narrator is is always well worth considering.

But unfortunately the horror of "naïve" reading that's inculcated in students of literature tends to create a barrier between those students and the literature they're studying. Whatever else the great novelists in English hoped their readers would notice about their work, they knew that their novels would acquire readers in the first place by telling a story about characters who are interesting—because they're like real people.

The great English novel of manners, of which Jane Austen's works are the consummate examples, begins with Samuel Richardson's *Pamela: Or Virtue Rewarded.* Pamela's a pretty, lively, and intelligent young servant girl living in the household of a young man with lax morals. She's bound to attract his notice, and she's not in a position to expect that his attentions will do her any good. It's out of the question that he'll think of marrying someone of her rank, but if she settles for anything less than marriage, it will be a disaster for her.

What keeps you turning the pages is your curiosity to see whether Pamela will win the contest of wills (and intellects, and principles) with her employer. But other powers of your mind are brought into play by Pamela's internal struggle, as well. Richardson set out to write an edifying book. Pamela struggles not just to escape seduction, and not just to improve her circumstances by marrying really well, but to act in such a way that she can approve of her own conduct. She's judging her own choices throughout, and Richardson invites us to judge them, too. It's an interesting question, to what degree Pamela lives up to her own standards, and how thoroughly she understands her own motives. (*Clarissa,* Richardson's second novel, sets up an even more complex and interesting psychological puzzle.)

In other words, the novel of manners calls into play the same mental faculties that we tend to squander in idle speculation about the personal lives of Hollywood celebrities, or the results of high-profile criminal trials. No one believes that your moral IQ gets a boost from reading the details behind the latest Hollywood breakup, or speculating about the truth of the accusations against Michael Jackson. Even with novels of manners, there's a fine line between the edifying and the prurient. (Henry Fielding—later the author of *Joseph Andrews* and *Tom Jones*—wrote a vicious parody of *Pamela* titled *Shamela,* in which all the worst possible motives on Pamela's part, and all the latent pornographic tendencies of Richardson's novel, are brought to the surface.) But the best novels offer opportunities to enjoy a great read while cultivating your moral intelligence.

Plenty of classic novels make perfectly good beach, airplane, or bedtime reading. But it does add to the interest to be reading along with friends, and—especially if you're at all intimidated by the thought of exchanging Danielle Steele for Jane Austen, or Tom Clancy for *Tom Jones*—it can be a help, getting started, to share what you're reading with other people. A book club is a good idea (as is the old-fashioned habit of reading aloud in your family), but so is just reading the same book at the same time as a couple of close friends. Almost any novel by Jane Austen is a great one to start with.

Mansfield Park is perfect if you want characters that you can think—and have interesting conversations with your friends—about. The heroine has her fans, but she has lots of detractors, too: readers who think her rival is the more attractive character, and wish the hero would marry her, instead. And the ending of the book is a real puzzle; Jane Austen's own sister, Cassandra, tried to persuade her to change it. There's much more pleasure and profit in gossiping about Jane Austen characters than about movie stars, or about your coworkers. You're not just indulging in idle or malicious curiosity; instead, you're testing your instincts and your principles against one of the greatest moral imaginations in the history of Western culture. You're sure to learn something.

And the beginning of this educational process is thinking and talking about the characters as if they really were people who can be judged by the same standards we use in real life. Jane Austen herself wasn't above talking about the characters in novels "as if they were real people." In a letter she wrote to her sister Cassandra from London, she chats about looking for portraits of "Mrs. Bingley" and "Mrs. Darcy" (Jane and Elizabeth Bennet in *Pride and Prejudice*) among the paintings she's seen. She'd found one of Jane, and was hoping to find one of Elizabeth at another exhibition: "Mrs. Bingley's is exactly herself—size, shaped face, features and sweetness; there never was a greater likeness. She is dressed in a white gown, with green ornaments, which convinces me of what I had always supposed, that green was a favourite color with her."

You could argue that Jane Austen was exercising the special privilege of an authoress with respect to her own creations. But she seems to have been happy for other people to treat her characters just like people, too. She collected impressions of *Mansfield Park* from readers—her family and friends, and their acquaintances—who felt that they'd gotten to know the characters as people they could approve or disapprove of. A gentleman was "Highly pleased with Fanny Price . . . Angry with Edmund for not being in love with her, & hating Mrs. Norris for teasing her." But a lady "thought [Fanny] ought to have been more determined in overcoming her own feelings, when she saw Edmund's attachment to Miss Crawford." Despite what your English professors would have you believe, it's not hopelessly naïve to treat the characters in novels as if they were real people, and chat with your friends about whether you like them or not. *That's just what Jane Austen did.*

NOTES

Introduction:

Why This Book Is Needed

1. Dympna Callaghan, ed. *A Feminist Companion to Shakespeare* (Malden, Massachusetts and Oxford: Blackwell Companions to Literature and Culture, 2000), 80-102, 208-25, 299-319, and 42-56, respectively. The "whether feminism needs Shakespeare" quotation is from the book's dust jacket. "Misogyny Is Everywhere" is especially interesting. It's actually a criticism of other scholars for exaggerating the oppression and passivity of Renaissance women, and it's full of amazing examples of what could accurately be described as feminist paranoia (my evaluation, not Professor Rackin's). As you read quotations from Rackin in Chapters 3 and 9 below, keep in mind that there are many feminists even more extreme than she is.

2. Megan Basham "A Modern Quest: How Sir Thomas Malory Changed My Life," *The Weekly Standard* 11, no. 4 (October 20, 2005): 49-51.

Chapter 1:

Old English Literature: The Age of Heroes

1. Until the nineteenth century, English literature wasn't generally considered a respectable subject for academic study. Students learned Latin and Greek and studied the literature in those languages; they read English poetry for fun, in their spare time. Including the Anglo-Saxon language in

the curriculum was part of the argument that English itself could be a real academic subject, like the classics.

2. The letter þ in þæt (that) was called a thorn (or þorn) and used where we would now use th. Because the th-sounds (there are actually two of them, the "unvoiced" consonant sound at the beginning of "think" and the "voiced" consonant sound at the beginning of "this") do not appear in Latin, the thorn was added to the Latin alphabet from the fuþorc—the runic alphabet used by Germanic peoples—for writing English in Latin letters. Sometimes ð (the eth, a modified version of the Latin letter d) was used instead.

3. Eileen A. Joy, "James W. Earl's *Thinking about Beowulf*: Ten Years Later," *The Heroic Age: A Journal of Early Medieval Northwestern Europe,* Issue 8 (June 2005) at: http://www.mun.ca/mst/heroicage/issues/8/forum.html (viewed August 30, 2006), referring to Clare A. Lees, "Men and Beowulf," *Medieval Masculinities: Regarding Men in the Middle Ages,* ed. Clare A. Lees (Minneapolis: University of Minnesota Press, 1994), 129-48.

4. See Evans-Pritchard, *The Nuer: A Description of the Modes of Livelihood and Political Institutions of a Nilotic People* (Oxford University Press, 1969).

5. The Old English poem *The Wanderer* is the classic statement of the hopeless misery of the man without a lord.

6. Clovis was baptized on Christmas day in the year 496, twenty years after the last Roman Emperor in the West was forced to abdicate. His great-granddaughter, as it happens, was Queen Bertha of Kent, the Frankish princess who married the then-pagan King Ethelbert of Kent and was instrumental in the conversion of the English to Christianity.

7. See J. C. Robertson, *Sketches of Church History. From AD 33 to the Reformation* (London: Society for Promoting Christian Knowledge, 1908), 142.

8. Terry Eagleton, "A Shelter in the Tempest of History," *Red Pepper* (a webzine devoted to "a classless society" and "the fusion of red, green, feminist, and other radical traditions" at http://www.redpepper.org.uk/ viewed 9/1/2006), February 2004, http://www.redpepper.org.uk/arts/x-feb02-eagleton.htm viewed 9/1/2006. Though Eagleton uses Freudian and deconstructionist as well as Marxist analysis, and even—in a coy, postmodernist sort of way—claims not to know what Marxism is, he continues to appeal

to Marx as an authority on "capitalist society" (see "The Roots of Terror" *Red Pepper,* September 2005, http://www.redpepper.org.uk/society/x-sep05-eagleton.htm, viewed 9/1/2006) and to look forward—albeit with some perfunctory hand-wringing—to a violent revolution that will over-throw that system.

9. J. R. R. Tolkein, "Beowulf: The Monster and the Critics," *Modern Critical Interpretations: Beowulf,* ed. Harold Bloom (New York and Philadelphia: Chelsea House, 1987), 28.

10. The Old English idiom for "each and every day" translates literally "of all days each."

11. See *The Ruin,* an Anglo-Saxon's poem about a Roman British city in ruins in his day.

12. Terry Eagleton, "A Shelter in the Tempest of History" (see note 10 above). Eagleton's suggestion that it "*would* take a revolution" to achieve these "remarkably modest" goals ought to astonish—nay, horrify—anyone with a rudimentary knowledge of modern history. Marxist revolutions haven't been noticeably successful at ensuring universal nutrition, let alone "freedom, dignity and the like." This fact doesn't seem to have made much of an impression on Professor Eagleton: "I think it's a mistake to think that the current crisis of the left has anything much to do with the collapse of communism."

13. Professor Leaños reproduces and defends the poster on his website, http://www.leanos.net/ at, http://leanos.net/Tillmantext.htm, viewed 9/1/2006.

Chapter 2:
Medieval Literature: "Here Is God's Plenty"

1. This is "accentual-syllabic" verse, a kind of hybrid between French and Italian rhyming "syllabic verse" and the native tradition of alliterating stress-measured lines. English verse, like the English language itself, has a mixed pedigree.

2. Margaret Atwood, *The Handmaid's Tale* (New York: Anchor, 1998).

3. See http://www.cariboo.bc.ca/atwood/publications.htm for a bibliography and http://www.mscd.edu/~atwoodso/, the current site of the Margaret Atwood Society, both viewed on 7/3/2006.

4. See Professor Brians's introductory remarks to his "Common Errors in English" webpage at http://www.wsu.edu/~brians/errors/, viewed September 1, 2006, in which he addresses such frequently asked questions as "Does it oppress immigrants and subjugated minorities to insist on the use of standard English?"

5. At http://wsu.edu/~brians/science_fiction/handmaid.html, viewed December 12, 2005.

6. Preface to *Fables, Ancient and Modern.*

7. Take, for example, the scene in which Will, the narrator, is speaking with Abraham. Both Will and Abraham, seeking Christ, meet on the road to the Crucifixion, and Abraham tells Will the latest news: "I have heard recently that a man, John the Baptist, has baptized Him. And this man has told the souls in hell, the patriarchs and the prophets, that he has seen the Lord, who will save us all, walking on this earth." Will listens to Abraham with great interest, but as he listens he also becomes curious about the patriarch's "ample garments": "For there was something which he carried in his bosom and blessed continually as he spoke. So I had a look, and saw a leper lying there, with a host of prophets and patriarchs all making merry together"—which is exactly the kind of scene you'd expect to see, if you thought about it, in "Abraham's bosom." After all, Abraham's bosom is where Jesus says, in the Bible, that the poor man, Lazarus, who used to beg for scraps at the rich man's gate ended up after death, while the rich man went to hell. William Langland, *Piers the Plowman,* trans. J. F. Goodridge (New York: Penguin, 1959), 205-06.

8. Polyphonic music, invented in the Middle Ages, is another parallel. In polyphony, different voices sing different melodies at the same time. These different melodies complement one another, and there are times when the harmony between a note held by one voice and one sung by another voice may be very beautiful. But every voice has an intrinsically interesting melody. No singer's part consists entirely of notes written only to harmonize with another singer's melody.

9. It makes sense to think of medieval literature as pre-classical, even though it took place long after classical times—that is, after ancient Greek and Roman art and literature had given rise to classical criticism—because the Middle Ages saw the birth of a new Christian culture and aesthetic. The systematic application to English literature of the classical rules of the

ancient critics, and the emergence of a native English critical tradition, were still in the future. All art requires some selection or streamlining of life, of course, but the critical inquiry that reduces that selection to rules comes late in the development of an artistic tradition.

10. Just as people whose parents festooned their yards with pink flamingos or cheap statues of the Blessed Virgin Mary (or their kitchens with ceramic mushrooms and ducks) grow up to shop at Pottery Barn and Crate and Barrel.

11. C. S. Lewis, *The Allegory of Love: A Study in Medieval Tradition* (Oxford: Oxford University Press, 1959), 195-96.

12. Even today, the government of Communist China persecutes both Protestants who read the Bible outside the guidance of the government-approved religious authorities and Catholics who are loyal to the pope.

13. In *The Stones of Venice*.

14. "The Physician's Tale."

15. See how Pertelote in "The Nun's Priest's Tale" and the merchant's wife in "The Shipman's Tale" talk about the kind of man (or rooster, as the case may be) they find attractive. The author of *Piers Plowman* treats the same theme more graphically: When Will grows so old that the particular one of his members that his wife loved the best is no longer good for anything, she feels such pity for him, he says, that she wishes he were dead.

16. Emily, for example, in "The Knight's Tale," who prays to Diana, the goddess of chastity, to spare her from having to marry either one of her violently smitten lovers. But in "The Clerk's Tale" it's not Griselda, that paragon of female virtue, who seems to have a constitutional aversion to marriage, but her very difficult husband Walter.

17. See "The Wife of Bath's Prologue," "The Miller's Tale" (in which a young wife and her lover dupe her old husband and, when he fortuitously discovers how he's been deceived, manage to convince the neighbors that he's out of his mind), and "The Shipman's Tale" (in which the merchant's wife finds a very smooth, and very sexy, way out of the problem she's created for herself by spending more money on clothes than her husband will allow her).

18. At least he was until quite recently: twenty or thirty years ago (when girls didn't go out for football or off to war), hitting a girl was thought to be the most cowardly thing a boy could do.

19. His gown very short and his sleeves very long and wide, according to the style denounced in "The Parson's Tale."

20. Of course, we can always assume that Chaucer, being male and therefore, *ex hypothesi*, an agent of "the patriarchy"—that nefarious conspiracy to keep the female half of the human race in perpetual servitude—wrote his poetry to hypnotize women into believing that chivalry, really a new tool for their oppression, was to their advantage. Or that "the patriarchy" itself was somehow ratcheting male dominance up to a new level, and Chaucer was its unwitting tool. But if we dismiss conspiracy theories, we're left with the fact that Chaucer's poetry contains realistic and convincing portraits of women who were happy to have their husbands treating them according to the rules of courtly love (or who thought they would be happier if their husbands did).

21. See the introduction to "The Man of Law's Tale." This awareness is what feminists call our ancestors' "virginity fetish."

22. Chaucer also wrote about that other ideal, in "The Clerk's Tale."

Chapter 3:

The Renaissance: Christian Humanism

1. Written for Matins (early morning prayer) in the Office for the Feast of Corpus Christi. See Thomas Aquinas, *Opera omnia* ed. E. Fretté, and P. Maré (Paris: Ludovicum Vives, 1876), 29: 336.

2. Shakespeare was born in the year of Michelangelo's death.

3. The reference to the ruins left when Henry VIII dissolved the monasteries and confiscated their property—"Bare, ruined choirs, where late the sweet birds sang"—in Shakespeare's 73rd sonnet is the most famous example.

4. Especially Edmund Spenser, whose epic poem *The Faerie Queene* is an elaborate (and delightful) attempt to read Reformation Christianity back into a purposely archaized, medieval-style allegorical England.

5. See *The Tempest*: "Oh brave new world..." and John Donne's "Elegy: To His Mistress Going to Bed": "Oh my America! My Newfoundland, / My kingdom, safeliest when with one man manned."

6. Marlowe named his protagonist after the robber, condemned to die by crucifixion, who was freed in the place of Jesus.

7. Or least substantial evidence from contemporary documents, including compellingly circumstantial testimonies by Marlowe's associates—who, it has to be admitted, are not the most credible witnesses: government informers who may have worked with Marlowe and a fellow playwright (Thomas Kyd, the author of *The Spanish Tragedy*) who testified that the blasphemous writing that government agents found among his own papers (and on account of which he had been put to torture) must be Marlowe's.

8. Tennesee Williams, *The Night of the Iguana* (New York, New Directions, 1962), 65-66.

9. Shannon's Freud-inspired picture of God as the senile patriarch whose imagined wrath is responsible for our sexual pathologies was a theme that had broad appeal at the time.

10. Jonson says that Shakespeare was "[o]f nature's family" and that "nature herself was proud of his designs / And joyed to wear the dressing of his lines" (First Folio). Dryden says in his *Essay of Dramatic Poesy* that Shakespeare "needed not the spectacles of books to read nature. He looked inwards, and found her there." According to Alexander Pope's preface to his Shakespeare edition, "Homer himself drew not his art so immediately from the fountains of nature . . . he is not so much an imitator as an instrument of nature; and 'tis not so just to say that he speaks from her as that she speaks through him. . . . His characters are so much nature herself that 'tis a sort of injury to call them by so distant a name as copies of her." In the preface to his edition, Dr. Johnson says, "Shakespeare is above all writers, at least above all modern writers, the poet of nature; the poet that holds up to his readers a faithful mirror of manners and of life."

11. Dryden's *Essay of Dramatic Poesy*, Coleridge's lecture on Hamlet, and Keats in a letter to his brothers, respectively.

12. *Biographia Literaria* XV.

13. Pope's Preface: "But every single character in Shakespeare is as much an individual as those in life itself."

14. Preface to his Shakespeare edition.

15. Mark van Doren, *Shakespeare* (New York: New York Review of Books Classics, 2005), xx, xxiii.

16. See, for example, Rachana Sachdev, "Sycorax in Algiers: Cultural Politics and Gynecology in Early Modern England" and Theodora A. Jankowski, ". . . in the Lesbian Void: Woman-Woman Eroticism in Shakespeare's

Plays," both in *A Feminist Companion to Shakespeare*, ed. Dympna Callaghan (Malden, Massachusetts and Oxford: Blackwell Companions to Literature and Culture, 2000), 208-25, 299-319.

17. In, respectively, *Othello, Henry V,* and *Measure for Measure.*

18. "For all these [Macbeth, Brutus, Othello, Romeo, Lear, and Antony], as for their author while he writes and the audience while they watch, death is the end: it is almost the frame of the picture. They think of dying: no one thinks, in these plays, of being dead. In Hamlet we are kept thinking about it all the time, whether in terms of the soul's destiny or the body's." C. S. Lewis, "Hamlet: The Prince or the Play?" *They Asked for a Paper* (London: Geoffrey Bles, 1962), 63-64.

19. Lecture on *Hamlet.*

20. From, respectively, President Clinton's defense in the Whitewater case, common wisdom (or the lack of it) heard every day, and Justice Kennedy's majority opinion in *Planned Parenthood* vs. *Casey.*

21. "Other Worlds Are Possible" is the title of a planned Radical Caucus panel at the 2006 Modern Language Association convention according to one of last year's panelists. See my report at http://www.humanevents.com/article.php?id=11375.

22. And, in a wider sense, at every way in which people compete with and compare themselves to each other: at sexual jealousy, but also at professional envy, racial prejudice, the value of a good reputation, and what it means to be a woman of ill repute.

23. *The Literary Remains of Samuel Taylor Coleridge Collected and Edited by Henry Nelson Coleridge.*

24. Preface to Johnson's edition of Shakespeare's plays.

25. See Evelyn's Waugh's August 1962 letter to Nancy Mitford in *The Letters of Nancy Mitford and Evelyn Waugh*, ed. Charlotte Mosley (Boston and New York: Houghton Mifflin, 1996), 457, quoting Hilaire Belloc.

26. Andrea Dworkin, it appears, never actually said and denies implying that "all sex is rape." But it seems a fair inference from what she has written. Here's an example from a book entitled *Intercourse* (New York: Free Press, 1997), 137: "This may be because intercourse itself is immune to reform. In it, female is bottom, stigmatized. Intercourse remains a means or the means of physiologically making women inferior: communicating to

her cell by cell her own inferior status, impressing it on her, burning it into her by shoving it into her, over and over, pushing and thrusting until she gives up and gives in—which is called surrender in the male lexicon." Sounds like rape to me. For marriage as slavery, see Chapter Six below on the writings of Mary Wollstonecraft.

27. See Auden's introduction to Shakespeare's *Sonnets* in the 1964 Signet paperback edition.

Chapter 4:
The Seventeenth Century: Religion as a Matter of Life and Death

1. John Donne's Third Satire.

2. Preface to *Biathanatos*.

3. Camille Paglia, *Break, Blow, Burn: Camille Paglia Reads Forty-Three of the World's Best Poems* (New York: Pantheon Books, 2005).

4. July 31, 2002, "Q & A with Andrew Sullivan," The Daily Dish. Google cache at http://72.14.209.104/search?q=cache:86I9LPT04dAJ:www.andrew-sullivan.com/interviews.php 1 %22andrew 1 sullivan%22 1 %22camille 1 paglia%22&hl=en&gl=us&ct=clnk&cd=1, viewed 7/22/2006.

5. Owen Keehen, "Coffee with Camille: Chatting with the Incomparable Camille Paglia," 1995 interview on glbtq: an encyclopedia of gay, lesbian, bisexual, transgendered & queer culture at http://www.glbtq.com/sfeatures/interviewcpaglia.html, viewed 9/9/2006.

6. Lords and Commons being the two houses of the English parliament.

7. David Renaker, "A Critique of Stanley Fish's Surprised by Sin," http://userwww.sfsu.edu/~draker/reviews/stanleyfish.html, The Atheist Seventeenth Century Website, http://userwww.sfsu.edu/~draker/, viewed 7/22/2006.

8. "Stanley Fish Replies to Richard John Neuhaus," *First Things* February 60 (1996): 38.

9. Milton himself called English "the language of men ever famous and foremost in the achievements of liberty" and reported that England was already famous for liberty among the inhabitants of the European continent.

10. Peter Singer, *Animal Liberation* (New York: HarperCollins, 2002), 18.

Chapter 5:

Restoration and Eighteenth-Century Literature: The Age of Reason

1. From the introduction to the Aphra Behn's "The Unfortunate Happy Lady: A True History," at http://www.pemberley.com/janeinfo/bhnufhpl.html on The Republic of Pemberley, (http://www.pemberley.com/index.html), viewed 7/22/2006.

Chapter 6:

The Nineteenth Century: Revolution and Reaction

1. This line is from the poem as revised by Wordsworth after its initial publication in 1800.

2. Virginia Woolf "Jane Austen," in *Jane Austen: A Collection of Critical Essays,* ed. Ian Watt (Englewood Cliffs, N.J.: Prentice-Hall, 1963), 24.

3. Virginia Woolf, *A Room of One's Own* (New York: Harcourt, Brace and Company: 1929), 4.

4. *Memoir* of J. E. Austen-Leigh.

5. *A Vindication of the Rights of Women.*

6. A Mrs. Mitford, quoted in Virginia Woolf, "Jane Austen," 16.

7. The single passage from the novels that's quoted over and over again by feminists in support of Jane Austen's supposed feminism mentions the fact that men have had more opportunity for education, but without suggesting that that fact is a result of some patriarchal plot—and without a hint of either anger or cattiness: "Yes, yes, if you please. No references to examples in books. Men have had every advantage of us in telling their own story. Education has been theirs in so much higher a degree. The pen has been in their hands. I will not allow books to prove anything." The speaker—Anne Elliot in Persuasion—is engaged in a friendly, equal, and rational discussion with a man, about the real differences between men and women. Anne mentions the "little bias towards our own sex" that both men and women naturally have, but she never suggests that the masculine version of that bias has done women any harm. She argues, in fact, that women's less public lives (which she doesn't blame on patriarchal oppression) help make them superior in a quality that both she and her interlocutor agree is admirable: faithfulness in love.

8. Virginia Woolf "Jane Austen," 22.

9. The most notorious example is Eve Kosofsky Sedgwick's "Jane Austen and the Masturbating Girl," *Critical Inquiry* 17 (Summer 1991): 818-837. Sedgwick simply announces that, reading scenes in *Sense and Sensibility*, "I find I have lodged in my mind" (827) a scene from an 1881 case history of "Onanism and Nervous Disorders in Two Little Girls"—from which she proceeds to argue.

10. See Deborah Kaplan, *Jane Austen among Women* (Baltimore: Johns Hopkins University, 1992), 201-05.

11. Kaplan, 201.

12. See, for example, Sandra M. Gilbert and Susan Gubar, "Shut Up in Prose: Gender and Genre in Austen's Juvenilia" in *The Madwoman in the Attic: The Woman Writer and the Nineteenth-Century Literary Imagination* (Yale University Press, 1979), 107-45.

13. From a bedtime prayer composed by Jane Austen.

14. From another bedtime prayer by Jane Austen.

Chapter 7:

The Twentieth Century: The Avant-Garde and Beyond

1. Evelyn Waugh, *Brideshead Revisited* (New York: Alfred A. Knopf by arrangement with Little, Brown: 1998), 38.

2. T. S. Eliot, *The Complete Poems and Plays* (New York: Harcourt Brace Jovanovick, 1971), 37.

3. Ibid., 39.

4. Ibid., 38.

5. Ibid., 39.

6. Ibid., 43.

7. Ibid., 38.

8. Ibid., 43.

9. Ibid., 44.

10. In the preface to a collection of essays published in 1928 under the title *Lancelot Andrewes: Essays on Style and Order*, reprinted in 1970 by Faber & Faber.

11. Evelyn Waugh, *Decline and Fall*, excerpted in *The World of Evelyn Waugh*, ed. Charles J. Rolo (Boston: Little, Brown and Company, 1958), 10.

12. Evelyn Waugh, *A Handful of Dust* (New York: Alfred A. Knopf, by arrangement with Little, Brown and Company, 2002), 147.

13. Waugh, *Brideshead Revisited*, 8.

14. Evelyn Waugh, *Sword of Honour* (Boston: Little, Brown and Company: 1961), 15.

15. Ibid., 788.

16. Ibid., 718.

Chapter 8:

American Literature: Our Own Neglected Canon

1. Robert Frost, *The Poetry of Robert Frost*, ed. Edward Connery Lathem (New York: Holt, Rinehart and Winston, 1969), 348.

2. *The Da Vinci Code* is actually taught in the University of Michigan's honors program for students seeking a curriculum that "focuses on writing and artistic expression, with a strong emphasis on developing critical thinking and writing skills." http://www.umich.edu/~regoff/timesched/winter/literature_science_arts/lloyd_hall_scholars_program_lhsp_.html, http://sitemaker.umich.edu/nesilver/syllabus, and http://www.housing.umich.edu/info/learncomm.html, all viewed 7/21/2006. The National Association of Scholars' study of representative English curricula found that Toni Morrison—certainly in a different class from Dan Brown, as a writer, but just as certainly not *the best* American writer—got more mentions in the 1997-98 course descriptions they surveyed than any other American writer, including William Faulkner, Henry James, Emily Dickinson, and Walt Whitman. Mark Twain didn't make it into the top 25. http://www.nas.org/reports/eng_maj/LosingTheBigPicture.pdf viewed 7/21/2006. Beat poetry is now a staple of the American literature curriculum in our universities.

3. Joseph Bottum, "On the Square," April 27, 2006, http://www.firstthings.com/onthesquare/?p=245 viewed 5/27/2006.

4. F. Scott Fitzgerald, *The Great Gatsby* (New York: Scribner, 1992), 154.

5. Full disclosure: I should say "We"—being a Southerner myself.

6. William Faulkner, *Absalom, Absalom* (New York: Random House, 1964), 355.

7. Ibid., 358.

8. Ibid., 378.

9. See, for example, Walker Percy, "Stoicism in the South," *Signposts in a Strange Land* (Picador, 2000).

10. Flannery O'Connor, *The Habit of Being: Selected Letters of Flannery O'Connor*, ed. Sally Fitzgerald (New York: Farrar, Straus and Giroux, 1979), 81.

11. Ibid., 131-32.

12. Flannery O'Connor, *The Complete Stories* (New York: Farrar, Straus and Giroux, 1971), 411.

13. Flannery O'Connor, *The Habit of Being*, 537.

Chapter 9:
How the PC English Professors Are Suppressing English Literature (Not Teaching It)

1. English 668A; #26663 READINGS IN MODERN LITERARY THEORY. PARADIGMS OF THEORY: MARXISM AND DECONSTRUCTION (Orrin Wang) University of Maryland, Fall 2004, http://www.english.umd.edu/courses/fall2004grad.html viewed 6/12/2006. English 180D Writing the Unhomely: the Afro-Caribbean Experience (Kaiama Glover), Stanford, Spring 2007 ("In this course, students will explore the idea of home(land) as it is configured in various fictional and theoretical texts of the Anglophone and Francophone Caribbean diaspora."), http://english.stanford.edu/courseDetail.php?course_id=1211 viewed 6/12/2006. English 598*/394 *WEIMAR GERMAN CINEMA: The Horror of Otherness* (Prof. Dan Gilfillan) Arizona State University, Fall 2005, http://www.asu.edu/english/courses/F2005x.html viewed 6/12/2006. English 25001 45001 Jewish Latin American Literature (Achy Obejas), University of Chicago, Spring 2006, http://english.uchicago.edu/courses/grad_spring06.shtml#10 viewed 6/12/2006.

2. English 276 Desire (Ellis Hanson), Cornell, Spring 2007 ("Topics for discussion will include pederasty, mysticism, hysteria, sadomasochism, pornography, cybersex, and other performative pleasures."), http://www.arts.cornell.edu/english/sp07u.html#Lit viewed 6/12/2006. English 692.01 Cultural Studies: Blues Theories, Histories, Legacies (Adam Gussow), University of Mississippi, Fall 2006, http://www.olemiss.edu/depts/english/courses/600-level.html viewed 6/12/2006. English W4670 Film Noir, Noir Nation (Ann Douglas), Columbia, Spring 2004, http://www.columbia.edu/

cu/english/courses_syllarchive.htm#Special%20Topics viewed 6/12/2006. English 142 American Film: The Western (Ken Fields), Stanford, Fall 2006, http://english.stanford.edu/courseDetail.php?course_id=1177 viewed 6/12/2006. English 22804 Chicano/a Intellectual Thought (Raul Coronado, Jr.) U. of Chicago, Fall 2005, http://english.uchicago.edu/courses/undergrad_autumn05.shtml#22804, viewed 6/12/2006. English 513 Asian American Literature and Theory 12071 (Y. Chang), George Mason University, Fall 2006 http://english.gmu.edu/temp/500.html viewed 6/12/2006. English 367: Studies in British Literature since 1930—"Black" British Literature (Lauren Onkey) Ball State University, Fall 2006 ("We will also consider how England's cultural changes register in a couple of feature films and in popular music."), http://www.bsu.edu/english/undergraduate/specialcourses.htm#367, viewed 9/22/2006. English 083S.002 Freshman Seminar: "Many Bodies, Many Minds" (Susan Squier), Penn. State, Fall 2006 ("In this course we will read memoirs, a detective novel, and several works of graphic fiction, to explore the varieties of human bodies and minds there are, and consider how we navigate the world we all share."), http://english.la.psu.edu/undergraduate/coursedesc.htm viewed 6/12/2006. English 220.001 Expository Writing: The Rhetoric of the Graphic Novel (Hallada), University of New Mexico, Fall 2005 ("Comic books are often regarded as mindless entertainment...."), http://www.unm.edu/~english/Courses/Archives/DescriptionsFall2005/220one.htm viewed 6/12/2006. English 394A *When Carrie Met Sula: Blurring the Line Between "Literary" and "Popular" Works with Toni Morrison and Stephen King* (Dr. Michael Perry), Arizona State University, Fall 2005, http://www.asu.edu/english/courses/F2005x.html viewed 6/12/2006.

3. All quotations are from the descriptions for jobs in English departments (at, respectively, Northwestern State University of Louisiana; Princeton; Niagra University; and Marshall University) advertised in the Modern Language Association's Job Information List for June 10, 2006. At that time, only a single job description—one for a job as an assistant professor of English at Hardin-Simmons University, "an institution affiliated with the Baptist General Convention of Texas," for which a "philosophy of teaching in a Christian context" was required—mentioned Shakespeare. The search category "Renaissance or early modern" yielded one advertisement, for an instructorship or assistant professorship at the University of North Ala-

bama, in "Early Modern Studies." That position was "open to a broad range of specialties including, but not limited to, colonial, gender, global, international, and postcolonial approaches to early modern literature and culture." http://www.mla.org/cgi-shl/docstudio/docs.pl?jil_login&xurl=jil_search_eng&edition=eng viewed 6/10/2006.

4. William Croyle, "Lawmaker Wants Prof Fired: English Teacher Urged Students to Ruin Right to Life Display," *Cincinnati Enquirer,* April 16, 2006, http://news.enquirer.com/apps/pbcs.dll/article?AID=/20060416/NEWS0103/604160375/1058/NEWS01 viewed 6/13/2006. For the course Professor Jacobsen was teaching on the evening of the incident, see the literature course listings at the Northern Kentucky University website at http://www.nku.edu/~litlang/spring06.htm viewed 6/12/2006.

5. Joyce Howard Price, "College Probes Teacher Who Urged Fragging by GIs," *Washington Times,* November 20, 2005, A2. On the current (sorry) state of composition instruction in college, see Nan Miller's "Inquiry No. 24: English 101: Prologue to Literacy or Postmodern Moonshine?" a study released by the John William Pope Center for Higher Education Policy on June 19, 2006, and available at http://www.johnlocke.org/acrobat/pope_articles/english101.pdf (viewed 6/23/2006).

6. See LIT 49906 Seminar: Marxism and Literature (N. Rao), College of New Jersey Department of English, Spring 2006 (according to the course description, "Marxism offers us not only the tools to analyze and critique established structures of oppression and inequality, but also a way of approaching literary and cultural texts from a radical, liberatory perspective."), http://www.tcnj.edu/~english/courses/062litlng.htm viewed 6/12/2006; English 987a Psychoanalysis and Literature (Pericles Lewis), Yale, Fall 2006 http://www.yale.edu/english/courses.htm viewed 6/12/06; English 262 American Literature after 1914: Unsettling Texts of the Americas (Desireé Martín), University of California at Davis, Spring 2006, http://wwwenglish.ucdavis.edu/grads/S06_grad_courses.htm viewed 6/13/06; and English 171 Studies in Literature and Culture: Intercultural Autobiography (David Leigh, SJ), Marquette, Spring 2006, http://www.marquette.edu/english/courses/englishcoursesspring2005.shtml viewed 6/13/06.

7. Other bodies of knowledge just don't pose the same kind of threat. PC history professors can simply rewrite the history. In the introductory courses, they tell the story their way. And as their students begin to do

research with primary sources, the professors can steer their attention away from texts toward inarticulate material records. Philosophy and theology, on the other hand, aren't to everyone's taste. It may be true that, as Aristotle says, every man by nature desires to know. But it's abundantly clear that not every man desires to subject what he thinks he knows to the kind of rigorous examination that theologians and philosophers engage in.

8. Several of these terms have complicated histories in the various bodies of thought that "literary theory" draws on. But they're now used even by professors and students who aren't committed to those particular schools of thought. As far as the teaching of (or failure to teach) English literature is concerned, the real significance of, for example, binary opposition in Ferdinand Sassure's structuralist linguistics, matters less than how (and why) people in English departments today actually use "binaries" in their jargon. What I hope this chart suggests is how some of the jargon used in English departments limits what you can say about literature, and what's attractive about that jargon, and those limits.

9. Dympna Callaghan, ed. *The Feminist Companion to Shakespeare,* (Malden, Massachusetts, and Oxford: Blackwell, 2000), xi-xxiv.

10. Judith Butler, *Excitable Speech: The Politics of the Performative* (Routledge, 1997).

11. Kay Stanton, "'Made to write "whore" upon?': Male and Female Use of the Word 'Whore' in Shakespeare's Canon," *The Feminist Companion to Shakespeare,* ed. Dympna Callaghan, (Malden, Massachusetts, and Oxford: Blackwell, 2000), 80-102.

12. Callaghan, xii-xiii.

13. Ibid, xiii.

14. Ibid., op. cit.

Chapter 10:

What Literature Is *For*: "To Teach and Delight"

1. Margaret Soltan, "No Field, No Future," InsideHigherEd.com, December 6, 2005, http://www.insidehighered.com/views/2005/12/06/soltan viewed 6/9/2006.

2. Even Shakespeare's stock fluctuated wildly over the centuries. John Donne's poetry was neglected through the eighteenth and nineteenth centuries only to become wildly popular in the twentieth—at the same time that Milton's valuation crashed.

3. The American Council on Education (ACE)'s *Minorities in Higher Education Annual Status Report* released October 8, 2003, showed that "African-American college enrollment grew by 56 percent" from 1980-81 to 2000-01. For the ACE press release about the report, see http://www.acenet.edu/AM/Template.cfm?Section=Search&template=/CM/HTMLDisplay.cfm&ContentID=3719 viewed 6/29/2006.

4. John Donne, "Air and Angels."

Chapter 11:

How to Get Started (Once You Realize You're Going to Have to Read the Literature on Your Own)

1. This chapter is for readers who have even a little time to devote to the actual *study* of literature. If you don't, read in Chapter Twelve about how you can still make English and American literature an important part of your life.

2. I have to admit that I never gave this particular line a second thought until I read *Shadows of Ecstasy* (Grand Rapids, Michigan: Eerdmans, 1980), a popular novel in which Charles Williams, an amateur literary critic from the first half of the twentieth century, has his protagonist, a "professor of applied literature," think some of the things in my discussion below about it (4, 78-79).

3. For other reasons that this picture of Milton can't be accurate see the discussion of Milton (in Chapter Four) and of dictionaries (in Chapter Five) above.

4. Robert Frost, *The Poetry of Robert Frost,* ed. Edward Connery Lathem (New York: Holt, Rinehart and Winston, 1969), 222.

5. T. S. Eliot, *The Complete Poems and Plays* (New York: Harcourt Brace Jovanovick, 1971), 35.

Chapter 12:

Learn the Poetry by Heart—See the Plays—Gossip about the Novels (That's Just What Jane Austen Did)

1. W. H. Auden, "Reading," *The Dyer's Hand and Other Essays* (New York: Random House, 1962), 10.

2. See John Carey's *What Good Are the Arts?* (New York: Oxford University Press, 2006), 245.

3. Jane Austen, *Northanger Abbey*.

4. Natalie Tyler, *The Friendly Jane Austen* (New York: Viking Penguin, 1999), xviii.

ACKNOWLEDGMENTS

Heartfelt thanks to everyone who helped with this book. First to Jeffrey M. Rubin, the "onlie begetter" of the Politically Incorrect Guide™ series, and a man with an extraordinary talent for nurturing other people's talents; if not for him, this book would certainly not have been written.

And I wouldn't have known English and American literature well enough to write it without many diligent, expert, and inspiring teachers. Among them I must thank (or, in a few cases, remember with gratitude) at least Mary Hills Baker Gill, Joan Daniel, Lois Strock, Lee McMahon, Mark L. Reed, Ritchie D. Kendall, Theodore H. Leinbaugh, Jerry Leath Mills, Thomas A. Stumpf, William Harmon, Chrisopher Armitage, Harold I. Shapiro, Richard D. Rust, Jeanne Moskal, Joseph Viscomi, George Lensing, Thomas Prufer, and Richard Kennington—not all of whom will approve of what I've written here, but to all of whom I'm deeply grateful. I am also grateful to the Andrew W. Mellon Foundation (and to the Woodrow Wilson Foundation, which administered the program) for the Mellon Fellowship in the Humanities that paid for my graduate study in both philosophy and English.

Thanks also to all the wonderful folks I'm lucky enough to work with at Eagle Publishing, many of whom gave me useful criticism and advice, and all of whom helped make it possible for me to do my day job and also get this book finished. I'm in debt to (and in awe of) the consummate professionals at Regnery—from editors to designers to publicists to the sales force. I owe my editor, Harry Crocker, gratitude for his many useful suggestions at each stage of this project and my copy editor, Kate Morse, thanks for her careful attention to every detail of the manuscript. Paula Currall, Regnery's managing editor, also made many improvements for which I'm grateful. The multi-talented Kristina Phillips not only designed this book and its cover but also checked my translations from the Old English. And Jim Zerr (who, naturally, has to be thanked in advance) will, I know, do his usual magnificent job of getting this book manufactured to high standards on a tight schedule.

Many friends contributed ideas and assistance. Scott Carson checked my translations from the Latin and Greek. Leslie and Robert Spencer offered valuable advice and encouragement. Stephen Pimentel helped me track down the source of an elusive quotation; Maggie Wynne hosted many dramatic evenings that inspired material in Chapter Twelve; and other members of the St. Bonaventure Society offered insights from their extensive reading, and helpful responses to my thinking. Of course none of my teachers, editors, or friends is responsible for any errors of fact or failures in judgment in the book; they're mine.

Harcourt generously granted permission to reprint poetry from T. S. Eliot, *The Complete Poems and Plays 1909-1950* (San Diego, New York, and London: Harcourt Brace Jovanovich, 1971), 36-39, 43-44, 295, 381. Copyright © 1971 by Esme Valerie Eliot. Copyright 1930, 1939, 1943, 1950, © 1958, 1962 by T. S. Eliot. Copyright 1934, 1935, 1936, 1952, by Harcourt, Brace & World. Reproduced by permission of Penguin Books Ltd., to whom I'm also very grateful, are passages from the novels of Evelyn Waugh: *A Handful of Dust,* excerpted in *The World of Evelyn Waugh,* ed. Charles J. Rolo (Boston and Toronto: Little, Brown and Company,

1958), 10. Copyright 1928, 1929, 1939, 1932, 1934, 1942, 1944, 1945, 1948, 1954, 1955, 1957, by Evelyn Waugh. © 1958, by Charles J. Rolo. *A Handful of Dust* (New York and Toronto: Alfred A. Knopf, 2002), 147. This edition published by arrangement with Little, Brown and Company (Inc.). (*Brideshead Revisted* (New York and Toronto: Alfred A. Knopf, 1993), 8, 138. Copyright © 1944, 1945 by Evelyn Waugh. Copyright renewed © 1972, 1973 by Mrs. Laura Waugh. Published by arrangement with Little, Brown, Inc. Reproduced by permission of Penguin Books Ltd. are also passages from J. F. Goodridge's translation of William Langland, *Piers the Plowman* (Harmondsworth, Middlesex: Penguin Books Ltd., 1980), 205-06. Copyright © J. F. Goodridge, 1959, 1966. I've made every good faith effort to credit the proper sources, to comply with "fair use" and "fair dealing" in quotation, and, where necessary, to obtain permission to reprint copyrighted material. If I've omitted proper credit in any case, please notify Regnery in writing so that future printings of this work may be corrected.

I am also grateful for the enormous range of materials and the expert staff at the Library of Congress, the fine collection and helpful librarians at the John K. Mullen of Denver Library at the Catholic University of America, and the longsuffering folks in the Arlington County, Virginia, interlibrary loan program. I owe a great debt to the public benefactors at Project Gutenberg for making thousands of works in the public domain available on the internet, and another to many generations of my ancestors for being great collectors of novels and poetry. (I should note that for easier reading I've freely modernized spelling, punctuation, italics, and capitalization when quoting works that are out of copyright.)

My son Billy was a great sport throughout this project: how many eleven-year-olds would put up with *The Rime of the Ancient Mariner* for bedtime reading? And Jeff Kantor—the only man I know who's read *Finnegans Wake* from cover to cover—has been at once a friend with whom I could discuss the literature and the structure of the book with pleasure (and always to my profit), and an extraordinarily patient husband.

All that remains to be said is that writing this book has brought home to me, once again, the truth of the Psalmist's words: "Except the Lord build the house, they labor in vain that build it."

INDEX

A

Astrophel and Stella (Sidney), 78, 81

As You Like It (Shakespeare), xvii, 49

"The Atheist Seventeenth Century Website," 96

At War with the Word: Literary Theory and Liberal Education (Young), 200

Atwood, Margaret, 27, 30

Auden, W. H., 81, 154, 229

Austen, Jane, 30, 120, 126, 192, 209; English literature, suppression of and, 189; female characters of, 140–45; feminism and, xiii, 135–37, 145, 147–49; male characters of, 145–47; marriage and, 137; misogyny and, 141–42; "patriarchal values" and, 137–40, 144–45, 148; PC English professors and, 135; postmodernism and, 138, 139; reading, 229, 230, 239, 240–41; religion and, 137; Shakespeare, William and, 135; what they don't want you to learn from, 137, 141, 144, 146, 148

avant-garde literature. *See* twentieth-century literature

B

Babbit (Lewis), 173

Bacon, Francis, 51

Baines, Richard, 56

Balzac, Honoré de, 179

Bartholomew Fair (Jonson), 71

Basham, Megan, xvi–xviii

The Battle of Maldon, 3, 18–21, 231

Beardsley, Aubrey, 158

Becket, Thomas, 38

Behn, Aphra, 103–4

Beowulf, 207; courage in, 9–10; as elegy, 15; heroism in, 3, 6–11, 11–12, 13; honesty and, 10; language of, 3–4; nostalgia and, 14; Old English language and, 3–4;

Beowulf (continued)
  PC English professors and, 6; plot
  of, 4–5; postmodernism and, 6;
  what they don't want you to
  learn from, 8, 11, 14
Bible, 12, 31, 35, 93
Biographia Literaria (Coleridge),
  120, 215, 217
Blake, William, 96, 119, 124, 126
Bleak House (Dickens), 151
Boccacio, 196
Bosch, Hieronymus, 32
Boswell, James, 104, 116
Bottum, Joseph, 168
*Break, Blow, Burn: Camille Paglia
  Reads Forty-Three of the World's
  Best Poems* (Paglia), 90
Brians, Paul, 29
Brideshead Revisited (Waugh), 154,
  159, 161, 163–64
Brontë, Charlotte, 149
Brontë, Emily, 149
Brown, Dan, 60, 167
Browne, Thomas, 85
Browning, Robert, 120, 123, 149
Brueghel, Pieter, the Elder, 32
Bunyan, John, 85
Burke, Edmund, 114
Butler, Judith, 200
Byron, George Gordon, 120, 124,
  130, 132–33, 143

C

Caedmon's Hymn, 3
Cain, 12, 14
California, University of, Berkeley,
  202
Callaghan, Dympna, 200–201

The Canterbury Tales (Chaucer), 23,
  26, 32; chivalry and, 41–47; "The
  Clerk's Tale," 46; "The Franklin's
  Tale," 45, 47, 230; "The Friar's
  Tale," 35; *The Handmaid's Tale*
  vs., 27–29; language of, 24; marriage in, 42, 44–47; "The Merchant's Tale," 27, 36, 41–42, 46;
  meter and, 25–26; "The Miller's
  Tale," 26, 46; "The Monk's Tale,"
  33; "The Nun's Priest's Tale," 27,
  36, 39–40; "The Pardoner's Tale,"
  35; "The Parson's Tale," 37; "The
  Physician's Tale," 46; "Prologue,"
  25; "The Reeve's Tale," 46; "The
  Tale of Melibee," 37, 40; what
  they don't want you to learn
  from, 42; "The Wife of Bath's
  Tale," xvii, 26, 45
Cantos (Pound), 168
Carlyle, Thomas, 149
"The Cask of Amontillado" (Poe),
  171
Catholicism, 50; O'Connor, Flannery and, 182–83; Wilde, Oscar
  and, 157, 158
"Channel Firing" (Hardy), 153
Charles I, King, 92
Charles II, King, 106
Chaucer, Geoffrey, xiv, xvii, 23, 29,
  30, 33, 44, 192, 227; language of,
  24; medieval tragedy and, 33–34;
  meter and, 25; what they don't
  want you to learn from, 47. *See
  also The Canterbury Tales*
  (Chaucer)
chivalry: *The Canterbury Tales*
  (Chaucer) and, 41–47; feminism

and, 41, 43, 44, 45–46; women's happiness and, 47

Christabel (Coleridge), 124

Christian Humanism, Renaissance literature and, 49–52

Christianity: chivalry and, 43–44; as civilizing force, 6, 11; heroism and, 11–12; PC English professors and, 85; political correctness and, 85; seventeenth-century literature and, 85; twentieth-century literature and, 157

Churchill, Winston, 207, 209

Clairmont, Jane ("Claire"), 131

Clancy, Tom, 239

Clarissa (Richardson), 104, 239

Clinton, Hillary Rodham, 122

Clovis, King of the Franks, 11

Coleridge, Samuel Taylor, 61, 66, 71, 119–21, 124, 125, 128–29, 133, 215, 217, 237

colonialism, xvi, 61

Colorado, University of, Boulder, 53

"Composed upon Westminster Bridge" (Wordsworth), 128

Comus (Milton), 93–94

Confessions of an Opium-Eater (de Quincey), 123–24

Congreve, William, 117

A Connecticut Yankee in King Arthur's Court (Twain), 175

Conrad, Joseph, 153, 196

Cornell University, 191

Corral, Wilfrido, 194

Counter-Reformation, 50

courtly love. *See* chivalry

Crews, Frederick, 202

Cromwell, Oliver, 92

Crucifixion, 11, 12–13, 89–90

Cultural Logic, 193

D

Daily Mail, 110

David Copperfield (Dickens), 120

da Vinci, Leonardo, 50

The Da Vinci Code (Brown), 55

Davis, Lennard J., 196

Dead White Males: Dryden, John, 29–31, 32, 61, 103, 104, 106–8; Johnson, Samuel, 61, 63, 72, 86, 103–5, 114–16; Pope, Alexander, 104–6, 108–11, 117–18; Swift, Jonathan, 103–6, 111–14

Decline and Fall (Waugh), 162–63

deconstruction, xv, 4, 190

Dee, Ivan R., 190

Defense of Poesy (Sidney), 49, 204

de Mann, Paul, 192–93

de Quincey, Thomas, 123–24, 216–17

Dickens, Charles, 120, 126, 149, 150–52

Dickinson, Emily, 168, 190

Dictionary of the English Language, 115

Doctor Faustus (Marlowe), 49, 53–54, 56, 57–60

Don Juan (Byron), 120, 132–33

Donne, John, xvii, 85, 86–91, 230

"Do Not Go Gentle into That Good Night" (Thomas), 154

Douglas, Lord Alfred, 157, 158

Douglass, Frederick, 28, 167, 175

"Dover Beach" (Arnold), 121

The Dream of the Rood, 3, 11–13

Dryden, John, 29–31, 32, 61, 103, 104, 106–8, 133

D'Souza, Dinesh, 190

Duke University, 29

"Dulce et Decorum Est" (Owen), 154

Dunbar, William, 23

The Dunciad (Pope), 104, 108–9

E

Eagleton, Terry, 6, 13, 16

eighteenth-century literature. *See* Restoration and eighteenth-century literature

"Elegy Written in a Country Churchyard" (Gray), 104

Eliot, George, 120, 149

Eliot, T. S., 154, 159–62, 209, 224, 230, 235

Ellis, John M., 200

Emerson, Ralph Waldo, 173–75

Emma (Austen), 141–45

Emmett, Hilary, 177

Endymion (Keats), 134

"Energized by Pulpit or Passion, the Public is Calling: 'Gospel Grapevine' Displays Strength in Controversy over Military Gay Ban" (Milton), 93

English literature: civilizing power of, 204–5; "close reading" and, 215–17; eighteenth-century, 103–18; medieval, 23–47; nineteenth-century, 119–52; Old, 3–21; purpose of, 203–11; reading, 215–27; renaissance, 49–83; Restoration, 103–18; seventeenth-century, 85–102; suppression of, xiv, 189–202; twentieth-century, 153–66; Victorian, 149

English professors. *See* PC English professors

Enlightenment, 99, 105, 106

Epipsychidion (Shelley), 131

Essay on Man (Pope), 117–18

Euripides, 70

Evans-Pritchard, E. E., 8

Eve, Adam and, 12, 95–96, 102

"The Eve of St. Agnes" (Keats), 134

Everyman, 34–35

Every Man in His Humor (Jonson), 71

"Everything That Rises Must Converge" (O'Connor), 168, 183–84

Excitable Speech: A Politics of the Performative (Butler), 200

F

The Faerie Queene (Spenser), 49, 78, 93, 226–27

Far from the Madding Crowd (Hardy), 153

Faulkner, William, xv, 168–69, 170, 178–82, 203, 207, 208

feminism, xiv, 3, 17; Austen, Jane and, xiii, 135–37, 145, 147–49; chivalry and, 41, 43–46; marriage and, 45–46; sex differences and, 67–68, 73, 76, 77; sexuality and, 53; Shakespeare, William and, xv–xvi

A Feminist Companion to Shakespeare (Callaghan), xv–xvi, 200

"Feminist History, Theory, and Practice in the Shakespeare Classroom" (Lublin), 73

"Fern Hill" (Thomas), 154

Fielding, Henry, 104, 239

Finnegans Wake (Joyce), 162

Fish, Stanley, 99

Fitzgerald, F. Scott, 168, 169, 174

Frankenstein; or the Modern Prometheus (Shelley), 129–30, 133, 238

Frantzen, Allen J., 5

French Revolution, 119–20, 121–23, 136, 151

Freud, Sigmund, xiii, 189, 191

The Friendly Jane Austen (Tyler), 238

Frost, Robert, 168, 190, 223

Furr, Grover, 193

G

Gawain and the Green Knight, 23, 24

gender, as social construct, 67, 137

gender studies: sex differences and, 73; Shakespeare, William and, 74, 77

Germania (Tacitus), 7

Ginsberg, Allen, 124, 167

Godwin, Mary, 131

Godwin, William, 131

Goldsmith, Oliver, 161

"Goodfriday, 1613. Riding Westward" (Donne), 89–90

"A Good Man Is Hard to Find" (O'Connor), 183

Gray, John, 158

Gray, Thomas, 104

The Great Gatsby (Fitzgerald), 168, 169, 174

"Greenleaf" (O'Connor), 183

Gulliver's Travels (Swift), 104, 112–14

H

Hamlet (Shakespeare), 49, 62, 64–65, 66, 206

The Handmaid's Tale (Atwood), 27–29, 29–31, 41

Hanson, Ellis, 191

"The Happy Prince" (Wilde), 155

Hard Times (Dickens), 151

Hardy, Thomas, 149, 153

Hawthorne, Nathaniel, 167, 168, 171–73

Heart of Darkness (Conrad), 153, 196

Hemingway, Ernest, 123, 168, 173–74, 196

Henry Esmond (Thackeray), 223

Henry IV (parts I and II) (Shakespeare), 49

Henry V (Shakespeare), 49, 64, 65

Herbert, George, 85, 231

heroism: *The Battle of Maldon* and, 20–21; in *Beowulf*, 3, 6–11, 11–12, 13; Christianity and, 11–12; military, 6–9; Milton, John and, 93–98; modernity and, 3; obedience and, 97–98; Old English literature and, 3; temptation and, 93–98

Hill, Anita, 17

Hitler, Adolf, 68

Hitler Youth, 20

Hoffman, Abbie, 123

Holmes, Oliver Wendell, 223

Holy Sonnets (Donne), 85

Holy Sonnet XIV (Donne), 90

Holy Sonnet XIX (Donne), 89

Homer, 7, 14, 15, 109, 207, 217

homophobia, xvii, 16

homosexuality, 81

Hopkins, Gerard Manley, 121, 149

Horowitz, David, 190

Housman, A. E., 153, 154, 223

Howl (Ginsberg), 124

Huckleberry Finn (Twain), 168, 169, 175–78

human nature: Marxism and, 67, 68; PC English professors and, 66–67, 72–73; postmodernism and, 67; Shakespeare, William and, xvi, 60–68, 68–70, 70–78

Huysmans, Joris-Karl, 158

Hyperion (Keats), 134

I

I, Rigoberta Menchu, 191

An Ideal Husband (Wilde), 155, 157

Idler, 115

Iliad (Homer), 7, 15, 109

Iliberal Education: The Politics of Race and Sex on Campus (D'Souza), 190

Illinois, University of, Chicago, 196

The Importance of Being Earnest (Wilde), 121, 155, 157

In Memoriam (Tennyson), 120

"It Is a Beauteous Evening" (Wordsworth), 128

Ivanhoe (Scott), 23

J

Jackson, Jesse, 189

Jackson, Michael, 239

James, Henry, 168

James I, King, 88

Jankowski, Theodora, xv

Jaudon, Toni Wall, 177

Jesus Christ, 36, 50; Crucifixion of, 11, 12–13; Incarnation of, 49; obedience of, 97–98

The Jew of Malta (Marlowe), 49, 53, 56

Johnson, Samuel, 61, 63, 72, 86, 103–5, 114–16

Jonson, Ben, 60, 71–72

Joseph Andrews (Fielding), 239

Joyce, James, 154, 162, 179

K

Keats, John, 61, 120, 121, 124, 133–35, 235

Kimball, Roger, 190

King, Stephen, 190

King Lear (Shakespeare), 50, 69–70

Klages, Mary, 53

Kubla Khan (Coleridge), 120, 124

Kyd, Thomas, 55

L

"La Belle Dame Sans Merci" (Keats), 134

Lacqueur, Thomas, 201

"The Lady of Shalot" (Tennyson), 223–24

Lady Windermere's Fan (Wilde), 155

"The Lame Shall Enter First" (O'Connor), 183

Langland, William, 23, 24

Language, Sign, and Gender in Beowulf (Overing), 17

Laud, William, 92

Leaños, John Jota, 18–19, 21
Leaves of Grass (Whitman), 168
Lewis, C. S., 34
Lewis, Sinclair, 173
liberalism, 99
Life of Johnson (Boswell), 104, 116
Lincoln, Abraham, 168, 207
literary theory, xiv–xv; deconstruction, xv, 4, 190; English literature, suppression of and, 192–94; Old English literature and, 3; postmodernism and, 55; queer theory, 53, 55, 67–68; reality-denial and, 199–202; resistance theory, 192–93
Literature Lost: Social Agendas and the Corruption of the Humanities (Ellis), 200
Lives of the Poets (Johnson), 86
London Review of Books, 6
Longfellow, Henry Wadsworth, 168
"The Lovesong of J. Alfred Prufrock" (Eliot), 154
Lublin, Robert I., 73
Lucifer, 12
Lycidas (Milton), 235
Lyrical Ballads (Wordsworth and Coleridge), 124, 127, 128

M

Macbeth (Shakespeare), xiii, xvi, 50, 61, 67, 68
MacFlecknoe (Dryden), 104, 107
Machiavelli, Niccolo, 51, 53, 55
"Made to write 'whore' Upon?: Male and Female Use of the Word 'Whore' in Shakespeare's Canon" (Stanton), xv

Main Street (Lewis), 173
Malory, Sir Thomas, xvii–xviii, 23, 93
Manfred (Byron), 133
Mansfield Park (Austen), 140–41, 146–47, 240
Marlowe, Christopher, 49, 51–52, 52–60, 226; atheism of, 52, 55, 57; *Doctor Faustus*, 49, 53–54, 56, 57–60; homosexuality of, 52, 55; *The Jew of Malta*, 49, 53, 56; *The Massacre at Paris*, 54; PC English professors and, 52; *Tamburlaine the Great*, 52–53; villain-heroes of, 53–55; what they don't want you to learn from, 58, 100
marriage: Austen, Jane and, 137; feminism and, 45–46; Shakespeare, William and, 72–77
Marriage of Heaven and Hell (Blake), 96
Marvell, Andrew, 85, 161
Marx, Karl, 6, 121
Marxism, xiii, xv, 3, 16, 67, 68, 189, 190, 191
Mary, Blessed Virgin, 43
Massachusetts, University of, Boston, 73
The Massacre at Paris (Marlowe), 54
Maud (Tennyson), 226
medieval literature: aestheticism and, 32, 33; allegory in, 34–36; alliterative verse and, 24–25; authority and, 39–41; *The Canterbury Tales* (Chaucer), 23, 26, 27–29, 32; chivalry and, 41–47;

medieval literature (continued):
Christianity and freedom and,
36–38; church and state, separation of and, 38–49; *Gawain and
the Green Knight*, 23, 24; language of, 24; morality and,
34–36; *Morte D'Arthur* (Malory),
23; *Piers Plowman* (Langland),
23, 24–25, 26, 32, 35, 37; political incorrectness of, 26–27;
Shakespeare, William and,
60–83; teaching, 29–31; tragedy
in, 33–34; what they don't want
you to learn from, 26, 40
Melville, Herman, 167, 168
The Merchant of Venice (Shakespeare), 49, 61, 64, 65–66
Meredith, George, 149
"Michael: A Pastoral Poem"
(Wordsworth), 127–28
Michelangelo, 50
Middlemarch (Eliot), 120
Mill, John Stuart, 98
Milton, John, xiv, 87, 91–102, 190,
207, 226, 230, 235; Christianity
of, 91–102; *Comus*, 93; *Paradise
Lost*, 85, 91–92, 95–97; *Paradise
Regained*, 95; public affairs and,
92; *Samson Agonistes*, 95;
speech, freedom of and, 98–101;
temptation and, 93–98; use of
words by, 218–21; what they
don't want you to learn from, 93,
96
misogyny, xvii, 196
"Misogyny Is Everywhere" (Rackin),
xv

Mitterrand, Francois, 151
MLA. *See* Modern Language Associ-
ation
Moby-Dick (Melville), 167, 168,
170–71
modernism, twentieth-century liter-
ature and, 158–66
Modern Language Association
(MLA), 29, 121
"Modest Proposal" (Swift), 111–12
Mohammed, 98
Montclair State University, 193
Morrison, Toni, 167
Morte D'Arthur (Malory), xvii–xviii,
23, 93
Mosses from the Old Manse
(Hawthorne), 167
multiculturalism, 176, 189, 190
"Musée des Beaux Arts" (Auden),
154
"My Last Duchess" (Browning), 120

N
Napoleon, 120
*Narrative of the Life of Frederick
Douglass: An American Slave*
(Douglass), 28, 167, 175
Newman, John Henry, 121, 149
New Organon (Bacon), 51
New Testament, 11
The Night of the Iguana (Williams),
56, 57
Niles, John D., 5, 6
nineteenth-century literature,
119–52; Austen, Jane, 135–37,
137–40, 140–45, 145–49;
Coleridge, Samuel Taylor, 124,

128–29; Dickens, Charles, 150–52; human consciousness and, 125–28; Keats, John, 133–35; psychology and, 125, 129; revolutionary spirit and, 120–24; Shelley, Mary, 129–32; Shelley, Percy Bysshe, 129–32; what they don't want you to learn from, 122, 131; Wordsworth, William, 124–28
Nixon, Richard, 96
nostalgia, 14
"Nothing Gold Can Stay" (Frost), 223

O

O'Connor, Flannery, 168, 182–85
"Ode: Intimations of Immortality" (Wordsworth), 119, 128
"Ode on a Grecian Urn" (Keats), 120, 134
"Ode on Melancholy" (Keats), 134
"Ode to a Nightingale (Keats), 120, 134, 235
"Ode to Psyche" (Keats), 134
"Ode to the West Wind" (Shelley), 120, 133
The Odyssey (Homer), 93
Oedipus Rex (Sophocles), 70
Of Covetousness (Dunbar), 23
Old English literature: *The Battle of Maldon*, 18–21; *Beowulf*, 4–11; *The Dream of the Rood*, 11–13; heroism and, 3, 6–11; literary theory and, 3; what they don't want you to learn from, 8, 11, 14, 20

The Old Man and the Sea (Hemingway), 168
Old Testament, 36
"On the Knocking at the Gate in *Macbeth*" (de Quincey), 216
Oroonoko (Behn), 103
Othello (Shakespeare), xvi, 50, 61, 62, 69, 175
Overing, Gillian, 17
Ovid, 40, 196
Owen, Wilfred, 154

P

Paglia, Camille, 90
Pamela: Or Virtue Rewarded (Richardson), 238–39
Paradise Lost (Milton), 85, 91–92, 95–97, 207, 218–21
Paradise Regained (Milton), 95, 97–98
Patai, Daphne, 194
Pater, Walter, 154, 156, 158
Paul, St., 39–40
PC English professors: American literature and, 167; Austen, Jane and, 135; *Beowulf* and, 6; Christianity and, 85; English literature, suppression of by, 189–202; human nature and, 66–67, 72–73; jargon of, 189, 194–99; Marlowe, Christopher and, 52; political correctness and, 29; politics of, xv; reality-denial and, 199–202; Restoration literature and, 103; Romantic poets and, 121; Shakespeare, William and, 61, 66–67, 72–73

Pearce, Joseph, 156

Pennsylvania, University of, 67

Pepys, Samuel, 116

Percy, Walker, 182

Persuasion (Austen), 142

Petrarch, Francis, 78, 79

The Picture of Dorian Gray (Wilde), 155–56, 158

"Pied Beauty" (Hopkins), 121

Piers Plowman (Langland), 23, 24–25, 26, 32, 35, 37

Pilgrim's Progress (Bunyan), 85

Plato, 81

plays, performing, 229, 236–37

Poe, Edgar Allan, 167, 171

Poems (Dickinson), 168

poetry: epic, 6; memorization of, 229, 231; metaphysical, 86–91; middle English, 24–26; old English, 4–11; "symbolist," 154–55

Polidori, John, 130

Pope, Alexander, 61, 103, 104–6, 108–11, 117–18, 133, 183

pornography, 190, 191

The Portrait of a Lady (James), 168

A Portrait of the Artist as a Young Man (Joyce), 154

postmodernism, xvi, xvii; Austen, Jane and, 138, 139; *Beowulf* and, 6; heroism and, 3; human nature and, 67; literary theory and, 55; PC English professors' jargon and, 194–99; Shakespeare, William and, 62

Pound, Ezra, 168

Preface to *Lyrical Ballads* (Wordsworth), 119, 126

The Prelude (Wordsworth), 119, 128

press, freedom of, 98–101, 207

Pride and Prejudice (Austen), 120, 140, 141, 142, 144, 146, 240

The Professors: The 101 Most Dangerous Academics in America (Horowitz), 190

Prometheus Unbound (Shelley), 133

Protestantism, 50

Protestant Reformation, 50–51, 92

psychology, nineteenth-century literature and, 125, 129

Puritanism, 100, 174

Q

queer theory, 53, 55, 67–68, 73

R

racism, xvi, xvii, 16, 103; *Huckleberry Finn* (Twain) and, 175–78

Rackin, Phyllis, xv, 67, 201

Rambler, 115

The Rape of the Lock (Pope), 104

Rauh, Miriam Joseph, 226

Reed, Mark L., 217–18

Reed's Rule, 217–18, 222

Religio Medici (Browne), 85

Renaissance literature: Christian Humanism and, 49–52; Marlowe, Christopher and, 52–60; Shakespeare, William and, 60–83

Renaker, David, 87, 96

"Resolution and Independence" (Wordsworth), 128

Restoration and eighteenth-century literature: Dryden, John, 29–31, 61, 103, 104, 106–8; Johnson,

Samuel, 32, 61, 63, 72, 86, 103–5, 114–16; Pope, Alexander, 104–6, 108–11, 117–18; satire and, 105, 106–8, 108–11; Swift, Jonathan, 103–6, 111–14

A Rhymed Lesson (Holmes), 223

Rich, Adrienne, xvii

Richard III (Shakespeare), xvii, 62

Richardson, Samuel, 104, 238–39

Rimbaud, Arthur, 154–55

The Rime of the Ancient Mariner (Coleridge), 119, 128–29

"The River Merchant's Wife: A Letter" (Pound), 168

"The Road Not Taken" (Frost), 168

Romantic literature. *See* nineteenth-century literature

"A Room of One's Own" (Woolf), 135

Rousseau, Jean-Jacques, 149

Rubin, Jerry, 123

Ruskin, John, 39, 149

S

Sadchev, Rachana, xv

Samson Agonistes (Milton), 95

San Francisco State University, 87, 96

The Scarlett Letter (Hawthorne), 168, 171

Scott, James, 106

Scott, Sir Walter, 23, 143

"The Second Coming" (Yeats), 154

"The Selfish Giant" (Wilde), 155

Seneca, 40, 41

Sense and Sensibility (Austen), 146, 147–48, 149

"The Sensitive Plant" (Shelley), 133

seventeenth-century literature, 85–102; Donne, John, 86–91; Milton, John, 91–102

sex differences: feminism and, 67–68, 73, 76, 77; gender studies and, 73; queer theory and, 67–68, 73

sexism, xvi, 16, 103

Shakespeare, William, xiv, xv, 49, 52, 192, 193, 209, 230; Austen, Jane and, 135; comedies of, 70–78; English literature, suppression of and, 189; feminism and, xv–xvi; gender studies and, 77; human nature and, xvi, 60–78; marriage and, 72–77; meter and, 25; PC English professors and, 61, 66–67, 72–73; poetic technique of, 63; postmodernism and, 62; *Sonnets*, 230; Sonnets of, 50, 78–83; tragedies of, 68–70; what they don't want you to learn from, 62, 69, 71, 80; women, domestication of and, xiii, 77

Shakespeare and Women (Rackin), 67, 201

"Sharon Stone Shows Instinct for Sex Appeal" (Simpson), 110

Shelley, Mary, 136

Shelley, Percy Bysshe, 120, 124

A Shropshire Lad (Housman), 153, 154, 223

Sidney, Philip, 49, 78, 81, 204, 205

Simpson, Richard, 110

Singer, Peter, 102

Society for the Study of American Women Writers, 177

Solzhenitsyn, Aleksandr, 28

Songs and Sonnets (Donne), 85, 86

Songs of Innocence and Experience (Blake), 119

Sonnets (Shakespeare), 50, 230; couplet in, 79–80; homosexuality and, 81; love and, 81–83; rhyme scheme of, 78–79; themes of, 80–81; what they don't want you to learn from, 80

Sophocles, 70

The Sound and the Fury (Faulkner), 168, 179

Soviet Union, xiii

speech, freedom of, 98–101, 207

Spenser, Edmund, xvii, xviii, 49, 78, 93, 226–27

Stalin, Joseph, xiii, 68, 193

Stanford, 191

Stanton, Kay, xv

Stark, Rodney, 37

Starr, Sandy, 202

Steele, Danielle, 239

Stone, Sharon, 110

"Stopping by Woods on a Snowy Evening" (Frost), 168

A Student's Guide to Literature (Young), 226

"Surprised by Joy" (Wordsworth), 128

"Sweeney among the Nightingales" (Eliot), 224

Swift, Jonathan, 103–6, 111–14

Sword of Honour (Waugh), 163, 164–65

"Sycorax in Algiers: Cultural Politics and Gynecology in Early Modern England" (Sadchev), xv

T

Tacitus, 7

A Tale of Two Cities (Dickens), 150–51

Tales of the Grotesque and Arabesque (Poe), 167

Tamburlaine the Great (Marlowe), 52–53

The Taming of the Shrew (Shakespeare), 49, 74–77, 219

"Taxation No Tyranny: An Answer to the Resolutions and Address of the American Congress" (Johnson), 115

"The Tell-Tale Heart" (Poe), 171

The Tempest (Shakespeare), xvi, 49, 51, 61, 67, 77, 94

The Temple (Herbert), 85

Tennyson, Alfred Lord, 25, 120, 149, 223–24, 226

Tenured Radicals: How Politics Has Corrupted Higher Education (Kimball and Dee), 190

Thackeray, William Makepeace, 149, 223

Thatcher, Margaret, 151

Theory's Empire: An Anthology of Dissent (ed. Patai and Corral), 194

Thomas, Clarence, 17

Thomas, Dylan, 154

Thoreau, Henry David, 174

Tillman, Pat, 18–19, 21

"Tintern Abbey" (Wordsworth), 119, 127

"To a Skylark" (Shelley), 120, 133

"To Autumn" (Keats), 120, 134

Tocqueville, Alexis de, 174

"To His Coy Mistress" (Marvell), 85

Tolkien, J. R. R., 14–15

Tom Jones (Fielding), 104, 239

Tres Riches Heures du Duc de Berry, 32

The Trivium: The Liberal Arts of Logic, Grammar, and Rhetoric: Understanding the Nature and Function of Language (Rauh), 226

Troilus and Criseyde (Chaucer), 33–34

Trollope, Anthony, 149

Twain, Mark, 168, 169, 175, 175–78

Twelfth Night (Shakespeare), 49

twentieth-century literature, 153–66; aestheticism and, 154, 155, 158, 159; Christianity and, 157; decadence and, 154; Eliot, T. S., 159–62; modernism and, 158–66; Waugh, Evelyn, 162–66; what they don't want you to learn from, 157; Wilde, Oscar, 154–58

Tyler, Natalie, 238

U

Ulysses (Joyce), 154, 162

"Ulysses" (Tennyson), 120

The Unmasking of Oscar Wilde (Pearce), 156

Updike, John, 62

V

The Vagina Monologues, 57

"A Valediction: Of Weeping" (Donne), 86–87

Vallon, Annette, 123

van Doren, Mark, 61

Verlaine, Paul, 154–55

The Victory of Reason: How Christianity Led to Freedom, Capitalism, and Western Success (Stark), 37

The Violent Bear It Away (O'Connor), 184

Virgil, 15, 204

Volpone (Jonson), 71

Voltaire, 98

W

Wake Forest University, 17

Washington Post, 93

Washington State University, 29

The Waste Land (Eliot), 154, 159–62

Waugh, Evelyn, 154, 159, 161, 162–66

The Way of the World (Congreve), 117

Weisskopf, Michael, 93

Westbrook, Harriet, 131

Wharton, Edith, 173

Whitman, Walt, 168, 174

Wilde, Oscar, xviii, 121, 153, 154–58, 162, 237

Williams, Tennessee, 56, 57

William the Conqueror, 23

The Winter's Tale (Shakespeare), 61

Wise Blood (O'Connor), 183

Wollstonecraft, Mary, 136, 137

A Woman of No Importance
(Wilde), 155

Woolf, Virginia, 135, 137, 137–38

Wordsworth, William, 25, 119, 121,
122–28, 133, 136, 209–10, 227,
230

"The World Is Too Much with Us"
(Wordsworth), 128

Wuthering Heights (Brontë), 238

X

Xenophon, 205

Y

Yale University, 29

Yeats, William Butler, 154

Young, R. V., 226

"Young Goodman Brown"
(Hawthorne), 171–73